This book was compiled as a celebration. It's filled with fiction and nonfiction, poetry, music, crafts, recipes, riddles, jokes, puzzles, and more. I hope you'll return to it again and again throughout the year. I hope, too, that what you find here will add to your understanding and enjoyment of our holidays.

David A. Adler

The Kids' Catalog of Jewish Holidays

by David A. Adler

The Jewish Publication Society
Philadelphia and Jerusalem

To the Hampton Bay's Shavuot Group: The families Berkowitz, Getreu, Goldstein, Goldwyn, Harary, Kramer, Mermelstein, Merriam, Schoenfeld, Sender, Sichel, Slomovits-Schreiber, Steinberg, and Wolf.

Acknowledgments: My thanks to my editor Bruce Black for his good sense and constant encouragement. Thanks also to Rabbi Harry Cohensen and Mrs. Arlene Spiller of the Board of Jewish Education, who helped get me started.

© 1996 by David A. Adler

Manufactured in the United States of America

Library of Congress Cataloging-in-Publication Data

Adler, David A.
The kid's catalog of Jewish holidays / compiled by David A. Adler.
        p.   cm.
    Includes index.
    Summary: Presents stories, poems, songs, recipes, crafts, and other activities for special days that are significant to Jews.
    ISBN 0-8276-0581-1
    1. Fasts and feasts—Judaism—Juvenile literature.   2. Jewish crafts—Juvenile literature.   3. Fasts and feasts—Judaism—Juvenile fiction.   4. Cookery, Jewish—Juvenile literature.   [1. Fasts and feasts—Judaism.   2. Handicraft.   3. Cookery, Jewish.]   I. Title.
    BM690.A37   1996
    296.4'3—dc20   96-17784
                                                                        CIP
                                                                        AC

Designed and typeset by Eliz. Anne O'Donnell

97 98 99 00   10 9 8 7 6 5 4 3 2 1

The publication of this book was assisted through a generous grant from the MAURICE AMADO FOUNDATION, whose mission is to perpetuate Sephardic heritage and culture.

Contents

An Appreciation
Sadie Rose Weilerstein (1894–1993)

Sadie Rose Weilerstein was the author of two of the stories included in this collection, "K'tonton Takes a Ride on a Chopping Knife" and "Size Isn't Everything," as well as *The Adventures of K'tonton, What the Moon Brought, Little New Angel, Molly and the Sabbath Queen, Dick, The Horse That Kept the Sabbath*, and many other stories on Jewish subjects for children. She was a pioneer, the matriarch of modern Jewish books for children.

I was fortunate not only to listen to and read Mrs. Weilerstein's stories as a child but also to have worked as her editor. Mrs. Weilerstein was already eighty-five years old when we began our author-editor relationship. She complained to me about the aches and pains of aging, but when she spoke about her beloved K'tonton ben Baruch Reuben, Jewish tradition, and the holidays, her eyes lit up like a young woman's. Her eyes lit up, too, when she spoke of her four children and her late husband, Rabbi Baruch Reuben Weilerstein, the spiritual father of K'tonton.

Mrs. Weilerstein told me how one evening she created K'tonton after her husband read aloud a story by S. Y. Agnon about Rabbi Gadiel Hatinok, a finger-sized rabbi who saves his people from a blood accusation. When her young son asked what his father was reading, Mrs. Weilerstein told him, "About a tiny person, so high," and she held up her thumb. He asked about the rabbi, and rather than tell such a young child about a blood accusation, she made up a story of her own, of a thumb-sized boy who took a ride on a chopping knife and wished he hadn't. And so K'tonton was born.

Before my first visit to Rockville, Maryland, to meet Mrs. Weilerstein, I searched my parent's house for our copies of *Little New Angel* and *The Adventures of K'tonton*. I found them both without covers and with numerous pages taped. I had planned to ask Mrs. Weilerstein to autograph the books, but I was embarrassed by their poor condition and never brought them along. Of course, I should have. A well-worn book is a great compliment to an author. I suspect that there are thousands of Jewish families with Weilerstein books also without covers and with pages taped, evidence of how much Mrs. Weilerstein and her stories were—and still are—loved.

Notes from the Publisher

A safety note about the crafts in this book:
Some of the crafts in this book call for the use of a hammer, scissors, or other potentially dangerous tools. Before beginning any craft, get either help or the "go-ahead" from a responsible adult. Read the directions and assemble all the materials you will need before you begin.

A safety note about the recipes in this book:
A kitchen can be a dangerous place. Watch out for splattering oil or boiling water. Some of the recipes in this book are intended only for older children. Before beginning any of the recipes, make sure an adult is available to help. Read the entire recipe and assemble all the ingredients and utensils (pots, pans, spoons, knives, and so forth) before you begin.

A note about the spellings in this book:
There are many ways to spell Hebrew words using the English alphabet. Ḥanukkah, for example, is frequently spelled *Chanukkah*. Some of the short stories, poems, recipes, and music in this book contained different spellings when they were originally published. Whenever possible, we have been faithful to the spellings used in the original publications.

The Kids' Catalog of Jewish Holidays

Introduction

The Seasons

Fall	Winter	Spring	Summer

The Months

Tishre	Tevet	Nisan	Tammuz
Ḥeshvan	Shevat	Iyar	Av
Kislev	Adar	Sivan	Elul
	(And in a leap year—Adar II)		

When the Holidays Begin

Tishre 1—Rosh Hashanah

Tishre 3—Tzom Gedalia (Fast Day)

Tishre 10—Yom Kippur (Fast Day)

Tishre 15—Sukkot

Tishre 22—Simḥat Torah-Shemini Atzeret

Kislev 25—Ḥanukkah

Tevet 10—Asara B'Tevet (Fast Day)

Shevat 15—Tu B'Shevat

Adar 13—Ta'anit Esther (Fast Day)

Adar 14—Purim

Nisan 15—Pesaḥ

Nisan 27—Yom Hashoah

Iyar 4—Yom Ha-Zikaron

Iyar 5—Yom ha-Azma'ut

Iyar 18—Lag B'omer

Iyar 28—Yom Yerushalayim

Sivan 6—Shavuot

Tammuz 17—Shiva Asar B'Tammuz (Fast Day)

Av 9—Tisha b'Av (Fast Day)

The Story of the Jewish Calendar

We are accustomed to seeing the calendar as a neat pad of squares and numbers hanging on the wall. But the calendar was not always as tidy an affair as this. Once it might have been a buffalo skin marked with Native American signs; some Native American tribes still plant corn when the oak buds are the size of a squirrel's ear. Or it may have been a clay tablet, a carved stone, or some other primitive object. Before these early calendars people told the time of year by the position of the sun and stars, by the new moon and by the habits of birds, plants, and animals.

The making of an exact calendar, however, had puzzled people for ages because the natural divisions of time do not fit squarely together. The day does not evenly fit into the moon month nor does any even combination of days or months exactly make up a solar year. The Egyptians were the first to realize that a calendar had to be a man-made device and the Egyptian year is still the basis of the year calendar as we know it. We now know that it takes about three hundred and sixty-five days for the earth to complete one trip around the sun. And because three hundred and sixty-five is not exactly right, we have a leap year every fourth year. That is when we add an extra day to the month of February to make the calendar agree with the sun year. This is the civil calendar. The Jewish calendar is based on both the moon and the sun. The months are moon months, but the year is a sun year. Since twelve moon months (of twenty-nine and a half days) add up to only three hundred and fifty-four days, while the sun year has three hundred and sixty-five days, something had to be done to make up this difference. So every few years, there is a Jewish leap year, when a whole month is added to straighten matters out. The Jewish calendar is arranged in cycles of nineteen years, and seven out of every nineteen years are leap years.

The day in the Jewish calendar begins with sunset and ends with sunset. The days of the week have no special names, but are known simply as the first day, second day, etc. Only the seventh day has a special name, Shabbat, and the sixth day is known as Erev Shabbat, the "Eve of Shabbat."

There was a time when Jews did not have names for all the months. In the earlier books of the Bible we find only a few months with names. Of these only the following four names are preserved: *Aviv*, which may mean an ear of corn or spring; *Etanim*, which means hardy fruit; *Bul*, which means rain; and *Ziv*, which means beauty.

The present names of the months of the Jewish calendar were taken from the Babylonians. The Jews became acquainted with these names when they were in exile in Babylon. The Hebrew months more or less describe the season of the year when they occur. The names of the months are Nisan (March-April), Iyar (April-May), Sivan (May-June), Tammuz (June-July), Av (July-August), Elul (August-September), Tishre (September-October), Ḥeshvan (October-November), Kislev (November-December), Tevet (December-January), Shevat (January-February), and Adar (February-March). In leap years another month is added, Adar Sheni, that is, Second Adar.

The Jews did not always have a fixed written calendar. In ancient Jerusalem people had to depend on actual observation of the new moon. In the days of the Second Temple those first to notice the slightest crescent in the sky would rush to inform the Sanhedrin, or Great Council. Then fires were lit on the highest hills in Jerusalem as signals for the neighboring cities. As soon as the signal was seen by the inhabitants of the next city, they in

turn lit a fire on their nearest hill, as a signal to the more distant communities.

Because Jews of far-distant countries like Egypt and Rome and Persia could not very well depend on fire signals and messages, which sometimes arrived too late, they found it necessary to observe two no-work festival days at the beginning and end of Pesaḥ, for Shavuot, the beginning of Sukkot, and for Simchat Torah/Shemini Atzeret. In the fourth century, Jews had become scattered over so many countries that a written calendar was absolutely necessary. Rabbi Hillel the Second (360–365 C.E.) wrote down the definitive rules for the calendar.

Calendar makers have used events great and small and the lives of kings and prophets to start their reckonings. The Romans counted time from the founding of their city. Christians date events from the birth of Christ. Jews, however, number the years from the time of Creation, as accounted for in the Bible.

The Jewish year begins with the month of Tishre. The first day of Tishre is the Jewish New Year. That is because the Creation is affirmed to have taken place on that day, and the Creation is the start of the Jewish calendar. It is also the beginning of the rainy season in Israel, which is so important to a people of shepherds and farmers such as our ancestors were.

But Tishre is still regarded as the seventh month, for the Bible commanded the Israelites to consider Nisan as the first of months, being the month of the great Exodus from Egypt. On the fifteenth of Nisan we celebrate Pesaḥ, our chief festival of springtime and freedom.

A long time ago, when Jews lived more or less apart from the general community, the Jewish calendar was used in the way the civil calendar is used today. Jewish businessmen would date their bills, notes, and records with Hebrew dates. Nowadays, the Jewish calendar is used mainly as a guide in our religious lives, in celebrating the holidays. As such, the Jewish calendar is important in every Jewish home and institution.

Rosh Ḥodesh

A New Month Begins

About Rosh Ḥodesh

The first commandment given in the Torah to the entire nation was to proclaim Rosh Ḥodesh. In ancient times fires were lit on the tops of mountains to signal the beginning of a new month. But some sixteen hundred years ago Rabbi Hillel the Second prepared a calendar. Since then the days of Rosh Ḥodesh and Jewish holidays have been set.

The Jewish calendar is a lunar one: it is based on the moon. The moon goes through phases. Toward the end of the Jewish month we see less of it, and then it's not visible at all. When some of it begins to be seen again, we celebrate Rosh Ḥodesh, the beginning of a new Jewish month.

For some months, those following a twenty-nine day Jewish month, Rosh Ḥodesh is celebrated for one day. For months following a thirty-day month, Rosh Ḥodesh is a two-day holiday. The two days are the thirtieth day of the preceding month and the first day of the new month.

Rosh Ḥodesh has special significance to many Jews because we as a people have been compared to the moon. Just like the moon, the Jewish people have lived through times of darkness and light.

"SHOW ME A FULL MOON . . . AND I'LL SHOW YOU A NIGHT LIGHT"

Although there are added morning prayers and a Torah reading, Rosh Ḥodesh is not a no-work day. Some families make the day special by having a festive meal. Traditionally, Jewish women don't do heavy work on Rosh Ḥodesh. It's their special holiday because they did not join the men in the sin of the Golden Calf. Some women get together for prayer and worship at Rosh Ḥodesh celebrations while others light a candle for Rosh Ḥodesh.

The day before Rosh Ḥodesh has been called Yom Kippur Katan, a little Yom Kippur. On this day some Jews fast and say prayers of repentance.

Mendel of Chelm Captures the Moon

by David A. Adler

Mendel the tailor was about to travel and needed advice, so he went to see Berel, the wisest of the Wise Men of Chelm.

Tap. Tap.

Mendel knocked on the front door of Berel's house.

Tap. Tap.

Mendel knocked again.

"It's no use knocking," someone standing behind Mendel said. "Berel isn't home."

It was Berel. He was standing there, right behind Mendel and he was holding a large bundle of clothes.

"I just came from the river," Berel said. "I was washing my clothes. I looked in the water and Berel was looking right back at me. I'll show you where he was. He's probably still there."

Mendel followed Berel to the river.

"This is where I saw him," Berel said as he looked into the water.

Mendel looked into the river and said, "You're right. There he is. And there I am, standing right next to him."

Mendel looked into the river and asked, "Dear, wise Berel, I am going on a long journey. The moon always shines right above the village of Chelm and I won't be here when we will bless the new moon. I'll be much too far away to see it. What should I do?"

Mendel waited for Berel to answer his question, but Berel's reflection didn't speak.

"He's thinking," the real Berel whispered.

Mendel and Berel stood there, waiting for Berel's reflection to speak.

After a while the real Berel whispered, "I don't know why he has to think so much. The answer is really quite simple. Fill a bucket with water and leave it out. At night you'll see the moon reflected in the water. As soon as you see it, quickly throw a cloth over the bucket. You'll capture the moon."

Berel smiled, "Then, take the bucket with you on your trip. When it's time to bless the moon, just take off the cloth. The moon will be right there waiting for your blessing."

What's closer, school or the moon?

The moon, of course. I can see it from here, but I can't see school.

8
Rosh Ḥodesh

A New Month Begins

A Rosh Ḥodesh Bummer

Being outside beneath a full moon and hearing strange sounds.

And that's what Mendel did.

He carried the bucket with him as he traveled far from Chelm. One night, Mendel was sitting under a tree and resting when he realized it was time to bless the new moon. He took the cloth off the bucket, but the moon was gone.

"Maybe you're there," Mendel said, "but I just can't see you because it's dark here under the tree."

Mendel put the cloth back on. Then he carried the bucket out by the road. There, under the light of the moon he took off the cloth.

"There you are," Mendel said to the moon's reflection. And Mendel said *Kiddush Levanah,* the monthly blessing of the moon.

Rosh Ḥodesh Recipe

Moon Crescent Cookies

Celebrate Rosh Ḥodesh with crunchy cookies shaped like the crescent moon. You can substitute one cup of your favorite chopped nuts for the almonds: try hazelnuts, peanuts, walnuts, cashews, or a combination.

2 cups flour
1/4 teaspoon salt
1 cup sweet margarine
1/2 cup confectioners' sugar
1 teaspoon vanilla
1 cup finely chopped almonds

Preheat the oven to 350 degrees.

Sift the flour into a bowl and stir in the salt. Set the bowl aside.

Beat the margarine with the sugar and vanilla in a second bowl and set the bowl aside.

Chop the almonds until they are very fine: you can ask a parent to grind them in the food processor.

After you have chopped the nuts, add them to the margarine, sugar, and vanilla mixture.

Add the flour and salt mixture to the margarine, sugar, vanilla, and almond batter, and stir.

Shape the dough into crescents.

Place the crescents on cookie sheets (not greased) and bake for 12–15 minutes or until crescent cookies are golden brown.

Immediately after taking the crescent cookies out of the oven, use a spatula to transfer them to a plate or to paper towels spread on the countertop.

While cookies are still hot, put several teaspoons of confectioners' sugar in a sifter and then sift the confectioners' sugar over the cookies.

Makes 30–50 cookies

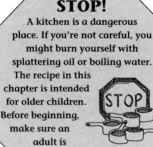

STOP!

A kitchen is a dangerous place. If you're not careful, you might burn yourself with splattering oil or boiling water. The recipe in this chapter is intended for older children. Before beginning, make sure an adult is available to help.

Rosh Ḥodesh Fun

Rosh Ḥodesh Puzzles *(Answers on page 270.)*

At lunch time 3 friends decided to celebrate Rosh Ḥodesh together. They each brought along sandwiches, drinks, and fruit. But only 2 of the friends brought along cookies. One brought 10 cookies. The other brought 5. The 3 friends shared the cookies equally. The third friend insisted on paying for her share of the cookies. She gave her 2 friends $1.50. How should the money be divided?

The Shared Cookies

Rearrange the letters in each group to form a Hebrew month:

A E E O W B H H N T M R

B A H R E M N O T H W E

H N M E B E A H R W O T

Hebrew Month Mix-up

which is heavier,
a quarter moon
or a full moon?

A quarter moon
because a full
moon is much
lighter.

Shabbat

A Taste of Heaven

About Shabbat

Shabbat, "a sweet taste of the heaven," begins each Friday at twilight and ends after sunset on Saturday night—every week. As soon as one Shabbat ends you can think about and look forward to the next one. It begins just six days later.

The source for the observance of Shabbat comes from the Ten Commandments: "Remember the sabbath day and keep it holy. Six days you shall labor and do all your work, but the seventh day is a sabbath of the Lord your God. You shall not do any work . . ." And work here is defined as the thirty-nine acts done in building the mishkan—the sanctuary—in the desert after leaving slavery in Egypt. Among the forbidden acts are writing, erasing, tearing, trapping, baking, building, making a fire, and putting out a fire.

Shabbat is a day for rest, study, prayer, singing, festive meals, family, and friends. For Sabbath-observant Jews the day is the high point of the week. According to legend, when the Jewish people forget their weekday worries their Shabbat soul insures them a day of peace and joy.

Shabbat begins in Jewish homes on Friday afternoon before sunset when candles are lit to welcome Shabbat. In certain Sephardic communities it is considered preferable to use oil and not candles.

At the very least there are two Shabbat lights, one reflecting the command in Exodus to "remember" Shabbat and the second reflecting the command in Deuteronomy to "observe" Shabbat. Some people have seven lights, one for each day of the week, and others have ten, one for each of the Ten Commandments. And in some homes there is a light for each member of the family.

In synagogues and temples, before the evening prayers, Kabbalat Shabbat, several psalms and a poem, "Lekha Dodi," are said. "Lekha Dodi" compares Shabbat to a bride. Her loving groom is the Jewish people.

"Come, my friend, to greet the bride,
let us welcome Shabbat . . .
Come, let's go to greet Shabbat,
For it is a source of blessing.
From the beginning

Shabbat was honored,
Last in creation,
But first in God's plan . . ."

On the Shabbat dinner table are two loaves of bread, ḥallah, a reminder of the double portion of manna found each Friday during the forty years the Jews wandered in the desert after leaving slavery in Egypt. The extra portion was for Shabbat, when no manna fell. The two loaves of bread are covered with a cloth, a reminder of the layer of dew that covered the manna.

Before the Shabbat meal kiddush, a blessing over wine, is said. In some homes before kiddush a little water is mixed into the wine. This Mezigah, or custom, is said to sweeten God's judgment of us. After kiddush parents gently place their hands upon the heads of their children and bless them.

In synagogues every Shabbat morning a different portion of the Torah is read. During the year, beginning with the first Shabbat after Simḥat Torah, the entire Five Books of Moses are read. A selection from the prophets is read, too.

There are special Shabbats. The one immediately before Pesaḥ is called Shabbat HaGadol, the Great Shabbat. Many people have the custom to read the Pesaḥ Haggadah on the afternoon of this Shabbat. In many synagogues there is a special Shabbat HaGadol afternoon sermon.

Shabbat Shuva is the one between Rosh Hashanah and Yom Kippur. In many synagogues on this Shabbat, too, a special afternoon sermon is given. The day gets its name from the first word of the haftorah, the reading of the prophets on that day. Shabbat Ḥazon, the one just before the fast of Tisha b'Av, and Shabbat Na Ḥaamu, the one following Tisha b'Av, also get their names from the first words of the days' haftorahs.

There are three Shabbat meals. The third meal, often eaten at sunset, is a farewell to Shabbat. Some people have the custom to prolong

this meal, the seudah shelishit, *with songs and words of Torah and thereby prolong the beloved Shabbat.*

Saturday, after nightfall, Shabbat ends with havdalah, *a prayer said over wine, fire, and sweet-smelling spices.*

In the Talmud (Pesaḥim 53:b) Rabbi Yehudah explained in the name of Shmuel that we say a blessing over lighting a fire at the end of Shabbat because fire was created at the conclusion of the first Shabbat.

According to Maimonides, the sweet-smelling spices are meant to bring joy to the soul saddened that Shabbat must end.

Some people have the custom to fill the cup of wine until it overflows in the hope that the coming week will overflow with good fortune. Others look into the wine hoping to see their reflections, an indication that God will protect them from harm in the week ahead. After havdalah, *some people place drops of wine behind their ears, on the backs of their necks, over their eyes, and in their pockets as a sign of their wishes for good health and success.*

The song "Eliyahu Ha-Navi"—Elijah the Prophet—is sung in some homes to express the hope that one day there will be peace. Some families also sing "Miriyam Ha-Niviah," Miriam the Prophet.

Shabbat in Jerusalem
by Yaffa Siegel

Sunday in Israel is a regular work day, so for most Israelis, Shabbat is the only free day in the week. Shabbat doesn't just mean a day off from work. It's a day which is so special and so different that in some places, it actually *looks* and *sounds* different from the rest of the week! This is what Shabbat is like in many neighborhoods in Jerusalem.

The difference starts on Friday afternoon when the streets suddenly become very empty. The buses all over the city return to the garages until Saturday night, and the stores close while everyone rushes home to wash up and get ready for Shabbat.

A long blast from Jerusalem's main air raid siren tells you that it's time to light the Shabbat candles. Now the streets fill up again—not with cars or trucks or buses, but with people going to the synagogue. The children are back outside playing while they try to keep their Shabbat clothes clean (at least for a little while!). At the Western Wall in the old City of Jerusalem, thousands of people come to welcome Shabbat every Friday night with dancing and singing, in addition to their Shabbat prayers. After services, if it's summertime when windows are open, you can hear a

"Shabbat concert" as you listen to each family singing *zemirot*—Shabbat songs—during their Shabbat meal.

On Shabbat morning, the streets bloom with people dressed up in their best, going to services. The men walk to the synagogue wearing their white *tallitot* over their jackets. The Chassidim wear special, elegant looking, wide fur-rimmed hats, and some of them wear long striped, silk Shabbat robes instead of their regular clothes. Jerusalem is filled with smiling, cheerful, holiday-looking people.

Jerusalem probably has more synagogues than any city in the world. There are hundreds of them tucked away in stores, shelters, and apartment buildings. There are big, modern synagogues, and tiny, ancient ones. Some pray according to eastern customs and melodies, and some sound just like services *you* are used to hearing.

Considering that Shabbat is a day of rest, it's really a pretty busy time! It's a day for inviting people to your home, and it's amazing how many Israelis open their homes (and their hearts!) to people they don't know, have never seen before and will probably never see again! There are committees in Jerusalem that will arrange for any visitor—soldier, student, tourist, or volunteer—to spend Shabbat with a Jerusalem family. Of course, Shabbat is an "eating day" when special foods and big meals are served. Jerusalem even has its own *kugel yerushalmi*—Jerusalem Kugel—made out of rice and oil and spices which are left to bake overnight until they turn into a big, round, brown, "hot" cake. You eat it with sour pickles and something cold to drink!

Shabbat afternoon is a good time to learn Torah, and so adults and children all over the city go off to a שִׁעוּר (*shi'ur*), or lecture. It's also time for boys and girls to go to their youth organizations and synagogue groups. And in between all these activities, you simply *must* find time for a Shabbat nap. In fact, lots of neighborhoods expect you to be quiet between 2 and 4 p.m.!

There are those Israelis who spend Shabbat the same way that Americans spend Sunday. They go to the beach or to a soccer game. They wash their cars or clean their houses. But if you want to make Saturday a *real* Shabbat and not let it become a day to wash the car or clean the house, you have to get the car washed and the house cleaned during the week. So what happens is that Israeli families often plan their week around Shabbat. The begin-

ning of the week is washing time, and laundry flaps on clothes-lines all around the country (very few Israelis have dryers). The next day or two is for cleaning, and Thursday is for shopping; the supermarkets and outdoor markets are jammed full of people carrying bags and baskets. Thursday is also baking time, when good smells float out of kitchens into the street. Friday morning is for cooking, and Friday afternoon is for bathing, dressing and last minute details. Before you know it, there goes the Shabbat-air-

The Sabbath: A Metamorphosis
by Chaim Berger

You might have heard about it . . . the Sabbath. It is a special metamorphosis that traditional Jews around the world experience one day each and every week, as another seven-day rotation of the earth ends with sunset.

An investment banker in New York checks the time and turns off her computer, as the sunlight turns golden on the World Trade Center's towers . . . an Israeli farmer rides his tractor home through his orange grove as the sun nears the horizon . . . a small group of people make their way through the gray streets of Moscow to the synagogue, now able to celebrate the Sabbath without fear for the first time in seventy years . . . They are all bound together by the metamorphosis to come.

Sabbath is the central hub of Jewish life. But what does it feel like? To quote the poet: "Let me count the ways . . ."

Sabbath is a time out from the rigors of day-to-day life. It is long, leisurely meals with family and friends, talking and singing. It is time spent actually communicating with parents, spouses, children, friends. It is experiencing a sense of gratitude for what you have. It is long Friday nights (in the winter) and long Saturday afternoons (in the summer) free from the "have-to" syndrome (but I have to . . .) to read, to talk, to walk, to think an elevated thought, to study a sacred text, to rest. Sabbath is a collection of moments in the synagogue, the center of Jewish communal life: moments to pray, unshackled from the

week's cares; moments to hear a sermon and think about it; moments to be with old friends, to experience community.

Sabbath is also a special silence. The cacophony of the phone, television, stereo is absent. It is a slower pulse, relaxed muscles. The Sabbath is the glow of candles, reminiscent of the first lights of creation. It is a place in time which the worries of the world cannot touch. Sabbath is reflection and perspective. It is time to think about life and priorities. Sabbath is peace, rest for the body, and rest for the soul.

Others may look at the Sabbath and see restrictions. The traditional Jew sees opportunities for familiar patterns and feelings which add glow to his or her entire week.

raid-siren again, and it's time to light the candles and wish everyone another *Shabbat Shalom*.

You needn't live in Israel to have a "real" Shabbat. You can make Shabbat special every week no matter where you live. But in Israel, and especially in Jerusalem, Shabbat is not only celebrated as a private holiday inside your home. It is a special public holy day which is celebrated both in your house and on the street by an entire country.

Reb Meir Bear
by David Einhorn

A stranger wandered into town leading a huge brown bear. The beast had an iron ring through his nose with a heavy chain attached to it. Every afternoon the stranger led the bear into the market place. Playing upon a flute, he put the animal through his tricks. The bear danced, stood up on his hind legs, waved his forelegs, begged money from passersby, and performed other antics for the amusement of the towns-people.

It was on a Friday afternoon when the bear, apparently hungry, refused to dance. The stranger beat him mercilessly but the bear did not budge. Among the townspeople who stood by watching was Rabbi Meir, the richest merchant in town, known for his piety, generosity and good deeds.

"Why do you beat this poor hungry animal?" he asked angrily.

"If you don't like it, you can buy the bear and feed him milk and honey," the stranger sneered.

"How much will you take for him?" asked Reb Meir.

"Twenty gold pieces," the stranger snapped, never thinking that the Jewish merchant would pay that sum.

"I will pay your price," the merchant replied.

Digging into his pocket, Reb Meir counted out twenty gold pieces, took hold of the chain and led the bear to his house.

"I have brought a guest for the Sabbath," Reb Meir told his astonished family, as he brought the bear into the courtyard.

A Shabbat Bummer

You've learned a new Shabbat song and your Dad doesn't know the tune, but he sings along anyway.

A Shabbat Bummer

Waking up in the middle of the rabbi's speech and he's looking right at you.

He tied the bear by the chain, went into the house to change his clothes and went off to attend the services at the synagogue. When he returned, he led the bear into the house, recited the Kiddush, washed his hands, pronounced the blessing over the halla, cut it into pieces and, as was his custom, distributed the pieces to all of the members of the family. The bear, too, was handed a large piece.

Thus it went for the entire Sabbath. The bear ate at Reb Meir's table, was treated like a member of the family, and in the evening, at the end of the Sabbath, the pious merchant led the bear out into the forest, removed the chain and said, "Go in peace, bear, and do no harm to good people."

Time passed and Reb Meir and his partner set out on a journey. For some strange reason, they lost their way in a forest. After wandering aimlessly for more than two days, Reb Meir suggested that since it was Friday night and the Sabbath was near, they should stop to rest. To this the partner would not agree. They decided therefore to divide their food and money. The partner took the wagon and the horse and went off, leaving Reb Meir alone in the forest.

As the sun went down Reb Meir began to recite the Friday evening prayers, welcoming Queen Sabbath. Suddenly a heavy paw descended on his shoulder. He turned and lo and behold!—there was a huge brown bear staring at him with mild, almost human eyes. Reb Meir immediately recognized his Sabbath guest of several years before.

"Good Sabbath," said Reb Meir to the bear.

The bear growled pleasantly, picked up Reb Meir's bags and carried them to a cave which was obviously his home. There Reb Meir spent the Sabbath as the guest of the bear.

On Saturday night after Reb Meir had recited the Havdalah, the bear again picked up Reb Meir's bags and led him out of the forest. As dawn rose they reached the edge of the woods. A strange sight met Reb Meir's eyes. He saw his partner tied to a tree. Near him a band of robbers was dividing his goods. Before Reb Meir had time to cry out, the bear swept down on the robbers, killing some and frightening away the others. Reb Meir untied his partner and within a few days they reached home safely.

From that day on, Reb Meir was known as Reb Meir Bear, and that name has remained with the family ever since.

K'tonton, the tiny hero of this story, is a Jewish boy no taller than your middle finger. Stories of his adventures have delighted children since their first appearance in print in 1930.

K'tonton Takes a Ride on a Chopping Knife
by Sadie Rose Weilerstein

It was Friday and K'tonton sat cross-legged on the kitchen table, watching his mother chop the fish for the Sabbath. Up and down, up and down went the chopping knife in the wooden bowl, chip, chop, chip, chop!

Now if there was one thing K'tonton loved it was a ride.

"If I could just reach that chopping knife," he thought, "I could sit down in the center of it with a leg on each side. It would be like riding horseback."

"Tap! Tap!" came a sound at the door. K'tonton's mother put down the knife. "Sit still until I get back, K'tonton. Don't get into mischief," she called as she went off to see who was knocking.

But K'tonton was too busy looking about him to hear her. How could he reach the top of that chopping bowl? Ah, there was a bag of sugar tied with a string! In a moment K'tonton had taken hold of the string and was climbing up, up to the very top. Then he sprang lightly to the wooden bowl, slid down the inner side and landed right in the center of the chopping knife. Just as he seated himself astride the blade, his mother returned. A neighbor's wife was with her. They were so busy talking that K'tonton's mother picked up the knife and began chopping away without even noticing that her little son was on it.

Up and down, up and down went the chopping knife, chip, chop, chip, chop! Up and down went K'tonton, holding fast to the blade.

"Gee-ap!" he shouted. "Gee-ap!" But the chop-chop of the knife was so loud, his mother didn't hear him.

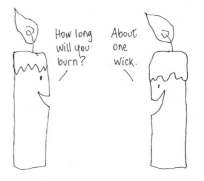

How long will you burn?

About one wick.

"This is a good ride! This is a jolly ride," thought K'tonton, bouncing up and down. "Why didn't I think of it before?" Suddenly, down on his head came a shower of pepper.

"Ketchoo!" sneezed K'tonton. "Ketchoo!"

Up to his nose went his hands and down into the bowl of fish went K'tonton. Ugh, how sticky it was! But the stickiness was the least of his troubles. Up and down, up and down the knife was going; and up and down and in and out jumped K'tonton, dodging the sharp blade.

"Help! Help!" he called, but his mother was still talking to the neighbor and didn't hear him.

"This is the end of me," thought K'tonton. "I know that Jonah was saved from the inside of a fish, but I never heard of anyone being saved from a bowl of chopped fish."

He was all covered with fish by this time. His legs were so tired he could hardly jump any more.

"I'd better say my *Shema*," said K'tonton.

But at that moment the chopping knife was lifted out of the bowl and K'tonton's mother was looking down into it.

"Ugh! There's a fly in the fish."

Down into the bowl went her spoon and up came K'tonton! Such a sputtering, struggling, sorry looking K'tonton!

"K'tonton!" cried his mother, "what have you been doing to yourself?"

"Taking a ride, Mother, a ride on the chopping knife."

"A ride? A ride on the chopping knife? God be thanked who preserves the simple!"

Then she picked K'tonton up in her two fingers, and held him under the faucet until there wasn't a bit of sticky fish left.

You may be sure K'tonton never rode on a chopping knife again.

Sabbath Candles

One by one in the windows
Facing our little yard,
The Sabbath candles are
    lighted,
And the evening gloom is starred.

And they shine in the deepening
    darkness,
Bright and holy and fair,
Like angels of faith and courage
In a world of war and despair.

Alter Brody

Shabbat

A Taste of Heaven

Shalom Aleikhem

Liturgy
S.E. Goldfarb

Moderately

Peace be upon you, angels of the Exalted One,
from the King of Kings, the Holy One blessed be He.
May your coming be for the sake of peace. Bless
me for peace; and may your departure as well be
with peace.

שָׁלוֹם עֲלֵיכֶם מַלְאֲכֵי הַשָּׁרֵת מַלְאֲכֵי עֶלְיוֹן

מִמֶּלֶךְ מַלְכֵי הַמְּלָכִים הַקָּדוֹשׁ בָּרוּךְ הוּא.

בּוֹאֲכֶם לְשָׁלוֹם מַלְאֲכֵי הַשָּׁלוֹם מַלְאֲכֵי עֶלְיוֹן

מִמֶּלֶךְ מַלְכֵי הַמְּלָכִים הַקָּדוֹשׁ בָּרוּךְ הוּא.

בָּרְכוּנִי לְשָׁלוֹם...

צֵאתְכֶם לְשָׁלוֹם...

Shabat Shalom

S. Secunda

Bim bam bim bim bim bam bim bim bim bim bim bam

Sha-bat sha-lom Sha-bat sha-lom sha-bat sha-bat sha-bat sha-bat sha-lom

sha-bat sha-bat sha-bat sha-bat sha-lom sha-bat sha-bat sha-bat sha-bat sha-lom

sha-bat sha-lom sha-bat sha-lom sha-bat sha-bat sha-bat sha-bat sha-lom

A peaceful Sabbath.

שַׁבָּת שָׁלוֹם

Tzur Mishelo

Moderato

Tzur mi - she - lo_____ a - khal - nu ba -
r' - khu e - mu - nai sa - va - nu v' - ho -
tar - nu kid - var A - do - nai_____ sa -
va - nu v' - ho - tar - nu kid - var A - do - nai

Let us bless the Lord whose food we ate.
Let us thank him with our lips chanting;
There is no one holy like our Lord.

צוּר מִשֶּׁלּוֹ אָכַלְנוּ בָּרְכוּ אֱמוּנַי
שָׂבַעְנוּ וְהוֹתַרְנוּ כִּדְבַר יְיָ

Shabbat Crafts

Pushke (charity box)

One of the best ways to experience the joy of Shabbat is to make something to help celebrate the holiday. Not only will you have the satisfaction of your work, but you'll also be a partner in making the day more beautiful.

A *pushke* is a container for *tzedakah,* giving to those in need. Before Shabbat can begin, we should remember the poor and provide for them. A *pushke* can be made from anything, but metal containers seem to be traditional. Perhaps it's due to the pleasing jingle the coins make when they fall into the can.

Every Friday, before shabbat, add a coin or two to the box. It can be either the family *pushke* or yours alone. When it's full, you can take it to a synagogue, where the money will be given to needy people.

This *pushke* requires the use of a hammer and a screwdriver, so be sure to ask a parent or another adult to help you.

MATERIALS

newspapers
1 metal Band-Aid container
permanent-ink marker pen
safety glasses or goggles
screwdriver
hammer
1 piece of fine sandpaper
1 can of gold spray paint
blue self-adhesive paper (such as Contact paper)
scissors

1. Cover your work area with newspapers.

2. Draw a line 1-1/2 inches long across the top (the lid) of the container with the marking pen.

3. Brace the container between two heavy objects so that it doesn't move when you touch it. You can use a real vise—the kind people have in their workshops—or you can create your own by placing the container on the floor and wedging it between the wall and a heavy object.

4. Put on safety glasses or goggles.

5. Position the screwdriver with the blade on the line. While moving the screwdriver from one end of the line to the other, use the hammer to tap gently on the screwdriver until it penetrates the metal. This will make the

STOP!
Some of the crafts in this chapter call for the use of a hammer, scissors, or other potentially dangerous tools. Before beginning any craft, get either help or the "go-ahead" from a responsible adult.

slot for inserting money. (It must be large enough for both coins and folded bills.)

6. Open the lid and tap gently on the hammer to flatten the inside jagged edges of the slot. If they are still rough after hammering, cover them with cloth tape.

7. Sand the outside of the container to prepare it for spray-painting.

8. Take the can outside or, if you must work inside, be sure that you're in a room with an open window. Shake the can of spray paint for at least a minute, and spray the container from at least 12 inches away.

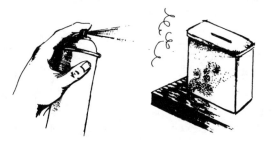

9. While the container dries, prepare designs for the *pushke* with the adhesive paper. Write PUSHKE on it, or *tzedakah* in Hebrew:

צדקה

Make a few circles traced from coins, or create any Shabbat design you like. Draw the designs and write the letters on the nonsticky side of the adhesive paper. Then cut them out, peel off the paper, and stick them on the coin box.

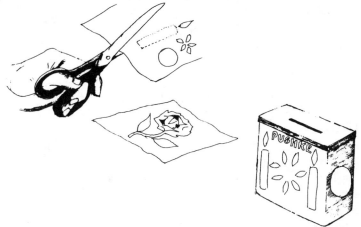

Candlesticks

Here is a simple way to make candlesticks that will last for years. These directions call for four flat stones, but you can also use unpainted seashells instead. You won't need to paint the seashells because their lovely natural color will be enough.

MATERIALS

newspapers
4 flat stones
2 screw-on bottle caps
white or epoxy glue
1 can of spray paint in any color

1. Place old newspapers on your work surface.

2. Find 4 flat stones that can be easily stacked on top of one another. Figure out which 2 will look best together.

3. Place 1 bottle cap on top of 1 pair of stones and place the other bottle cap on top of the other pair of stones.

 4. Glue them in place with white or epoxy glue. Be sure to use an epoxy glue if you want to wash the melted wax off the candlesticks later without having them come apart.

5. Let the glue dry for an hour.

6. After the glue is dry, hold the spray can of paint 12 inches away, and spray the candlesticks with a metallic color or any color that appeals to you. If you have paint left over from the *pushke,* you can use that.

Besamin Box

Many besamin boxes take the form of little houses or castles.

MATERIALS

2 empty raisin boxes
3 different colors of self-adhesive paper
a manila folder or construction paper the size of a manila folder
white glue
scissors
straight pin

1. Glue the boxes together, back to back.

2. Cover all 4 sides, but not the bottom or top, with adhesive paper.

3. With the scissors, cut out windows and a door from the adhesive paper and stick them onto the sides. You can make your little house a cottage or an apartment building, depending upon how many and what size windows you choose.

4. Make the pieces for the roof by cutting out the 4 triangles from the manila folder or construction paper. Measure the base of the triangles to fit the long sides of the roof before you start cutting. Then fit the 4 triangles together to form a pyramid which will be the roof.

5. Tape the 4 pieces together to make a roof.

6. Tape the roof to the house, and cover with the last color of adhesive paper.

7. Punch at least 20 holes in the house with a straight pin.

8. Open the flaps on the bottom to insert sweet spices, such as whole cloves and pieces of cinnamon bark.

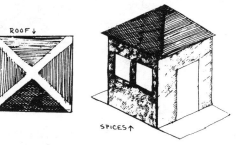

Shabbat Recipes

Chicken Soup (Eastern Europe)

This is a great dish to make ahead because chicken soup tastes even better the day after it was made.

8 cups of water
1 chicken (about 3 pounds) in parts
2 carrots
1 onion
4 celery tops with leaves
1 bay leaf
2 teaspoons salt
1 teaspoon pepper

GRANDMA'S HOUSE

Put the 8 cups of water in a large cooking pot.

Add the chicken to the pot of water.

Peel the vegetables, and add them to the soup.

Put the pot on the stove and turn on the burner. Bring the soup to a boil. Once the soup is boiling, lower the heat of the burner, cover the pot, and simmer the soup for 1-1/2 hours until the chicken is tender.

When the chicken is tender, remove the chicken and vegetables from the soup and put them on a plate or cutting board. Save the chicken pieces for chicken salad.

Pour the soup through a strainer into another large pot or jar.

Cut the carrots into pieces and return them to the soup.

Refrigerate for several hours.

Remove the layer of fat on top of the refrigerated soup.

Reheat the soup before serving it.

Serves 10–12

WHY WAS THERE A PUDDLE ON THE KITCHEN FLOOR?

THERE WAS A LEEK IN THE CHICKEN SOUP.

Sopa de Avas (Greece)
Bean Soup

In Kastoria and Salonika, beans were generally served on Friday night. A favorite in many homes, it was a convenient dish to serve again on the following day (Shabbat) when no cooking was done. In those distant times and places, beans in one form or another became the entrée. Here in America, they are still served as a one-dish meal, but more often as a soup course or an accompaniment.

1 pound onions
2–3 tablespoons oil
4 quarts water
1 can Italian tomato paste
1 pound Great Northern beans (unsoaked)
1/2 cup parsley, chopped
1 clove garlic (optional)

2 tablespoons sugar
salt and pepper to taste
1-1/2 pounds stewing beef (optional)

Slice the onions and sauté them in oil in a saucepan. When the onions are slightly brown, transfer them to a large pot and add water and tomato paste.

Bring the mixture to a boil and then add beans that have been rinsed in cold water, parsley, and garlic.

Bring the soup to boil again and then turn down the heat to let the soup simmer for 2-1/2 to 3 hours. When the beans are almost done, add sugar, salt and pepper to taste. Add more water if necessary.

This recipe can be made with 1-1/2 pounds of chuck or stewing beef, cut in large pieces and browned with the onions.

Serves 8–10

This nutritious dish tastes great on a hot summer day.

Tabooli (Egypt)
Cracked Wheat Salad

1/2 cup cracked wheat or bulgur
3/4 cup water
1/2 cup minced parsley
1/4 cup minced mint leaves
1/4 cup finely chopped green onion
1 diced tomato
3 tablespoons olive oil
1–2 tablespoons lemon juice or to taste
1 teaspoon salt
pepper and allspice to taste
lettuce leaves and sliced tomatoes for the garnish

Soak the cracked wheat in water in a bowl for 4 hours or until the water is absorbed and the wheat is tender.

Add parsley, mint, onion, and diced tomato to the wheat. Mix these ingredients by tossing them with a salad fork and spoon.

In a separate bowl, combine oil, lemon juice, salt, pepper, and allspice to taste. Add this to the wheat mixture and refrigerate it until it has been chilled.

Serve on lettuce and garnish with sliced tomatoes.

Serves 4–6

Ḥallah

According to Jewish law, if a large amount of dough is made (approximately 3-1/2 pounds or more), then a piece the size of an olive is separated and burnt in the oven while the ḥallah is baking. Before the separation a special blessing is recited.

1 package (1/4 ounce) active dry yeast
1 cup warm water
1/4 cup sugar
1 teaspoon salt
2 tablespoons softened margarine
1 egg, beaten
3-1/4 to 3-1/2 cups flour
1/3 cup raisins (optional)
1 egg yolk
poppy or sesame seeds

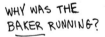

HOW DO YOU MAKE A ḤALLAH ROLL?

PUSH IT DOWN A HILL.

In a mixing bowl, dissolve the yeast in the warm water.

Stir in the sugar, salt, margarine, egg, and 2 cups of flour. Beat with a wooden spoon or by hand until smooth.

Add the raisins to the dough.

With spoon or by hand, work in the remaining flour until the dough is easy to handle and is not sticky. Knead the dough for 5 minutes.

Grease a bowl and place the dough in it. Turn the dough over so that the greased part of the dough is on top to prevent it from drying. Cover tightly with foil and refrigerate overnight, or up to 5 days.

Divide the dough in half. Then divide each half into 3 pieces.

On a floured board, use your hands to roll each piece of dough into a strand, tapering the ends. Braid three strands together, pinching the ends to hold them together. Lay the braided ḥallah on a greased pan.

Braid the other three strands together, pinching the ends to hold them together. Place the second braided ḥallah on a greased pan.

Cover the shaped ḥallah with a clean towel and allow it to rise in a warm place for 2 hours or until double in bulk.

Preheat the oven to 375 degrees.

Beat the egg yolk with a teaspoon of water. Brush the tops of each ḥallah with the egg yolk mixture, and sprinkle with poppy or sesame seeds.

Bake for 25 to 30 minutes or until the ḥallah sounds hollow when tapped on the bottom. Remove from oven and allow to cool away from drafts.

The ḥallah dough can be used to make rolls of any shape desired.

2 medium ḥallah loaves

WHY WAS THE BAKER RUNNING?

THE ḤALLAH RECIPE SAID "TAKE ONE EGG AND BEAT IT!"

Roast Chicken

This chicken dish is easy to make and tastes good with many different vegetables. After the chicken has been roasting an hour, put some whole potatoes in the oven to bake. Remember to poke holes in the potatoes to let the steam escape as they cook.

4-pound roasting chicken
salt to taste
1/2 teaspoon pepper
1 teaspoon paprika
1/2 teaspoon garlic powder
1/2 teaspoon onion powder
1/2 teaspoon thyme
1/2 teaspoon powdered ginger

Preheat the oven to 325 degrees.

Clean and tie together the legs of the chicken. Salt and pepper it well, and sprinkle with the paprika, garlic powder, onion powder, thyme, and powdered ginger.

Lay the chicken in a roaster or pot that is not too large (chicken or any meat will dry out if the utensil used is too large).

Roast the chicken in the oven for about 2 hours, depending on the tenderness of the chicken, or until nicely browned and tender.

6 servings

WHY IS MAX
FLYING SO LOW?

HE ATE
CHOLENT.

Cholent

Cholent gets its rich flavor from simmering overnight.

a few beef bones (about 1 pound)
2 large onions
12 medium potatoes
1 pound large lima beans
2 bay leaves
1/2 teaspoon peppercorns
2 garlic cloves
1/2 tablespoon paprika
salt and pepper to taste
1/2 pound large pearl barley

A Shabbat Bummer

Cold cholent.

1 medium onion
3 tablespoons margarine or chicken fat
3 pounds flank (flanken) meat
3 pounds brisket

Slice the onions and place them with the bones in a very large roaster.

Peel the potatoes and wash the lima beans. At one end of the roaster put the potatoes, and at the other end, the beans. Scatter the spices all around; salt and pepper the potatoes and beans.

Wash the barley and chop the onion. Take a piece of foil, and on it put the barley, onion, salt and pepper, and margarine or chicken fat.

Loosely close all sides of the foil like an envelope, leaving enough room for expansion. Place the foil envelope in the middle of the roaster on top of the bones and onions. Lay the flanken and brisket over the beans and potatoes. Salt and pepper the meat.

Put enough water in the roaster to cover the meat, but not so much water that the cholent boils over while cooking.

Cover the roaster with foil, securing it all around the pot, and then put on the cover of the roaster.

A few hours before the Sabbath, place the cholent in an oven set at 200 degrees. Bake overnight until lunchtime.

Before serving, remove the foil, and skim off the fat that has accumulated on top.

12 servings

Shabbat Fun

Shabbat Puzzles *(Answers on page 270.)*

Six people meet on Shabbat and each shakes hands with each of the others and says "Shabbat Shalom." How many hand shakes and how many "Shabbat Shaloms" are said?

Shabbat Shalom

Which Shabbat candle burns brightest?

Candle Puzzle

On Friday afternoon, just before Shabbat, someone rides from his home to his local synagogue at a rate of 15 miles an hour. After services he walks home at the rate of 3 miles per hour. He spends 18 minutes traveling to and from the synagogue. How far from the synagogue does he live?

How Far?

Two Shabbat candles are the same size and are lit at the same time, yet one burns for 1 hour and 15 minutes and the other only burns 75 minutes. Can you explain why?

Two Shabbat Candles

1. What's brown, yellow, and jumpy?

Ḥallah Riddles

2. Why would anyone baking a ḥallah mix shoe polish with the yeast?

3. Which is the left side of a ḥallah ?

4. What's the best thing you could put into a ḥallah?

5. Which of our fifty states is filled with white bread and bathing suits?

Rosh Hashanah

"May It Be a Sweet New Year"

About Rosh Hashanah

"Leshanah tovah tikatavu: *May you be inscribed for a good new year*" is the traditional Jewish New Year greeting. We like to wish all our family and friends the best in the year ahead.

Rosh Hashanah, the Jewish New Year, is a fall holiday, celebrated on the first and second days of the Hebrew month of Tishre (September/October). Many Reform congregations celebrate only one day of Rosh Hashanah.

According to tradition, many important events happened on Rosh Hashanah: The six days of creation were completed; Abraham and Jacob were born; Sarah, Rachel, and Hannah, after years of wanting and praying for children, conceived Isaac, Joseph, and Samuel; and Joseph was freed from prison.

If you play with the letters of the first word of the Torah, Bereshit, which means beginning, you can form א׳בתשרי, which means the first of Tishre, the day of the world's beginning.

Rosh Hashanah is also called Yom Ha-Din, *the Day of Judgment.* It's the day people are judged by God, and their fate for the coming year is decided.

In synagogues, during morning prayers, a shofar is sounded one hundred times (except when Rosh Hashanah falls on Shabbat). The sounds are a wake-up call to repentance. Most often the shofar is made from a ram's horn, a reminder of the time Abraham took his son Isaac to be sacrificed, but used a ram instead. The traditional Yemenite shofar is made from an antelope's horn.

On the afternoon of the first day of Rosh Hashanah, a prayer of forgiveness, Tashlikh, is said near a body of water. Following the prayer it is customary to throw bread crumbs into the water, where they are swallowed up in the hope that like the bread, our sins will be swallowed up, too. If the first day of Rosh Hashanah is Shabbat, Tashlikh is said the next day.

On the second night of Rosh Hashanah it is a custom to eat a new fruit, one not yet eaten that season, so that when the blessing—she-heḥeyanu—is said, it can apply to the fruit as well as to the holiday.

On Rosh Hashanah many Jews dip ḥallah and apple in honey and

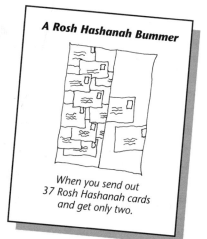

A Rosh Hashanah Bummer

When you send out 37 Rosh Hashanah cards and get only two.

ask God to grant us a sweet new year. Some dip the ḥallah in sugar and eat only sweet foods at the Rosh Hashanah meals.

Rosh Hashanah ḥallahs are not the usual rectangular or oval shape. They're round, the shape of a crown, because on Rosh Hashanah we remember that God is our King.

Rosh Hashanah is a good time to look back at the past year and ahead to the year that's just beginning.

Leshanah tova tikatavu—May you be inscribed for a good year.

The Rabbi of Nemirov
by I. L. Peretz

The week before Rosh Hashanah. Pious Jews rise at dawn and hurry to the synagogue to chant the Selichoth. The air is filled with mystery and the hearts of men with fear and hope. The Days of Judgment are near. And now the Almighty is reviewing the decisions He is about to hand down—and these decisions, affecting all of mankind, will be final.

In the crowded synagogues, men and women pour out their hearts in prayer. Through the beautiful words of the Selichoth they plead with the Master of the Universe for forgiveness, for relief from suffering. The Lord is just, they know, and merciful.

Yes, the Days of the Selichoth, are filled with mystery for all Jews but to the Jews of Nemirov in old Russia they bring still an added sense of awe. For it is during these mornings of the Selichoth that the Tsadik of Nemirov, that pious, saintly and learned Rabbi, disappears without a trace—as if he had never existed.

During that week members of his family rise, like everyone else, while it is still dark and hasten to the synagogue. The door of the house is left open. The Rabbi too would soon follow, they think. But no one ever sees the Rabbi, not in the street, not in the synagogue, not in the house of study, not anywhere.

Where is the Rabbi?

No one knows. But there are opinions. And in time these opinions are accepted as fact. The Rabbi goes straight up to Heaven, say the Jews of Nemirov. He goes up personally to tell the Lord Almighty of the needs of the Jews of Nemirov. This is the way, they feel, their Rabbi looks after his Jews. Not only does he plead for them, but in special cases he argues—and wins.

Year after year, the Jews of Nemirov tell each other the same story. It gives them a special confidence, a special faith in their future.

One day a stranger came to town, a Jew from Lithuania, and like most Jews of that country, he was a fine scholar, a master of the Talmud, but no believer in miracles.

And when this Lithuanian heard the stories about the Rabbi's trips to Heaven, he laughed. No living man ever went to Heaven and returned, said he. Not even Moses. To prove it, he quoted passages from the Talmud, and to clinch the argument, he declared that what Moses himself could not do the Rabbi of Nemirov would surely be unable to do.

The Lithuanian did not believe in miracles. Still the Rabbi must go somewhere when he disappeared. He made up his mind to find out.

That very day, before dark, the Lithuanian stole into the Rabbi's house, entered his bed chamber. There he spent the night, under the bed, while the Rabbi was in the bed. The Rabbi slept restlessly, frequently groaning as if in pity for the sufferings of his Jews. His uninvited visitor was silently repeating from memory page after page of the Talmud to keep himself awake.

Just before dawn the household began to stir. The Lithuanian heard the members of the Rabbi's family move about and leave the house one by one. In a few moments there was silence again.

Soon the Rabbi too rose from his bed. He washed his hands and opening a closet began to dress. Watching from under the bed, the Lithuanian's eyes grew wide with surprise. The Rabbi was putting on strange clothes indeed.

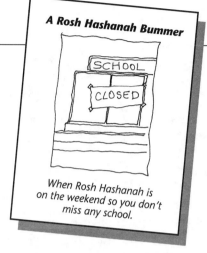

A Rosh Hashanah Bummer

SCHOOL
CLOSED

When Rosh Hashanah is on the weekend so you don't miss any school.

First the Rabbi put on a coarse peasant shirt, then a pair of broad peasant pants. The heavy boots he pulled on his feet reached almost to his knees. Finally, the Rabbi brought out a huge rough overcoat and a ragged fur cap. In a few moments he ceased to be the distinguished Rabbi of Nemirov and became a typical Russian peasant.

Rummaging in the closet a moment longer, the Rabbi finally brought out a large woodchopper's axe and a length of strong rope. With these in his hands, he turned and silently left the house. The Lithuanian crawled out from under the bed and followed.

They walked and walked—the Rabbi first and the Lithuanian following. Finally leaving the town behind, they reached the woods, which the Rabbi, without hesitation, entered. He took off his coat, picked up his axe and set to work to chop down one of the smaller trees.

One, two, three, four, five. The Rabbi chopped away at the tree until, with a crash, it fell to the ground. He then set to work to strip off the branches, cut the tree into logs and the logs into fire wood. With the rope he had brought he made a bundle of the wood, loaded it on his shoulder and set out to return to town. The Lithuanian still followed. Again that long tramp down the road and through the crooked streets of Nemirov. Suddenly, before a dilapidated shack, the Rabbi stopped. He knocked on a window and the Lithuanian heard a voice, that of a sickly old woman, calling out from inside, Who's there?

Vassil, the Rabbi answered in a rough peasant voice.

Vassil? Which Vassil? What do you want?

The Rabbi replied, still in that rough peasant voice, that he had a bundle of wood to sell cheap. And without waiting for an answer, he stepped over to the door and went inside.

The Lithuanian stole up to the window and looked in. By the bright light of the moon, he saw a small room and an old woman lying upon a rickety old bed.

Hoppy New Year

Rosh Hashanah

"May It Be a Sweet New Year"

ON ROSH HASHANAH, WHAT'S THE BUSIEST LETTER IN THE ALPHABET?

THE BEE. IT'S THE BUZZIEST, TOO!

The woman was speaking, How can I buy your wood, Vassil? I haven't any money.

The Rabbi told her that he was willing to trust her. The price was only six kopeks and he could wait for his money. But the old woman kept insisting that she could never pay.

She had no hope that she would ever have any money. It was then that the Rabbi in his peasant clothes laid his bundle down on the floor and raising himself to his full height spoke angrily, Oh, you silly old woman, here you are sick, miserable, and cold. I am willing to trust you. And you, a Jewish woman with a great God who watches over you—you refuse to trust Him or to believe that He will enable you to pay back a few pennies?

But who will make a fire in my oven? the old woman asked. I don't know when anybody will come to take care of me.

The Rabbi told her that he would light the fire for her and set to work.

As he put the first few pieces of wood into the stove, the Rabbi began to hum the first verse of the Selichoth. As he lit the fire, he hummed the second verse. After the fire was under way and the Rabbi of Nemirov was closing the door of the stove, he finished the last verse of the Selichoth. The Lithuanian, clinging to the outside of the window with frozen fingers, let out his breath with a fervent Amen.

The Lithuanian never laughs these days when he hears the Jews of Nemirov tell each other how their Rabbi goes up to Heaven during the days of Selichoth. Instead, muttering under his breath, he is apt to say, Heaven, who knows? Maybe even higher.

The Shofar Call

Within the synagogue the light is dim;
The air is hushed around;
Even the silence seems to pray until
We hear the shofar sound.
O Shofar, tell our souls we need not fear,
Though long and hard the way;
O Shofar, bind us with thy sacred strain,
Till each young heart will echo Israel's
    pain,
And, like a trumpet clear,
Sound to the world the vow we pledge
    anew—
To bear all-worthily the name of Jew,
Throughout the coming year!

E. C. Ehrlich

Amein Sheim Nora

May the almighty God bless His people this day and let us all say Amen.

אָמֵן שֵׁם נוֹרָא
אֵל אַדִּיר נוֹרָא וְאָיֹם
לְעַמְּךָ תְּנָה פִדְיוֹן
וִיבָרֵךְ אֶתְכֶם הַיּוֹם
וְאָמַר כָּל הָעָם אָמֵן

Avinu Malkeinu

Andante religioso

Liturgy
Folktune

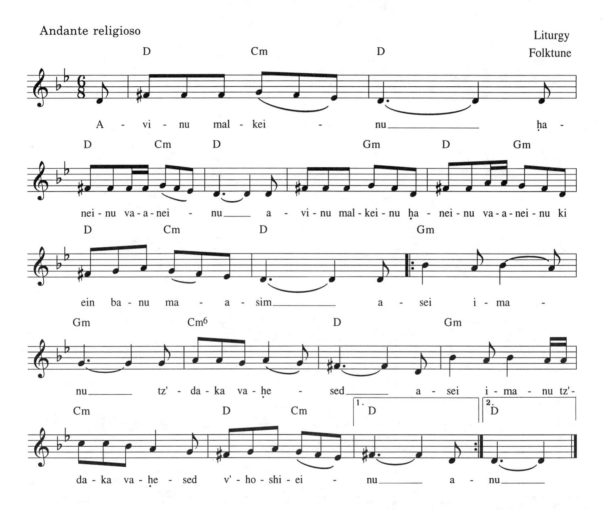

Our Father, our King, be gracious unto us and answer us, for we are unworthy; deal with us in charity and lovingkindness and save us.

אָבִינוּ מַלְכֵּנוּ חָנֵּנוּ וַעֲנֵנוּ
כִּי אֵין בָּנוּ מַעֲשִׂים
עֲשֵׂה עִמָּנוּ צְדָקָה וָחֶסֶד
וְהוֹשִׁיעֵנוּ

Just as clocks mark the minutes and hours of the day, calendars mark the days and months of the year. Every new year, the old calendar—filled with important days from the previous year—comes down from the wall. A fresh new one, waiting for its own special days to be marked, replaces it. Making a calendar can be the first new thing you do for the new year. You can make it special by designing something fancy for your own important days, such as your birthday and favorite holidays.

Your calendar should be two calendars in one—a Jewish and a general calendar. This is less complicated than it sounds. First, find a Jewish calendar for the coming year. Some banks and kosher butchers give them away for free. The Jewish calendar looks like an ordinary calendar except for two things. It begins in September instead of January, and it gives two dates for each day: the general date and the date according to Jewish tradition. Use this calendar as a guide for your own calendar.

MATERIALS

1 piece of blank 8-1/2 × 11-inch paper
ruler
pencil or pen
12 sheets of construction paper at least 12 × 18 inches
white glue
paper punch
1 piece of yarn 12 inches long

Rosh Hashanah Crafts

Rosh Hashanah Calendar

STOP!
Some of the crafts in this chapter call for the use of a hammer, scissors, or other potentially dangerous tools. Before beginning any craft, get either help or the "go-ahead" from a responsible adult.

1. Take a piece of blank paper—typing paper is good for this—and, holding it horizontally, draw a line across the page two inches from the top.

2. Draw 4 more lines, 1-1/2 inches apart, underneath. Then draw 6 vertical lines, 1-1/2 inches apart, as shown in the drawing, to make 35 squares—7 across and 5 down.

3. Take this page to a copying machine—most libraries and post offices have one—and make 11 copies.

4. Beginning with September, copy the dates from each month of the Jewish calendar onto your copies. Write the name of each month at the top of the page and be sure that you mark the first day of the month in the right square.

Rosh Hashanah

"May It Be a Sweet New Year"

5. Then paste each page of the calendar onto a separate piece of construction paper.

6. Decorate the top half of each page with pictures of things that remind you of the month. You may want to leave extra space for adding things later during the month itself. Here are some picture ideas for each month.

September: a shofar for Rosh Hashanah and Yom Kippur.

October: *sukkah,* pumpkins, and gourds for Sukkot.

November: turkeys and Indian corn for Thanksgiving; books for Jewish Book Month.

December: a *ḥanukkiyyah* and a *dreidel* for Ḥanukkah.

January: a snowman or a ski scene.

February: a bare tree for the New Year of the Trees, Tu B'Shevat.

March: *grager* (noisemaker) and pictures of Queen Esther or Haman for Purim.

April: Elijah's cup, matzah for Pesaḥ (Passover); flowers for spring.

May: a flag of Israel for Yom ha-Azma'ut, Israeli Independence Day.

June: a tablet of the Ten Commandments for Shavuot, the festival which celebrates Moses' receiving the Law, and fruit, since it's also a harvest festival.

July: an American flag for the Fourth of July.

August: a tent for camping; a sailboat on a lake.

You might also include photographs of friends or relatives in their birthday months, or pictures of your favorite rock group or sports team in the months they'll be on television or in your city.

7. Punch two holes 5 inches apart on the top of all the pages and put a piece of yarn, 12 inches long, through the holes. Tie the yarn, and hang the calendar on a nail.

A Rosh Hashanah Bummer

When you mail a bunch of Rosh Hashanah cards and you forget who you mailed them to.

New Year Cards

New Year cards are fun to make, and they help you keep in touch with friends and family who live far away. Pressed flowers can be glued to the surface to make a beautiful and unusual card. Flat flowers such as pansies, honeysuckle, or even dandelions are the easiest to use. Most of these flowers will still be blooming in late August, which is when you should start making the cards.

MATERIALS

square piece of paper
flowers and leaves
waxed paper
2 or 3 heavy books
watercolor paint brush
white glue

1. Make an envelope by folding a square piece of paper along the dotted lines as shown in the drawing.

2. Lay the flowers, along with a few leaves from the plant, between waxed paper and put them in a heavy book, such as a telephone directory. Place several heavy books on top and leave them like this for two weeks.

3. Gently remove the flowers from the book. They should be flat and dry, and their colors should still be vivid.

4. With a watercolor brush, paint the backs of the flowers with white glue. Then center the flowers on the front of the card and press lightly. After the glue is dry—in a couple of hours—open the card and write in Hebrew, *Leshanah Tovah*

לְשָׁנָה טוֹבָה

or in English, May you have a good and sweet year.

WHY DID REB SHLOMO BLOW HIS SHOFAR ALONE?

HE WAS A PRIVATE TUTOR.

Rosh Hashanah Recipes

Halva (Greece)
Farina Cake

Bring in a sweet new year with halva sweetened with honey syrup. You can substitute 1 cup of walnuts for the almonds.

CAKE

1/4 pound margarine
1/2 cup sugar
3 eggs
1 cup farina or semolina
1 teaspoon baking powder
1 cup almonds
1/4 cup pine nuts
1/2 teaspoon cinnamon
1 tablespoon vanilla extract

SYRUP

3/4 cup sugar
3/4 cup water
1 stick cinnamon
4 cloves
1/4 cup honey
1 tablespoon vanilla extract

Preheat the oven to 375 degrees.

Cream the margarine and the sugar.

Separate an egg, putting the egg white in one bowl and the yolk in the bowl with the margarine and sugar. Separate the remaining eggs, one at a time. Put the egg whites in the bowl with the first egg white and put the egg yolks, one at a time, into the margarine and sugar mix. When all the egg yolks are in the bowl, beat the mixture until it is fluffy.

In a separate bowl, mix the semolina or farina with the baking powder.

Ask an adult to grind the almonds in a blender or food processor and add them to the semolina or farina.

Add the pine nuts and the cinnamon and stir.

Stir the semolina or farina mixture into the margarine mixture. Add the vanilla extract.

Beat the egg whites and fold them into the batter.

Pour the batter into a well-greased 9 × 9-inch pan. Bake for 30 minutes.

While the cake is baking, make the syrup. Put the sugar, water, cinnamon, and cloves in a saucepan and cook it on medium heat for 15 minutes.

Add the honey. Remove the cinnamon stick and the cloves.

Add the vanilla extract.

Remove the saucepan from the stove and let the syrup cool. Pour it over the cooled cake.

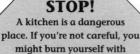

STOP!

A kitchen is a dangerous place. If you're not careful, you might burn yourself with splattering oil or boiling water. The recipes in this chapter are intended for older children. Before beginning, make sure an adult is available to help.

STOP

20 small pieces

Carrot Tzimmes
(Eastern Europe)

When eating carrot tzimmes on Rosh Hashanah, the Ashkenazi traditionally say "May it be Thy will that our merits will be increased." They slice the carrots into circles to represent coins in the hope of a prosperous new year.

1 pound carrots
1/4 cup margarine
1/2 cup brown sugar
salt to taste
1 teaspoon powdered ginger
orange juice

Scrape the carrots, and slice into rounds. Place the carrots in a pot with the margarine, brown sugar, salt, and ginger.

Add orange juice to cover the mixture, and bring to a boil. Lower the heat, and continue to cook until the carrots are soft and glazed.

4 servings

Honey Cake
(Eastern Europe)

Sweet cakes have a long history. The custom of eating sweet cakes on Rosh Hashanah can be traced all the way back to King David!

4 cups flour
1 teaspoon baking soda
2-1/2 teaspoons baking powder
1 teaspoon cinnamon
1/2 teaspoon powdered ginger
1/2 teaspoon allspice
1/2 teaspoon nutmeg
1-1/2 cups sugar
2 tablespoons brown sugar
1/2 cup margarine
4 eggs
1 pound honey
3/4 cup strong coffee

Preheat oven to 350 degrees.

Sift the flour together with the baking soda, baking powder, and the spices.

Cream the sugars with the margarine until fluffy. Add the eggs, one at a time, mixing well. Add the honey.

Stir the flour and spices together with the coffee into the sugar, margarine, and honey mixture. Mix well.

Pour the batter into a greased and floured 9 × 12-inch pan.

Bake the cake for 15 minutes. Reduce the oven to 325 degrees, and continue to bake the cake for 45 minutes longer or until golden brown.

Raisin Cake

Another sweet cake variation involves raisins, which were popular in biblical times. You can substitute 1 cup of dates or figs for the raisins if your taste buds would like a change.

1 cup raisins
1 cup water
1 cup brown sugar
1/2 cup margarine
2 cups flour
2 teaspoons baking powder
1/2 teaspoon baking soda
1 teaspoon cinnamon
1 egg
1 lemon
confectioners' sugar

Preheat the oven to 350 degrees.

Put the raisins, water, brown sugar, and margarine in a saucepan, and bring to a boil. Lower the heat, and simmer for 5 minutes, then allow the raisin mixture to cool.

Sift the flour together with the baking powder, baking soda, and cinnamon. Add the dry ingredients to the cooled raisin mixture.

Beat the egg in a separate bowl, and then add the egg to the raisin mixture.

Roll the lemon back and forth on a hard surface several times. This will make the lemon juicier.

Cut the lemon in half and squeeze the lemon over the raisin mixture or ask your parents to help you extract the juice with a juicer. Either way, be sure to pour the lemon juice over the raisin mixture.

Peel the lemon and use a grater to grate the peel into small pieces. Add the grated lemon peel to the raisin mixture. Mix it well.

Pour the batter into a 9 × 9-inch greased pan. Bake for 1 hour.

Allow the cake to cool before removing it from the pan, then sift confectioners' sugar over the top of the cake.

1 cake

A Rosh Hashanah Bummer

Getting too much honey on your apple.

Rosh Hashanah Fun

Rosh Hashanah Puzzles (Answers on page 270.)

Rearrange the letters in each group, using all the letters, to form a Rosh Hashanah word or name.

Rosh Hashanah Anagrams

1. LEAP P

2. OF RASH

3. YEAR RP

4. E WEST

5. TEN ERP

Two people were walking to synagogue. One is the father of the other's son. How are the two people related?

A Relative Puzzle

Donnie bought an apple and a jar of honey for Rosh Hashanah. He paid 35¢ less for the apple than for the honey and $1.75 in all. How much did he pay for the apple? How much did he pay for the honey?

Apples and Honey

To find out what we all wish for every Rosh Hashanah add 32464 and 22714 on a calculator. Then turn the calculator upside down and read.

Rosh Hashanah Calculator Fun

To find out what we should all resolve not to do in the year ahead subtract 896 from 1213 on a calculator. Then turn the calculator upside down and read.

Yom Kippur
A Day for Fasting, Prayer, and Forgiveness

About Yom Kippur

Leshanah tovah tikatavu v'tikatemu—*May you be inscribed and sealed for a good new year.*

Yom Kippur is a solemn day for fasting, prayer, reflection, and repentance. It's observed on the tenth day of the Hebrew month of Tishre. We pray that God will forgive our sins of the past year and grant us good fortune in the year ahead.

According to the Talmud, the obligation to eat on the day before Yom Kippur is as strong as the obligation to fast on Yom Kippur. Therefore, a holiday meal is served just before the fast. Some people have the custom to eat throughout the day.

It is a custom to wear white on Yom Kippur as a sign of purity. In some congregations only the rabbi and the cantor wear white. Traditional Jews don't wear leather shoes, bathe, or put on perfumes.

In our prayers are viddui, *confessions,* of our sins.

In the afternoon services, the book of Jonah is read to remind us of how the people of Nineveh repented from their evil ways and were forgiven by God.

Neilah, *the concluding prayers of Yom Kippur, are said as the sun is setting. During* Neilah *the curtains and doors to the* Aron Kodesh—

the cabinet that holds the Torahs—are open. In some congregations, people have the custom to smell sweet spices or rose water during Neilah so that they can make the appropriate blessing. At the end of Neilah three basic statements of faith are called out: the Shema, "Hear O Israel, the Lord our God, the Lord is one;" "May God's name be blessed forever and ever;" and "The Lord is God."

Lashon hora is evil speech.

46

At the end of Yom Kippur a shofar is sounded once and we pray that in the coming year we will all be together in the rebuilt city of Jerusalem.

There is a custom to begin the building of the sukkah for the coming holiday of Sukkot after the breaking of the Yom Kippur fast.

Leshanah tovah tikatavu v'tikatemu—*May you be inscribed and sealed for a good new year.*

J onah was a reluctant prophet. He refused to obey God's command that he go to the Gentiles in the city of Nineveh and bring them God's promise of forgiveness, if they repented of their sins. Jonah did not believe them worthy of God's love, nor did he think they were capable of repenting. Hence, Jonah had to be taught the lesson of God's universal love for all mankind.

The Book of Jonah was not written by Jonah, but about him. According to tradition, its author was one of the "Men of the Great Synagogue" who lived during the days when the Jews returned from the Babylonian exile. It is understandable that, after the suffering and humiliation of the exile, many Jews became hostile to the non-Jewish world, because of their national tragedy. In their anguish they questioned whether the Gentiles were capable of receiving the lofty message

The Story of Jonah
adapted by Mortimer J. Cohen

of God's forgiveness, and perhaps even denied their worthiness to receive God's love and compassion.

This attitude, however, was itself unworthy of the true Jew. For the whole spirit of Judaism, enlarged and enriched by the prophets of Israel, was that all people are God's children, and therefore are capable of knowing God and worthy of receiving God's divine blessings. It was to teach this lesson that the Book of Jonah was written.

As Israel prayed for deliverance from the depths of the exile and was rescued, so Jonah was saved from the belly of the fish that he might continue on his mission to Nineveh.

So noble is the message of the Book of Jonah, that God is one and humankind is one, our Sages made it part of the Synagogue's service. On Yom Kippur at the afternoon service (Minḥah), Jews throughout the world read how God's love and mercy are not confined to Israel but embrace all mankind.

Jonah's Flight

The word of the Lord came to Jonah, the son of Amittai, saying:

"Arise, go to that great city, Nineveh, and proclaim against it; for their wickedness is known to me."

But Jonah started to flee to Tarshish from the presence of the Lord. He went down to Joppa and found a ship going to Tarshish; so he paid the fare and embarked on the ship to go in it to Tarshish from the presence of the Lord.

But the Lord caused a furious wind to descend upon the sea. The ship was in danger of breaking into pieces. The sailors became afraid, and each man cried for help to his own god; and they threw into the sea the wares that were in the ship, to lighten it. But Jonah had gone down into the innermost part of the ship. He lay there and was fast asleep. Then the captain of the ship came and said to him: "How is it that you are asleep? Arise and call upon your God; perhaps God will think of us, so that we may not perish."

The sailors said to one another:

"Come, let us cast lots, that we may know on whose account this evil has come upon us."

They cast lots, and the lot fell upon Jonah. Then they said to him, "Tell us, what is your occupation, and where do you come from? What is your country, and to what people do you belong?"

Jonah said, "I am a Hebrew, and a worshipper of the Lord, the God of heaven, who made the sea and the dry land."

The men were exceedingly afraid, and asked "What should we do to you, that the sea may be calm for us?" For the sea grew more and more stormy.

Jonah told them, "Take me up, and throw me into the sea, and the sea will be calm for you, for I know that on account of me this great tempest has overtaken you."

But the men rowed hard to get back to the land. They could not, however, for the sea grew more and more stormy ahead. Therefore, they cried to the Lord and said, "We beseech Thee, O Lord, we beseech Thee, let us not perish for this man's life, nor let us be guilty of shedding innocent blood, for Thou art the Lord; Thou hast done as it pleased Thee."

Then they took up Jonah and threw him into the sea, and the sea became calm. The men feared the Lord exceedingly, and they offered a sacrifice and made vows to Him.

Jonah Swallowed by the Fish

Now the Lord had prepared a great fish to swallow Jonah; and Jonah was inside the fish three days and three nights. Then Jonah prayed to the Lord his God, saying:

> *"Out of my trouble I called unto the Lord,*
> *And He answered me;*
> *For Thou hast cast me into the depths,*
> *Into the heart of the sea.*
> *I will sacrifice to Thee with the voice*
> *Of thanksgiving;*
> *What I have vowed, I will pay.*
> *Deliverance belongeth unto the Lord!"*

Then the Lord commanded the fish, and it threw Jonah out upon the dry land.

The word of the Lord came to Jonah a second time, "Arise, go to that great city Nineveh, and proclaim to it the message that I bid you."

Jonah started for Nineveh, as the Lord commanded.

A Yom Kippur Bummer

When you're fasting and have to feed your baby brother.

Yom Kippur

*A Day for Fasting, Prayer,
and Forgiveness*

A Yom Kippur Bummer

GULP...

...OOPS!

*When you forget it's
Yom Kippur and take
a drink of water.*

Nineveh was a great city, three days' journey across. And Jonah went through the city a day's journey, and he proclaimed, "Forty days more and Nineveh shall be overthrown!"

The people of Nineveh believed God and they proclaimed a fast and put on sackcloth, from the greatest to the least of them. And when the word came to the king of Nineveh, he rose from his throne, took off his robe, dressed in sackcloth, and sat in ashes. And he made this proclamation and published it in Nineveh:

*"By the decree of the king and his nobles!
Man, beast, herd and flock shall not taste
anything; let them not eat nor drink water;
but let both man and beast put on sackcloth,
and let them cry earnestly to God,
and turn each from his evil way and from
the acts of violence which they are doing.
Who knows but that God may relent and turn away
His anger, that we may not perish."*

When God saw that they turned from their evil ways, He relented of the evil which He said He would do to them, and did not do it.

The Angry Prophet

This displeased Jonah exceedingly and he was angry. And he prayed to the Lord, and said:

"Ah, Lord, was not this that I said when I was still in my own country? It was what I wished to prevent by fleeing to Tarshish; for I knew that Thou art a God, gracious and merciful, patient, and abounding in love, and relenting of evil. Therefore, O Lord, take now, I beseech Thee, my life from me; for it is better for me to die than to live!"

But the Lord said, "Are you doing right in being angry?"

Jonah left the city, and on its east side he made a booth for himself and sat under it, until he might see what would become of the city. And the Lord prepared a gourd (a large leafy plant) and made it grow up to shade Jonah's head from the hot sun. The shade of the gourd gave Jonah great comfort. But at dawn the next day God prepared a worm which injured the gourd, so that it withered.

When the sun rose, God prepared a hot east wind and the sun beat upon Jonah's head, so that he was faint and he begged that he might die, saying, "It is better for me to die than to live."

God said to Jonah, "Are you doing right in being angry about the gourd?"

He replied, "I am right in being greatly angry!"

And the Lord said, "You have pity on a gourd which has cost you no trouble and which you have not made grow, which came up in a night and perished in a night. Should I not have pity on the great city, Nineveh and its people."

In the land of Holland, a Jewish fisherman named Satye lived in a half-sunken hut on the edge of the sea. A descendant of generations of fishermen, he had spent days, months and years by the sea. Satye caught fish, his wife mended nets and kept house. Their children played in the sand.

Perhaps Satye was named after his great-grandfather Saadie, but of that he knew very little. In fact, he knew very little of his ancestry and of his Jewishness. His was the only Jewish family in the fishing village. How much could he have known of his Jewishness?

When Satye went to sea with other fishermen and storms endangered his life, neither he nor his family could cry out even the "Shema Israel" prayer: "Hear, O Israel! The Lord is our God, the Lord is One." Satye would look silently at the sky, his wife would clutch her head and throw angry looks toward Heaven. His children would throw themselves onto the sand and cry out, with other children of the village: "Sancta Maria! Sancta Maria!"

How should they have known better? Their home was much too far away for the family to make regular visits to a Jewish community. They barely eked out a living, and could not afford to ride. Besides, the sea did not allow them to get away. Satye's father, grandfather and great-grandfather had perished on the

Miracles on the Sea
by I. L. Peretz

*translated and adapted
by Esther Hautzig*

Yom Kippur

A Day for Fasting, Prayer, and Forgiveness

sea. And though Satye knew that the sea was his worst enemy, he loved it and could not tear himself away from it. He wanted to live by the sea and to die by the sea.

However, Satye and his family retained one Jewish custom. They always observed Yom Kippur, the day for fasting and atonement. Each year, early in the morning on the day before Yom Kippur, Satye and his family chose the biggest fish from their catch. Then they walked to town. Once in town, they gave the fish to the Jewish community's shochet, the kosher butcher, with whom they ate before and after the fast.

During the holy day of Yom Kippur, the whole family sat in the synagogue. They listened to the choir and the playing of the organ, and to the singing and the chanting of the cantor. They did not understand a single word of the service. Satye and his family looked at the Holy Ark that held the Torahs, and at the rabbi in his golden skullcap. When the golden skullcap got up, they got up; when the golden skullcap sat down, they sat down. Sometimes, when Satye napped out of weariness, his neighbor poked him with his elbow.

All Satye knew about Yom Kippur was that he could not work, neither fish nor row, that he had to fast from sundown to sundown, and that he had to listen to the choir and the cantor in the synagogue. He did not know that even fish of the sea trembled on this day, that momentous things went on in Heaven.

Satye knew that after the final prayer of Yom Kippur, the Neilah, he would go to supper with the butcher. Perhaps even the butcher did not know more.

After supper and coffee, Satye and his family would say good-bye to the butcher and his family. They would wish each other good fortune for the year ahead. Then Satye and his family would leave and walk all night toward the sea. They did not say "home," but "to the sea!" It was impossible to keep them in town.

Sometimes the butcher and his wife chided Satye:

"You did not even see the town!"

"Hm, the town!" Satye would grimace. Satye did not talk much. The sea had taught him silence. But he did speak of his hatred for the town:

"It is crowded! Only a ribbon of sky between roofs! There is space by the sea, you can breathe by the sea!"

"But the sea is your enemy, your death," the butcher argued.

"But a good death it is!" Satye answered.

He wished for the same end that his father and grandfather and great-grandfather had had. To be swallowed healthy by the sea, not to be sick and stay in bed, and then be buried in the hard earth.

Brr! A chill would go through Satye when he thought of such a death. And so each year after Yom Kippur the family walked happily back to the sea—home to the sea.

Years went by. Fishermen came and went; the butchers also changed. But the Yom Kippur custom always remained the same. Satye fasted, listened to the choir and cantor, wished the butcher a good year and went home.

This was the only thread that held Satye to his Jewishness and his people.

It came to pass one morning that the eastern horizon was turning red and the sea was waking silently. Here and there a few birds fluttered against the blue sky. Beams of light floated above the sea. Golden rays slid over the yellow sand.

It was the morning before Yom Kippur. All the fishing huts were closed. Only one door creaked. Satye came out. His face was earnest, but his eyes sparkled. He was off to catch a fish for Yom Kippur. He untied the chains that moored his little boat. The chain rattled. At once voices were heard from all directions. Satye's neighbors were calling to him:

"Don't go, Satye, don't go!"

The wide sea lay peaceful and quiet, barely breathing, hardly audible. Smiles seemed to dance between its ripples, as on the wrinkled face of a kind old grandmother. But the fishermen knew the sea well. Today they did not trust it.

"Don't go, Satye, don't go!"

An old man with fluttering gray hair and a wrinkled face came out of his house. He went over to Satye and put his hand on Satye's shoulder.

"Look!"

The old man pointed to a little dot on the horizon, a tiny dot that only a fisherman's eyes could see.

"A cloud will grow from that dot! The sea will rock; its sparkling surface will break. The sea's playfulness will become

A Yom Kippur Bummer

When the seventh game of the World Series is played on Yom Kippur.

grim; the ripples will become huge waves that will swallow big and little boats as Leviathan swallows fish."

"I'll be home before it happens," Satye said. "I only have to catch one fish."

The face of the old man grew serious.

"You have a wife and children, Satye!"

"And God in Heaven, too!" answered Satye confidently. He pushed his little boat off shore and jumped in. Light as a feather the boat glided out to sea. The sea caressed it sweetly, lovingly. The old fisherman murmured on shore: "Sancta Maria, Sancta Maria."

Satye's boat moved swiftly over the sea. Skillfully he threw his nets into the water. They became heavy, and Satye pulled them up with all his might. In his nets he found all kinds of weeds, but no fish. Again and again he threw down the nets and pulled them up, to find only weeds.

The sea began to rock. The sun was still in the sky, but its radiance was becoming misty. A crying sun. Like a brown snake the little dot on the horizon sidled up to the sun. Nearly half the day was gone, and Satye had not caught a fish.

"God must not want me to catch a fish this year. He does not want me to perform my good deed for Yom Kippur."

Satye decided to return home and turned his little boat toward shore. At that instant his face was splashed with water. A big golden fish was cavorting on the waves, splashing water with its shiny fins.

"Oh, I must catch this fish!" said Satye. He decided that God, after all, willed him to have a fish. He turned his boat back out to sea and gave chase to the golden fish.

The sea foamed and waves rose ever higher. The sun was almost completely hidden. The golden fish swam on the crests of waves, and Satye's boat pursued it swiftly. As suddenly as it had come, the golden fish disappeared from view. An enormous, sky-high wave rose between the fish and Satye's boat.

"This fish is playing tricks on me!"

Satye turned his boat again to shore, and at that very moment the wave subsided. The golden fish appeared near the boat and looked at Satye, as if pleading:

"Take me, take me!"

Again Satye chased the fish. Again the fish disappeared. The furious sea came between the fish and Satye. As if afraid, the sun hid behind the clouds. The wind seemed to have waited for the disappearance of the sun. Now it lashed out with immense power. The sea thundered as if thousands of bass viols were playing in its depths and pounded as if thousands of drums were beating in its waves.

"I must go home!" Satye's heart was beating wildly. He pulled his nets into the boat and grasped the oars with all his might. The veins in his hands seemed about to burst.

Like an empty nutshell the little boat was thrown about by the waves. As Satye rowed toward shore, the sky went black and the sea turned an angry brown.

Suddenly Satye saw a woman swimming toward him. Her floating hair was black, like his wife's hair. Beneath her hair he saw white hands. His wife had such hands. A voice called out: "Help!" It was the voice of his wife, the mother of his children. She must have followed him in their second boat. Now she was drowning, calling for his help. He turned the boat to reach his wife, but the sea would not allow it. Waves rose, the storm screamed and howled. In all this noise Satye still heard the woman's voice: "Help, Satye, help!"

With his last ounce of strength Satye rowed to her, but when he was near the spot, he could not see her any more. A huge wave rose and hurled the boat one way and the woman another.

"A mirage!" Satye remembered that the same thing had happened to him with the golden fish. Suddenly he turned his gaze toward shore and realized that it was sundown. The lights were lit in all the fishermen's houses.

"Yom Kippur has begun!" He let the oars drop from his hands. "Do with me as You wish," he cried toward Heaven, "but on Yom Kippur I will not row."

The wind raged on. Enormous waves pummeled the boat. Satye sat peacefully in his boat and looked up toward Heaven. Suddenly he remembered a melody the temple choir had sung, and he began to hum. The sky got ever darker, the wind blew ever more sharply. A wave tore an oar from Satye's hand and threw it away. Another wave chased the little boat as if with open jaws. In the midst of all this uproar Satye sang a melody. Perhaps Satye's silent soul could only speak to God through song?

"SHOW ME SOMEONE WHO ENDS YOM KIPPUR EARLY ... AND I'LL SHOW YOU A FAST FASTER."

His boat turned over. Satye wanted to die singing, but he was not destined to die yet. Two figures, with flowing hair and glowing eyes, came out of the mist and walked over the waves toward Satye. They picked him up, placed him between them and walked with him over the waves, as if over hills and dales. They led him, arm-in-arm, through wind and tumult. He tried to speak, but they would not let him.

"Sing, Satye, sing! Your song will overcome the anger of the sea."

Walking over waves toward the shore, Satye heard his little boat following them. He turned around and saw his nets all tangled up in the boat. The golden fish was in his nets. The two figures put Satye down on shore and disappeared.

In his house, Satye met the butcher and the butcher's wife talking to his wife and children. There had been a fire in town, so they had come to visit Satye and his family.

They ate the fish and celebrated Yom Kippur together, as always.

Atonement

*Day by day, through all the year
In the Book that none may read
All my thoughts and deeds appear;
Now I count with hope and fear
Every thought and deed.*

*Day by day, through all this year
That is coming clean and new,
Let my heart Thy precepts hear,
And on the written page appear
Worthy of a Jew.*

Jesse E. Sampter

Yom Kippur Craft

Tooled Prayer Book Cover

STOP!
Crafts may call for the use of a hammer, scissors, or other potentially dangerous tools. Before beginning any craft, get either help or the "go-ahead" from a responsible adult.

MATERIALS

prayer book (maḥzor for Rosh Hashanah and Yom Kippur)
1 piece of lightweight cardboard (size of front cover, exclusive of binding)
paper slightly larger than the cardboard
pencil
household aluminum foil, 36-gauge tooling aluminum, or tooling copper (from craft store), 2 inches higher and 2 inches wider than front cover, exclusive of binding
cellophane tape
1 blunt-tipped, soft-lead pencil or ballpoint pen
newspapers
tooling tool (blunt-tip pencil, wooden popsicle stick, or tongue depressor split in half lengthwise)
filler for tooled indentations (instant papier-mâché, clay, or liquid lead)
white craft cement
Optional: fine-grade steel wool, black spray paint, rag or paper towels

1. To make the pattern for your prayer book cover, place the cardboard on the paper and draw a line around it. Draw a simple design for the prayer book cover within this outline.

2. Center the pattern on the foil, tape it down, and trace around the lines with a pencil or ballpoint pen. Your tracing should leave an impression on the foil (figure A). Remove the pattern.

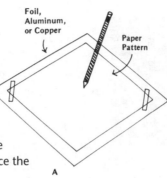

Foil, Aluminum, or Copper

Paper Pattern

A

3. Turn the foil over and place it face down on a pile of newspapers. Gently rub over parts of the design with the tooling tool until those areas become indented. Turn the foil face up and retrace the outline to define it even more.

4. Some sections of the drawing, as well as the entire background, may be textured by gently pushing down with the point of a pencil or ballpoint pen.

5. If you are using papier-mâché as the filler, mix a small batch according to package directions. To prevent the raised portions from being pushed in, add the filler to the indentations (figure B). Let dry.

B

6. Place the tooled aluminum foil on the cardboard with the raised side on top. Fold back the excess foil over the edges of the cardboard.

7. You may lightly rub the surface of the foil with steel wool to clean the foil and add a shine.

8. You may spray the tooled foil with black paint. Before the paint is thoroughly dry, wipe it off the raised areas with a rag or crumpled paper towels. Let dry.

9. Glue the panel to the cover of the prayer book (figure C).

C

Sukkot

Gather in the Sukkah *with Family and Friends*

About Sukkot

The days after Yom Kippur are no time to rest. It's time to prepare for the joyous holiday of Sukkot. The sukkah must be built and decorated. The arba minim—the lulav (palm branch), etrog (citron), hadassim (myrtles), and the aravot (willows)—must be bought.

Sukkot is a week-long holiday beginning five days after Yom Kippur, on the fifteenth of the Hebrew month of Tishre. In Israel, the first day is celebrated as a full-festival, no-work day, followed by six semi-holiday days. Outside Israel, traditionally, the first two days are full-festival days followed by five semi-holiday days. Reform and Reconstructionist Jews follow the Israeli calendar. Sukkot is followed immediately by Shemini Atzeret and Simḥat Torah.

The sukkah is a temporary dwelling, with walls made of any material and a roof made of some once-growing thing such as tree branches or bamboo. It's a reminder of the protection God gave the Jews while they lived in temporary homes during their forty years of wandering in the desert upon leaving slavery in Egypt. The holiday of Sukkot comes in the fall, the time of the harvest. It is also a holiday of thanksgiving for all God's gifts. For some people, the sukkah is a reminder of the temporary huts Jews set up in the fields during the time of the harvest.

But why is Sukkot a fall holiday? The Jews escaped slavery in Egypt in the spring, during the month of Nisan. Among the reasons our rabbis give for this seasonal switch is that Sukkot is a joyous holiday and what

better time for joy than after Yom Kippur when we know we have repented and are free of sin.

Sukkah decorations are both fun and a reflection of a family's customs. Among the many items traditionally hanging in sukkot are the sheva minim—the seven fruits of Israel—small containers of oil and flour to remember the Temple offerings, round pastries called biscochos and cranberry chains. It is a custom among Moroccan Jews to cover the walls with rugs and to hang a chair or stool from one wall. This kisei Eliyahu, the chair for the prophet Elijah, is reserved for the legendary

protector of the Jewish people, especially the children.

There is a custom to invite Abraham, Isaac, Jacob, Joseph, Moshe, Aaron, and David, the ushpizin, as symbolic invisible guests in our sukkot. Some families also invite Sarah, Rachel, Rebecca, Leah, Miriam, Abigail, and Esther. The command to take a lulav, etrog, hadassim, and aravot on Sukkot comes from the Torah. It is said that these arba minim—four species—are symbolic of all growing things. They are held, carried, and waved during the morning services on Sukkot. According to our rabbis, the four species are a reflection of the Jewish people. The etrog has both taste and fragrance. The lulav, which comes from a date palm, has only taste. The hadassim have only fragrance, and the aravot have neither taste nor fragrance. Similarly there are Jews with both good deeds and wisdom. Some have wisdom without good deeds, or good deeds without wisdom. And some have neither. Just as we hold the arba minim together on Sukkot, all Jews must act as one people, helping one another.

The seventh day of Sukkot is Hoshanah Rabbah, another day of atonement for our sins. The night is a time for Torah study, preferably in the sukkah. In the morning we walk around the synagogue seven times while carrying the arba minim and saying prayers. After the seventh circuit, along with special prayers, a bunch of aravot (willows) are beaten on the ground, the new year's last destruction of our sins.

Sukkot, along with Pesaḥ and Shevuot, is one of the pilgrimage festivals. During ancient times Jews traveled to the Temple in Jerusalem for the holidays.

Battletime Bar Mitzvah

by Barbara Soferr

"One more game, Hotshot," Tzvi pleaded.

"Sorry. I've got to go. Another time, Champ," Uri answered, tossing the basketball to his best friend. He had to shower and get dressed for Shabbat in time to go to the synagogue with his father.

Uri rarely had a chance to be alone with his father, a busy Jerusalem physician, and he looked forward to their weekly visit to the synagogue. About a year before, when his parents had begun planning his Bar Mitzvah, Dr. Michaeli, who hardly ever entered a synagogue, announced that they would go together every Friday night until the Bar Mitzvah. He mumbled something about his having gone to the synagogue with his own father.

Uri knew better than to ask why. Unlike his friends' parents who loved to tell stories about their pasts, Uri's father did not like to talk about his life in Poland and the aunts and uncles who had died there.

"You're always talking about the Bar Mitzvah," Uri's sister Orna complained during dinner that evening. "Maybe I'll get some attention when it's over."

"That won't be long now," Mother comforted her. "Rosh Hashanah is next week and the Bar Mitzvah is on Sukkot, about two weeks later. It's the first Shabbat after Yom Kippur."

The Michaelis had decided to put up a sukkah this year, in honor of the Bar Mitzvah. Their apartment had a balcony perfect for a sukkah, but they had never thought about building one before. Dr. Michaeli had bought a metal frame for the sukkah and had promised to build it the night after Yom Kippur.

"Going to the synagogue with Dad, making Orna jealous, building a sukkah—maybe this Bar Mitzvah is worth all the trouble," Uri thought to himself.

Of course, on the other hand, he did have to go to Mr. Berg's house twice a week to practice reading the *Haftorah*. Mr. Berg was the father of one of Dr. Michaeli's patients and had been hired to prepare Uri for his Bar Mitzvah. Uri's reading was *Zechariah* 14, and it was difficult to understand. Mr. Berg explained that it was the prophet's picture of the future, a prophecy.

"You're not the only one who can't understand it, Uri," Mr. Berg told him again and again. "Scholars have been puzzling over it and arguing about its meaning for centuries."

"What's that to me?" Uri had asked himself. He didn't dare ask Mr. Berg that. Mr. Berg wasn't much older than his father, but he seemed to have been around for centuries.

Rosh Hashanah passed, and the day of the Bar Mitzvah approached. After Uri's reading in the synagogue, his parents were planning a family dinner and a big party. When he entered the synagogue on the evening of Yom Kippur he pictured himself the star of a great performance the following week.

Jerusalem is very quiet on Yom Kippur. There are no television or radio programs and many people do not drive their cars. Uri remembered being bored in the synagogue in the past, but this year, because he was more familiar with the prayers, he became absorbed in the chanting. He almost did not notice when a man approached his father and tapped him on the shoulder.

"Dr. Michaeli," he said. "Report to your unit."

At first Uri did not understand the words. His father leaned over to him.

"I've got to go into the army. It's probably nothing. It must be a holiday alert. Tell Mother and Orna that I left. I'll phone as soon as I get a chance."

Men and women sat in separate sections of the synagogues and Uri's mother and sister did not see Dr. Michaeli leave. When they came downstairs after the service, they were alarmed to find him missing.

"Dad was called up," Uri explained. "He says it's probably nothing."

But when the air raid sirens blasted on Yom Kippur Day, Uri was only half-surprised. Something in his father's voice had warned him that this was more than a routine call-up.

Within minutes of the sirens' blasts the streets were filled with men seeking transportation to their units. Dr. Michaeli called that evening, just managing to say he was going "somewhere" and he would get in touch soon.

It was school vacation, but Uri and his classmates volunteered for the squad that painted car headlights blue so that they would conform to the blackout rules. There were garbled reports of tank

A Sukkot Bummer

When you have more bees in your sukkah than people.

and air battles. Uri tried to enforce the government call for confidence at home.

"Dad would be building the sukkah if he were home," Orna said.

The sukkah. Uri thought a minute and phoned Tzvi. Could he come over? Something important.

The two boys worked until 2 a.m. When they finished, a colorful, leaf-covered hut stood on the Michaelis' balcony.

"I've never done anything like that before," Tzvi confessed. "I bet we could do it more easily now that we know how. We can go into the sukkah business." He smiled.

"That's not a bad idea," Uri said.

"Are you kidding? Go into the business? How could we do that?"

Uri suggested that they advertise as sukkah builders, offering their services to other families in which the father was not around to build the sukkah. In the morning they found they were not the only young people with the idea. They joined a crew of children who answered requests for sukkot.

At one home, an old couple who had expected their son to help them wanted to give the boys money. Their son was away driving a tank.

ON WHICH SIDE
OF YOUR HOUSE
SHOULD YOU
BUILD A SUKKAH?

THE OUTSIDE.

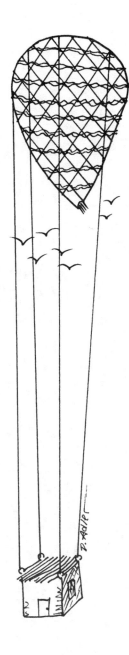

"Give it to the Soldiers' Fund," the boys suggested, not wanting to embarrass the older people.

The question of what to do about his Bar Mitzvah remained. Mrs. Michaeli cancelled the party but wondered if Uri should have his Bar Mitzvah with his father away. She wanted to discuss it with her husband, but he had not called again and she was worried.

Uri thought he would cancel the whole Bar Mitzvah, but something told him that it was the wrong thing to do. He announced to his mother that he would read the *Haftorah* in the synagogue. He would prepare the rest alone because Mr. Berg was also in the army, but he would go on.

Orna, his mother, cousins, and friends sat in the synagogue on Shabbat morning when Uri was called to read. He walked to the platform and his voice shook a little as he recited the blessings. There was one moment when he almost laughed as he thought of Mr. Berg in a soldier's uniform. His voice got stronger as he got to the *Haftorah* reading.

*"Behold, a day of the Lord cometh,
When thy spoil shall be divided in the midst of thee.
For I will gather all nations against Jerusalem to battle;"*

Uri realized that he was understanding the verses for the first time.

*"And this shall be the plague wherewith the Lord will smite
All the peoples that have warred against Jerusalem."*

His friends shook his hand when the service ended and Uri walked home with his mother and sister. The next day, while, eating lunch in the sukkah he had built, they heard the phone ring.

"It's for you," his mother said in a shaky voice.

Uri picked up the phone. It was his father.

"Happy holiday, son," he said. "How does it feel to be a man?"

Wings

by Lamed Shapiro

My father never built a sukkah for Sukkot; but nevertheless, our family still had a sukkah for the sacred festival—and what's more, a beautiful one. All year long our sukkah was simply a plain pantry room, where one could find a host of things: a sack of potatoes, a string of onions, a barrel of borscht, and all sorts of other foodstuffs.

The pantry room bore not even the slightest trace of holiness, and no one in his wildest dreams thought ever that it could serve as a sukkah. If anyone would have taken the trouble to look up to the ceiling, he would have seen a clever device that could convert the pantry to a sukkah: the ceiling was made of bars and gratings . . . But for what good reason would anyone glance up to the ceiling in the middle of the year? Therefore, everyone thought it was simply a pantry.

Despite all this, on the day before Sukkot the pantry-room became a sukkah. My older brother climbed up on the roof, fussed with something, and suddenly two big black wings opened up above the pantry. The bars were immediately covered with green boughs and thatching, the potatoes and onions vanished, a white cloth was draped over the borscht barrel, and a table, chair, and couch were brought in. My father faithfully fulfilled the *mitzvah* of residing in the sukkah—he ate, drank, and slept there. The entire house, usually higher than the pantry, was now lower than it. The pantry now proudly spread its wings over the house as though to say, "I'm a sukkah," seemingly ready to fly up to the blue sky and toward the bright sun.

A Sukkot Bummer

When leaves fall into your soup.

The first day of the Sukkot festival passed without incident. The sukkah felt like home: we ate and slept in it; we lived there. Most importantly, the sukkah was privileged to hear sacred discussion concerning itself. My father and brother recited and reviewed the laws concerning the sukkah—how high it may be, what shape it should have, with what it may be covered, etc. The sukkah heard all this and no doubt thought that it could even satisfy the most pious Jew. And it was absolutely right.

But the second day of the festival brought misfortune.

From early morning a huge dark cloud hung low and heavy over the sukkah, as though about to crash down on it and crush it. The wind moved the sukkah's wings and they squealed softly and plaintively. Everyone in the house was vexed. Father kept looking gloomily and anxiously through the window, shaking his head.

Nevertheless, we ate lunch in the sukkah. We were still hopeful. But in the midst of the meal we heard some sort of noise on the roof, as if a tiny creature were scampering around on the thatching. We looked up and then silently stared at our own plates. Everyone ate quickly and quietly. A minute later one of us wiped his cheek . . . Then something wet and shiny splashed down into a bowl, followed by another drop, and a third. Father rose.

"It's no use! Moishe, lower the wings."

My brother stood and untied the rope that hung down from the ceiling. A creaking noise—and then with a slam something fell over our heads.

A gray workaday shadow entered, expanded and covered the entire length and breadth of the sukkah. The snow-white tablecloth, the silver candelabra, and the entire festively-set table looked odd and strange, like new silver embroidery on a dirty prayer shawl. Near the wall, beneath its white covering, the borscht barrel seemed to mock us, like a saucy slave snickering at his humiliated master. And, avoiding one another's glances, we swiftly slipped out of the sukkah.

The sukkah had become a pantry-room again.

Gather in the Sukkah
with Family and Friends

Yom Tov Lanu

Allegretto

Em — Am — Em — Am — Em

Yom tov la - nu ḥag sa - mei aḥ y' - la - dim na - gi - lah na l' -

Am — D — Em

su - ka - tei - nu ba o - rei - aḥ Av - ra - ham a - vi - nu ba - rukh ha - ba

G — D⁷ — G

ya - ḥad ha - ḥag na - ḥog b' - lu - lav ha - das et - rog

B⁷ — Em Am B⁷ — Em

hoy he - aḥ nis - maḥ m' - od u - va - ma - a - gal nir - kod

All the world is rejoicing on this joyous holiday.
Abraham our father joins us in the Sukka. Welcome!
Together we will celebrate this holiday with Lulav
and Etrog. We will be joyful and dance in a circle.

יוֹם טוֹב לָנוּ חַג שָׂמֵחַ יְלָדִים נָגִילָה
לְסֻכָּתֵנוּ בָּא אוֹרֵחַ אַבְרָהָם אָבִינוּ בָּרוּךְ הַבָּא
יַחַד הַחַג נָחוֹג בְּלוּלָב הֲדַס אֶתְרוֹג
הוֹי הֶאָח נִשְׂמַח מְאֹד וּבַמַּעְגָּל נִרְקֹד

Sukkot Crafts

Sukkot Chain

For a beautiful chain that can be hung from the ceiling or along the walls of your sukkah *all you need are cranberries, peas, a large sewing needle, and strong thread. You could also make a chain from colored construction paper or pages from old magazines. Cut the paper into one-inch strips and use glue or staples to link them as shown in the picture. They can hang from the ceiling or along the walls.*

MATERIALS

large sewing needle
strong thread
whole raw cranberries
whole raw peas

1. Thread the needle and then knot the end of the thread.

2. Pierce a whole raw cranberry with the threaded needle. With your finger, push the cranberry all the way down to the knot.

3. Thread a raw pea the same way.

4. Continue, alternating peas and cranberries, until the thread is completely covered with cranberries and peas. Tie a knot at the end, and hang the chain in the *sukkah.*

Hanging Birds

The following craft is three hundred years old. In the days of the American colonies, Jews decorated their sukkot *with yellow, green, purple, and red ribbons pinned to the walls or hanging from the roof as streamers. They also tied the* lulav *in yards of colored ribbons. Another old idea comes from the Middle East. In Iraq, Jews made figures of birds out of hollowed-out eggs and hung them in memory of members of the family who had died. You can make these birds simply as* sukkah *decorations, even if they aren't meant for departed relatives.*

STOP!
Some of the crafts in this chapter call for the use of a hammer, scissors, or other potentially dangerous tools. Before beginning any craft, get either help or the "go-ahead" from a responsible adult.

MATERIALS

a large raw egg
1 straight pin
2 feet of white thread

1 piece of white paper
pencil
scissors
colored construction paper
scissors
cellophane tape

1. Gently poke a hole through each end of the egg shell. Make one hole slightly larger than the other by moving the pin around the edges of the hole.

2. Blow through the smaller hole to make the contents of the egg spurt out through the larger hole. Now you have an empty shell, which will be the body of the bird.

3. Cut a piece of thread two feet long, and tape it to the shell as shown here.

4. Place a piece of white paper over the drawings of the beak, wings, and tail and use a pencil to trace the pattern outlines onto the white paper.

5. Cut out the beak, wings, and tail from the white paper. Tape them to the construction paper and cut around them, leaving a space on each piece for taping to the shell. Fold the pieces along the dotted lines shown in the drawing, and tape them to the shell. The bird is ready for hanging from the roof of the *sukkah*.

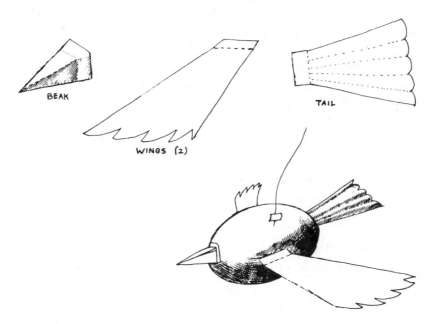

BEAK

WINGS (2)

TAIL

WHAT DID THE
LULAV SAY TO
THE ETROG?

LET'S
SHAKE, PAL

This is another hanging decoration that is a reminder of the "clouds of glory" that protected the Jewish people in the desert.

Clouds of Glory

MATERIALS

1 sheet of white construction paper
2 feet of blue ribbon
2 feet of white ribbon
1 sheet of red construction paper
about 20 cotton balls
a piece of string long enough to hang cloud
     from ceiling

1. Cut a large cloud, in any shape you wish, from the white paper.

2. Cut the blue and the white ribbons into 7 pieces of differing lengths and attach them to the cloud with white glue. Alternate the colors.

3. Cut 7 six-pointed stars from the red paper. A simple way to do this is to cut 14 equilateral triangles. Each side of each triangle should be 1 inch long. Then, with a little glue, attach 1 triangle on top of another.

4. Glue the stars to the tips of the ribbons, and glue the cotton balls to the white cloud. Punch a hole near the top of the cloud and put a string through it for hanging.

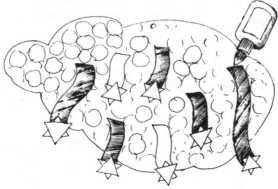

70
Sukkot
Gather in the Sukkah
with Family and Friends

A Sukkah in a Sukkah

How can you put one sukkah inside another? It's easy. Make a miniature sukkah to decorate the big sukkah.

MATERIALS

newspapers
green and white or yellow poster paint
shoebox (without the lid)
miniature table and chairs from a doll-
   house
construction paper in several different
   colors or modeling clay
blades of grass
string
orange seed
small branches from trees and bushes

1. Spread old newspapers across the
    table or counter where you will be
    working.

2. Using poster paint, paint the bot-
    tom of a shoebox green and the
    walls white or yellow. When the
    paint is dry, put in a miniature table and chairs from a dollhouse.

3. Cut out tiny fruits and vegetables from construction paper, and put them
    on the table. If you have modeling clay, you can use it instead to make
    attractive fruits.

4. Make a tiny *lulav* by tying a bunch of grass blades together with a piece of string, and make an *etrog* from the seed of an orange by painting it yellow. Little dolls, pictures of food cut from magazines, and copies of the Sukkot designs will make the toy *sukkah* look like the real one. Branches from small shrubs and bushes laid across the top of the shoebox make the sekhakh.

Even though each holiday has its own customs, the festivals of the year are linked to one another because together they celebrate the history of the Jewish people. The tradition is to carry part of one holiday to the next. An example of this is to begin building the sukkah *the night of Yom Kippur. In the same way, the* lulav *is saved to sweep away the bread crumbs of Passover in the spring. The etrog, too, can be saved, because it never rots. It just grows smaller and harder, and it turns black with age. It holds its fragrance for years.*

A Spice (Besamin) Ball

MATERIALS

1 *etrog*
cloves
toothpick

After Sukkot, put cloves into the *etrog* by first piercing the fruit with a toothpick. Then use the *etrog* for *havdalah* at the conclusion of Shabbat. Its fragrance will remind you all year of the pleasure of Sukkot.

*Gather in the Sukkah
with Family and Friends*

Sukkot Recipe

Easy Sukkot Vegetable Soup (North America)

Celebrate Sukkot with this hearty harvest meal. For variety, try substituting different vegetables, including peppers, peas, and onions.

2 medium size potatoes
10–15 string beans
2 medium size carrots
1 stalk celery
1 cup fresh or frozen corn kernels
salt to taste

Peel the potatoes and the carrots. Cut all of the vegetables into bite size pieces and place them in a medium-sized pot. Cover with water. Add salt to taste. Cook until vegetables are soft. Serve.

4 servings

STOP!
A kitchen is a dangerous place. If you're not careful, you might burn yourself with splattering oil or boiling water. The recipe in this chapter is intended for older children. Before beginning, make sure an adult is available to help.

Sukkot Fun

Sukkot Puzzles (Answers on page 271.)

If 2 families build 2 *sukkah*s in 2 hours, how long would it take 7 families to build 7 *sukkot?*

Sukkah *Building*

Each day Barry puts up 2 *sukkah* walls. Each night 1 wall falls down until all 4 walls are up. With all 4 walls up no walls fall down. How many days does it take Barry to build his *sukkah?*

How Many Days?

The Cohen family, Mr. and Mrs. Cohen and their children, are together in their *sukkah.* The Cohens have 4 sons and each son has a sister. How many Cohens were together in their *sukkah?*

The Cohen Family

"We had so many bees in our *sukkah*," Michael said. "They all flew in a line. We had 2 bees in front of 2 bees, 2 bees behind 2 bees, and 2 bees between 2 bees." How many bees were in Michael's *sukkah?*

So Many Bees

A Sukkot Bummer

SNAP

When the pitum (stem) of your etrog breaks.

Shemini Atzeret and Simḥat Torah

Days of Joy

About Shemini Atzeret and Simḥat Torah

"Sisu V'Simḥu b'Simḥat Torah—Rejoice, be happy with the Torah celebration."

Shemini Atzeret is described in traditional texts as a gift from God to the Jewish people. God, not wanting to have his guests leave at the end of the week-long Sukkot visit, gave them another holiday, Shemini Atzeret. A prayer for rain is said on Shemini Atzeret, marking the beginning of the needed winter rains in Israel.

Simḥat Torah celebrates the completion of the cycle of reading the Five Books of Moses done every Shabbat. It's the day the reading is completed, and also the day it is begun all over again. Everyone is called to the Torah, even the children.

Simḥat Torah is a day of marching and dancing with Torah scrolls and singing. In some synagogues, when the Torah scrolls are all taken from the ark, a lighted candle is placed inside—the light of Torah is temporarily replaced with the burning light.

In Israel and among Reform and Reconstructionist Jews everywhere both holidays are celebrated on the same day, the twenty-second of the Hebrew month of Tishre, the day immediately following the end of Sukkot. Among more traditional Jews outside Israel, the holidays are celebrated on separate days, the twenty-second and twenty-third of Tishre.

Gittel and the Bell
by Roberta Goldshlag Cooks

Nestled between two mountains, somewhere far from the sea, lay the tiny town of Kolodky. Like most Jewish towns of its size, Kolodky had one main street, with a butcher shop, a bakery that sold fresh Challah on Friday, a shoe repair shop, and an old wooden synagogue.

In the town square stood the famous Kolodky town bell. On important occasions, when the bell was rung, the whole valley sang with its magnificent sound.

Oddly, the winter had gone by without the bell ever ringing. But one morning, three days before Purim, the sound of the bell echoed through Kolodky. Whoever was able headed for the heart of town.

6

Everyone was asking the same questions.

"Who rang the bell?"

"Is it good news or bad?"

"I bet the cantor's son came back from the army," said Leybush, the pretzel-maker.

"Or another theft of a *kiddush* cup," said Riva Leya, the rabbi's wife.

Speculation continued until Reb Moishe, one of the town elders, mounted the podium. The crowd quieted. "Whoever has rung the bell step forward and tell the good people your news," he commanded.

When eight-year-old Gittel stepped up to the podium, everyone gasped. No child had ever rung the town bell before.

"Gittel," said Reb Moishe, looking very concerned. "What is it? Has your poor mother, Rachel Leah, taken sick?"

"Oh no," said Gittel. "She still has leg pains, but she's home taking her afternoon nap."

"Is there news about your poor father?" asked Reb Moishe.

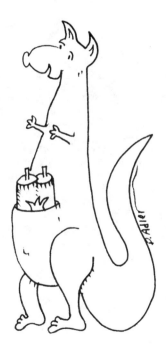

"No," said Gittel. "He's still far away with the Polish army. My mother fears he may never come back."

"Well then," said Reb Moishe. "Are *you* having some kind of problem?"

"Oh no," said Gittel, smiling brightly.

"Then why did you ring the bell?" asked Reb Moishe.

"Don't you notice my new hairdo? My mother says I look just like Queen Esther."

"Is that why you rang the bell?" cried Reb Moishe.

"Yes," answered Gittel calmly. "I thought you'd want to see how pretty I look."

"You do look pretty Gittel," said Reb Moishe, "only . . ."

But before Reb Moishe had finished his sentence, the whole crowd was laughing—the butcher, the town beggar, and even the rabbi.

"We understand you want to share your good news," said Reb Moishe when the laughter had quieted down. "But this bell must be rung only to announce something important."

A Simḥat Torah Bummer

Someone talks and talks to you while everyone else is dancing.

"This is important," said Gittel.

"Something *very* important," answered Reb Moishe patiently. "A matter of life and death."

"Life and death," repeated Gittel.

"Exactly," said Reb Moishe, hoping he had made his point.

A month went by. Passover arrived and with it spring. Every family in Kolodky recited the story of the Exodus and poured a cup of wine for Elijah.

Gittel loved the spring. Every morning, after she finished her chores, she'd go out with a pillowcase and hunt for treasures. Sometimes she'd bring vegetable peels to feed wild goats who lived by the lake.

As spring turned to summer, Gittel noticed that the goat she called Raysen was getting fatter. Instead of leaping, Raysen wobbled. One afternoon Raysen did not appear. Gittel searched the lakeside as the sky turned from rose to deep blue.

Finally, she heard a soft bleating. Hidden in the high grass, lay Raysen. Around her were three of the tiniest goats Gittel had ever seen.

Late that night, the Kolodky bell echoed once again. People were worried as they gathered in the town square. "Is it a fire?" they asked each other. "Or, heaven forbid, a gang of thieves?"

Reb Moishe stepped to the podium in his nightclothes. "Whoever has rung our bell step forward and tell the good people your news," he announced.

Up leaped Gittel, holding one of the baby goats. A hush fell over the crowd. Reb Moishe's face turned quite pink. "You've awakened our whole town," he warned Gittel. "I hope you have something important to report."

"It's just what you told me," said Gittel brightly.

"Just what I told you?" repeated Reb Moishe.

"A matter of life and death," she reminded him. "Raysen the mountain goat just had three babies. I brought them here for everyone to look at."

"Gittel," Reb Moishe said firmly. "We do not ring the bell for the birth of a goat."

"Three goats," said Gittel, as she bent down to stroke Raysen and her babies.

"Gittel," pleaded Reb Moishe. "I want to be sure you understand me. This bell must be rung only for something very, very important. An avalanche, or a plague, or a great discovery. Something that touches our whole town."

"An avalanche, or a plague, or a great discovery," Gittel repeated.

"I'm glad we finally understand each other," said Reb Moishe. He waved his hand to dismiss the grumbling crowd. Only the rabbi came over to admire Raysen and her kids.

The bell rang twice more that summer: once to announce good news—the birth of Reb Moishe's first great-great grandson, and once to announce bad news—the Torah, its silver crown, and its beautiful gold-embroidered cover had been stolen from the synagogue's ark.

When Rosh Hashanah came, the Jews of Kolodky did not feel like celebrating. The sacred Torah was still missing, and the rabbi was too upset to leave his bed.

Yom Kippur came, and then Sukkot. The Jews of Kolodky walked through the town with their heads bowed. In another week it would be Simchat Torah. How could they rejoice with the Torah when their Torah was gone?

Gittel was also feeling unsettled. There still was no word from her father. It was too cold to visit Raysen, and her mother's leg was acting up.

One gray day she decided to hunt for treasures. She had just found an old umbrella when Riva Leya, the rabbi's wife, came by.

"Gittel, you're getting dirt on your stockings!" said Riva Leya. "In my day little girls didn't play in the mud. They stayed at home learning manners."

"My mother says that too many manners make her sneeze," said Gittel, but Riva Leya had already walked off. Gittel turned back to her new umbrella. It opened perfectly. As she admired the shiny cloth, she noticed a paper tucked into the frame. She pulled it free and unrolled it. It looked like some kind of map.

Maybe it would lead to a palace of treasures, thought Gittel. She studied the scribbles and closed her eyes. When she looked again she saw that it was a map of Kolodky. A cow stood for the town butcher. A book stood for the Hebrew school.

Gittel followed the trail out of town until it stopped at a barn.

"Hello," she called out. No one answered. She pulled the barn door open. The barn was empty, except for a pile of hay.

Gittel searched carefully but found no treasures, not even a gold thread. She realized she was tired and lay down in the hay.

But everywhere she turned, she felt something hard and bumpy.

She started tossing aside armloads of hay, and then she saw it: the Torah wrapped in its gold-embroidered cover. In the dim light it glittered like jewels. She dug further and found the silver crown.

Gittel was excited. She ran as fast as she could back to Kolodky, filled with that wonderful urge to ring the bell and share her great discovery.

But as soon as her hand touched the rope, Gittel stopped. She imagined Riva Leya laughing at her. She thought of Reb Moishe shaking his finger in her face. She wondered if anyone in Kolodky would believe her. Sadly, she dropped the rope and started back home.

As Gittel walked past the butcher shop, she overheard Leybush, the pretzel-maker, talking to Reb Moishe.

"Our rabbi will not live until Simḥat Torah," said Leybush. "All day he spends praying for the missing Torah. He won't eat or sleep."

As soon as Gittel heard these words, she turned and ran to the rabbi's house.

"I've found the Torah," Gittel cried, as Riva Leya answered the door.

"Don't you know not to bother us!" said the woman. "The rabbi needs peace and quiet, not stories from rude little girls."

But, before she could slam the door, the rabbi appeared from his room, wrapped in his prayer shawl.

"You say you've found the Torah?" he asked in a weak whisper.

"Yes," said Gittel, staring. The rabbi looked like a ghost.

"Take me," said the rabbi. Together they hurried out of town.

When they reached the barn, Gittel began digging through the haystack. But she found no gold-embroidered Torah cover, no silver crown. She'd almost given up when the rabbi uncovered a plain parchment scroll.

"Our Torah!" he shouted. He wrapped the scroll in his prayer shawl, threw open the barn door, and carried it into the light.

Then, as Gittel watched in amazement, the rabbi started dancing, with tears rolling down his cheeks and the Torah high over his head.

"Rabbi," cried Gittel, running after him. "Why are you dancing? The silver crown and gold-embroidered Torah cover have been stolen!"

"Let the thieves keep all the gold and silver!" shouted the rabbi. "The Torah is our real treasure—our laws, our teachings, our history! All this is precious in a Jew's life!"

Just then Reb Moishe and Riva Leya came running.

"Rabbi, what are you doing?" cried Riva Leya.

"Gittel has found our Torah!" the rabbi exclaimed.

"A miracle!" shouted Reb Moishe. "A miracle for Simchat Torah! We must ring the bell and tell the whole town."

So the rabbi, Riva Leya, Reb Moishe, and Gittel all hurried back to the town square.

The rabbi mounted the podium and reached for the rope.

Then he stopped. "Gittel," said the rabbi, as he helped her up next to him. "This is something important."

"Something important?" Gittel repeated. Her heart was beating fast.

"Something very important," said the rabbi. He put the rope in her hand. The ring of the bell echoed through Kolodky. The whole valley sang with its magnificent sound.

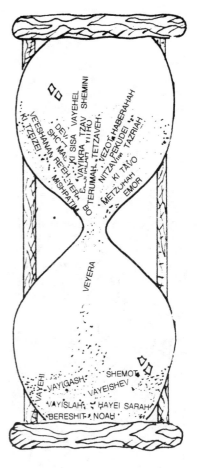

O nce upon a time, twin brothers inherited a very large fortune. Yet, these two brothers who were identical twins, differed in their character as well as in their business methods. One was stingy and tightly held onto his money, while the other was very kind and always donated his money to charities,

The "Worthless" Esrogim
(Based on a Midrash)

by Geshon Kranzler

and poor people. In no time at all, the kind-hearted one managed to give away practically his entire fortune for charitable purposes.

Finally, a small sum of money remained, and in the end only a few cents. On *Hoshanoh Rabboh,* his wife gave him the few cents and asked him to go to the market and buy food, inasmuch as it was *Erev Yom Tov,* and there was no food in the house to prepare for the coming *Shmini Atzereth* and *Simchas Torah* holidays.

The kind man took the money and went to the market. On the way he met the *"Gabbai Tzedoko,"* (official charity collector). "Good Morning, *Gabbai!* What are you doing in the market place on *Erev Yom Tov?"*

"Well, that shouldn't surprise you," replied the *Gabbai.* "I have come here on business. There are orphans in town. And they are ashamed to come to *Shul* on *Yom Tov,* for they haven't any decent clothing".

The kind man did not have to think twice. Immediately he gave the *Gabbai* the few cents he had. But now his worries really began. How was he going to purchase food for *Yom Tov?* How could he possibly face his family? Now, that *he was poor and worried*—was there anyone to whom he could turn for help?

Thus, walking through the streets dejected as he was in spirit, he approached the synagogue. Playing in the synagogue yard were many children, and all had the *Esrogim* which were given to them by their parents, inasmuch as they were no longer needed. As time passed the children tired of playing with the *Esrogim,* left them strewn all over the yard.

The kind-hearted man found a burlap bag and quickly filled it with the *Esrogim,* which were now completely useless. Then he walked the streets of the town trying to sell them to the different merchants. Of course everyone laughed at him and no one, not a single merchant, was interested in buying the worthless *Esrogim.*

Once again, worried and dejected the man walked alone. He walked down to the shores of the sea and sat down on a lonely rock for he dared not go home without food for his family.

It so happened that at this very moment, while the kind man was sitting on the lonely rock, the King was very sick. He had stomach trouble and could not eat any food. All the big doctors of the country had prescribed different medicines, but alas, not a single one helped him. That night the King had a dream. In that dream, he heard a voice tell him that if he should eat the fruits which the Jews had used during their most recent holiday, he would become healthy again.

That night the King could not sleep any more. Impatiently he waited for dawn and as the sun rose, the King ordered his servants and messengers to search the land for *Esrogim*. But, they could not find any.

After a day's search, two of these servants who were returning home, disappointed that they could not find the proper medicine for the King, suddenly noticed a lonely man sitting sadly by the seashore on a barren rock. One of the servants also noticed a sack near this lonely man. The servant asked him what he sold, but the man claimed that he had nothing to sell. Disregarding the answer, the servants opened the sack, and to their surprise found the sack full of *Esrogim*.

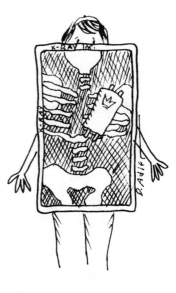

Quickly they took the man with the sack and brought him to the King. With all the King's doctors gathered around him the King began to eat some of the *Esrogim*. Much to their surprise, the fruits that the Jews had used during their recent *Sukkos* holiday helped the King immediately. And he felt no more pain.

The king summoned his advisers and asked them how to reward the man who had the *Esrogim*. After some thought, they decided that the best reward would be to fill with gold pieces the sack in which the *Esrogim* were brought and then present this sack to the only man in the Kingdom who had *Esrogim*.

In no time at all, the kind-hearted man returned home. Once again he was rich, and once again he was able to keep up his charitable work.

Thus God rewarded a most charitable man.

**Shemini Atzeret
and Simḥat Torah**

Days of Joy

Mipi Eil

Joyously

Ein a - dir____ ka - do - nai v'ein ba - rukh k' - ven a - m' - ram

ein g' - vi - rah ka - to - rah____ ein do - r' - she - hah k' - yis - ra - el

mi - pi Eil____ mi - pi Eil y' - vo - rakh____ Yis - ra - eil

*There is no one greater than God. There is no one
more blessed than Moses. There is nothing greater
than the Torah. There are no people as wonderful as
the people of Israel.*

אֵין אַדִּיר כַּאדֹנָי
וְאֵין בָּרוּךְ כְּבֶן-עַמְרָם
אֵין גְּבִירָה כַּתּוֹרָה
וְאֵין דּוֹרְשָׁהּ כְּיִשְׂרָאֵל
מִפִּי אֵל מִפִּי אֵל
יְבֹרַךְ יִשְׂרָאֵל

Sisu V'Simḥu

*Let us rejoice altogether on Simḥat Torah and give
honor to God's Torah.*

שִׂישׂוּ וְשִׂמְחוּ בְּשִׂמְחַת תּוֹרָה
וּתְנוּ כָּבוֹד לַתּוֹרָה

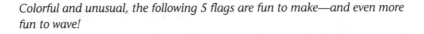

Simhat Torah Crafts

Simhat Torah Flags

Styrofoam Flag

STOP!
Some of the crafts in this chapter call for the use of a hammer, scissors, or other potentially dangerous tools. Before beginning any craft, get either help or the "go-ahead" from a responsible adult.

Colorful and unusual, the following 5 flags are fun to make—and even more fun to wave!

MATERIALS
7 × 9-inch styrofoam meat tray
pinking shears
piece of paper a little larger than the meat tray
pencil
heavy-duty pin or hole punch
cellophane tape
crepe paper streamer
13-inch narrow wooden dowel
white glue (optional)

1. Start with a styrofoam meat tray, about 7 × 9 inches. To make a scalloped border for the flag, cut around the edges of the tray with pinking shears.

2. Place the tray on a sheet of paper and trace around it. Remove the tray and draw a design on the piece of paper within the penciled outline.

3. Tape the drawing to the tray. With a heavy-duty pin or hole punch, poke holes through the outline of the design, piercing all the way through the styrofoam. Remove the taped paper and check to be sure all the holes went through the tray.

4. Tape or glue one end of a crepe paper streamer to one end of a narrow wooden dowel about 13 inches long (available at a craft or hobby store). Wind the crepe paper around the length of the dowel, gluing or taping down the end. Glue the dowel to the tray.

Styrofoam Flag

Paper-Cut Flag

MATERIALS

8-1/2 × 11-inch sheet of white typing paper
pencil
manicure scissors
white glue
8-1/2 × 11-inch sheet of construction paper
15-inch narrow wooden dowel

1. To make the paper-cut, fold the sheet of typing paper in half (figure A). Then fold in half again (figure B). Draw a design that touches all edges of the folded paper (figure C).

2. With manicure scissors, carefully cut out the design, making sure not to cut apart the folded side of the paper.

3. To mount the cut-out, carefully open the folded, cut-out paper. Glue the cut-out onto the construction paper.

4. To make the flag, glue the mounted paper-cut to a narrow wooden dowel about 15 inches long (available in a craft or hobby store), as shown in figure D.

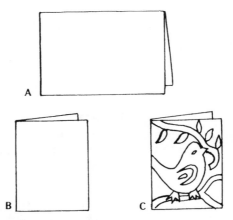

Paper-Cut Flag

Shemini Atzeret and Simḥat Torah

Days of Joy

Textured-Sand Flag

MATERIALS

8-1/2 × 11-inch sheet of construction paper
pencil
8-1/2 × 11-inch piece of cardboard
newspapers
white glue
colored sand or glitter
spoon
flat wooden stick 15 inches long
paint
tacks or stapler and staples

Textured-Sand Flag

1. Spread a batch of newspapers on your work surface. Draw a design on the sheet of construction paper and glue the construction paper to a piece of cardboard.

2. On the construction paper, apply white glue to all areas that will contain the first color of sand or glitter. Take a spoonful of colored sand or glitter and sprinkle it generously on the glued areas. Wait a few minutes for the glue to dry. Carefully tilt the flag to return excess sand or glitter to its container. Repeat for each additional color area of the flag.

3. Paint a flat wooden stick about 15 inches long (available at a hobby store or lumberyard). Let it dry. Staple or tack the flag to the stick.

Felt-on-Felt Banner

MATERIALS

ruler
11 × 14-inch piece of felt
pencil
scissors
scraps of felt in assorted colors
white glue
narrow wooden dowel 20 inches long

1. Lay a ruler along the top of the 11 x 14-inch piece of felt. Use your pencil to make 14 marks, each an inch apart. Draw a 2-inch line down from each mark (figure A).

2. Starting at the first drawn line, cut out every other strip (figure B). Fold over each remaining strip and glue down at the bottom only, forming eight loops (figure C). This is the back of the banner.

3. Turn over the felt. Cut scraps of felt in assorted colors into various shapes. Flowers, animals, and symbols make good choices. Glue the shapes in a design on the banner.

4. Insert a narrow wooden dowel about 20 inches long (available at a craft or hobby store) through the loops (figure D). To use as a flag, hold one end of the dowel at an angle. After using, you may hang the banner as a wall decoration.

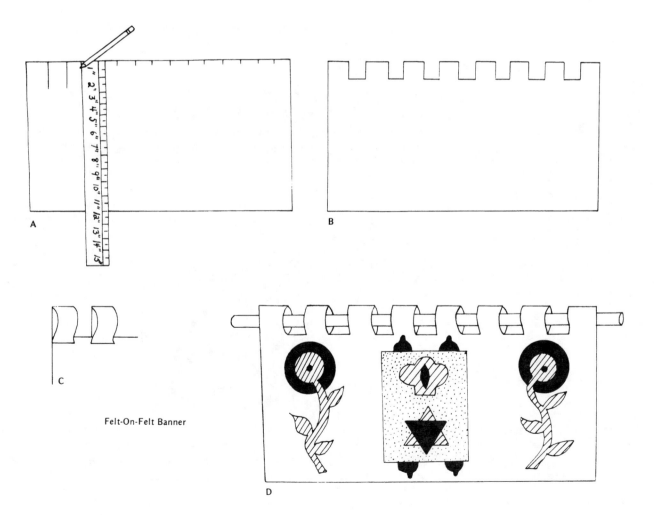

A

B

C

Felt-On-Felt Banner

D

Shemini Atzeret and Simḥat Torah

Days of Joy

Stenciled Flag

MATERIALS

1 large, deep box or box top
pencil
scissors or craft knife
newspapers
1 handkerchief or hemmed cloth
fabric spray paint (from craft store), any color
rags
1 narrow wooden dowel, about 15 inches long (craft or hobby store)
tacks or staple gun
apple

1. To make the stencil, draw designs or symbols for Simḥat Torah on the box or box top.

2. Cut out the shapes.

3. Cover the work surface with newspapers. Place the handkerchief or cloth on top of the newspapers. Place the stencil on top of the cloth.

4. To make the flag, hold the paint can about a foot away from the stencil and lightly spray back and forth over the cut-out holes (figure A).

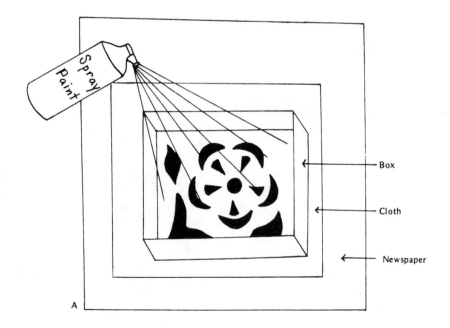

שמחת תורה

B

5. Carefully lift the stencil straight up and wipe the back of the box with rags to clean it. If the cloth is large, move the box stencil to another area of the cloth and spray again. Continue until the whole cloth is printed. Let dry.

6. Tack the flag at least 1 inch down from the top of the wooden dowel, as shown in figure B.

7. Push an apple onto the top part of the dowel (figure B).

Simḥat Torah Fun

Simḥat Torah Puzzles (Answers on page 271.)

Party Time

For their Simḥat Torah party, Betty and Jake baked 3 rectangular cakes. If they sliced each cake separately and evenly, how many slices did they have to make to get 27 slices of cake?

Simḥat Torah Candy

Can you spend exactly $1?

How Many Grandchildren?

For Simḥat Torah, Grandpa Sol baked cookies for his grandchildren. He planned to give each of them 5 cookies leaving 2 for himself and 2 for his wife. His wife said, "Why don't you give each of us the same number of cookies?" And he did. Each of the grandchildren and their two grandparents got 4 cookies. How many grandchildren does Grandpa Sol have?

Art Puzzle

Look at the 2 drawings. Can you tell what is being prepared for Simḥat Torah?

Unscramble each set of letters to form the names of four people from the Torah (including Prophets and Writings). Write each unscrambled name in the squares and circles to the right of the letters, one letter to each. Then unscramble the circled letters to form the answer to the riddle.

Simḥat Torah Scramble

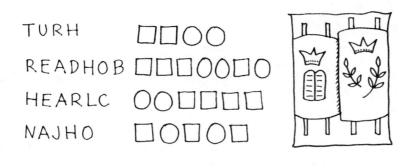

TURH □□○○

READHOB □□□○○□

HEARLC ○○□□□□

NAJHO □○□○□

Riddle: **What's a popular Simḥat Torah dance?**

Answer: A _ _ _ _ _ _   _ _ _ _ _

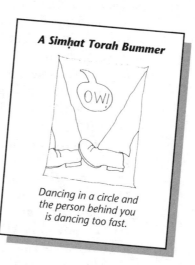

A Simḥat Torah Bummer

OW!

Dancing in a circle and the person behind you is dancing too fast.

Ḥanukkah
Holiday of Lights

About Ḥanukkah

Ḥanukkah is the Holiday of Lights. It brightens every winter with lights, parties, games, and often gifts.

Ḥanukkah, an eight-day holiday beginning on the twenty-fifth of the Hebrew month of Kislev (November-December), celebrates the victory of the Maccabees over the Syrian-Greeks more than two thousand years ago. The Syrian-Greeks desecrated the Temple in Jerusalem. The Syrian ruler, Antiochus Epiphanes, commanded that sacrifices to idols be offered there. The Hasmonean family led a three-year-long revolt against the mighty Greek-Syrian armies and conquered Jerusalem. According to the Talmud Shabbat (21b), only a small quantity of pure consecrated oil could be found for the menorah, enough to burn just one day. But the oil burned and burned for eight days until more oil could be prepared.

Each night of Ḥanukkah we light candles or oil lights to commemorate the miracle. On the first night one light is lit. One is added each night until the eighth night of Ḥanukkah when eight candles are lit. The menorah is lit by a window to publicize the miracle.

In Ashkenazi homes, the hymn "Ma-Oz Tzur" ("Rock of Ages") is sung. In Sephardic homes, the thirtieth psalm is read. It is customary for women not to work while the Ḥanukkah lights are burning.

In many families gifts and gelt (coins) are exchanged on Ḥanukkah. The traditional game of dreidel is played. Latkes (potato pancakes) and sufganiyot (Israeli doughnuts) are served because both are made in oil.

The Ḥanukkah menorah (ḥanukkiyyah) has nine branches,

one for each night of the holiday and one for the shammash, *the helper candle or oil wick. The shammash is lit first and then used to light the other candles. There is a specific order to the lighting of the Ḥanukkah menorah. On the first night one candle is placed at the very right of the menorah and lit. On the second night two candles are placed from right to left in the two spaces at the right of the menorah (one, then two). The candles are lit from the left (two, then one). The pattern is continued until the eighth night, when eight candles are placed in the menorah from right to left and then lit from left to right.*

Chanukah in Yemen
by Leah Abramowitz

"Chanukah in Yemen was a children's holiday," says Rabbanit Kapach, the wife of a famous Jerusalem rabbi. "Every night we had a party. It was very gay."

Rabbanit Kapach is known all over Jerusalem for her charitable activities. Her house is a center for *tzedakah* (charity) and good deeds. She collects and distributes food parcels and clothing to needy families, she sends volunteer students to care for lonely, old people, and she visits invalids. But Rabbanit Kapach is also a storehouse of Yemenite customs and lore. (Yemen is a small country south of Saudi Arabia. Until the Arabs forced the Jews to leave, it had a large and famous Jewish community.)

She recalls the way she celebrated Chanukah in Yemen fifty years ago. Each family placed a mosaic plate or marble menorah containing vials of oil on the wide, black stone staircase of its three-story building, the kind of house in which most city dwellers lived. They lit them out in the open to fulfill the *mitzvah* of *Pirsumei Nissa* (publicizing the miracle). (The weather is calm enough in Yemen to make that possible. In our northern climates, the winter wind would blow out the flames.) Only the father or

1944

A true story by Ruth Minsky Sender

Ḥanukkah 1944. I was in a German concentration camp. We were 50 girls in a crowded room lined with triple decker wooden bunks. A table and a few benches stood in the center. Each night we were left in this room after a hard day in a German factory. We were hungry and bruised and we would crawl into our dark cubicles to cry, and to dream of freedom and food.

One night, weak and hopeless, we were all lying on our sacks of straw. A head poked out from the narrow opening of the bunk on the other end of the room. Sara, one of the older girls, looked toward the little window and the barbed wires beyond. She sighed and said softly, *"Kinder, es is Chanuke"* (Children, it's Ḥanukkah). For a few moments there was silence. Then, one by one, more heads slipped out from the cubicles. Memories of Ḥanukkah with mothers, fathers, sisters and brothers started coming back. *"Oy vey,"* said Rose, *"if I had my mama's latkes right now,"* and with tears in her voice, she added *"... if I had my mama ..."*

From the top bunk we heard the whisper of a Ḥanukkah song: *O, ir kleine lichtelech* (O, you tiny little candle lights). Somehow strengthened by an inner flame, we all joined in, singing together with tears in our eyes: *Ir Dertseylt fun mutikayt, wunder fun amol* (You tell of bravery and wonders long ago. Jews, there were battles you waged, Jews there were victories. All so hard to believe.)

At that moment the German guard outside the room began to bang on the door with her rifle. *"Stop that or I will come in,"* she shouted. We stopped, but I smiled and whispered to my friend, *"We have just won a victory. We are still alive, we will survive!"*

Today, when I think back to that Ḥanukkah night, I see another great miracle before me. I see the children, who according to Hitler's master plan should never have been born.

But here we are: myself, a survivor, who teaches the children to be proud of their Jewishness, and the new generation who will learn, I hope, to draw strength and courage from the Maccabees of long ago and the Maccabees of our own time.

grandfather lit and made a *brachah*. After the adults retired, all the children gathered on the staircase and, sitting on mattresses, rugs, and pillows, they would make merry around the flickering menorahs all night long.

In the middle of the staircase, we put a table laden with *jalla* (goodies). There were fruits of all sorts, carrots, almonds, popcorn, sweets, nuts, baked peas, and a tasty homemade drink made from apricot pips. They sang special Ḥanukkah songs and danced as long as the menorah was burning. The oil burnt much longer than those little wax candles some people use nowadays. There were no dreidels, but the boys used to make wooden tops and hammer in a nail, and set them spinning with a string.

Later the children had a festive meal of their own, still on the staircase. Every night they would gather at someone else's home and each night they would eat something different.

The adults also had family gatherings on Chanukah, but inside their houses. They, too, ate a good meal and sat around a *jalla* table, singing and telling stories. Some Yemenite immigrants continue this custom in Israel as well.

In Yemen, as in many Eastern countries, people sat on rugs or pillows on the floor around a low, round table. Everything they ate was homemade. Even today, many Yemenite residents in Israel buy few finished products if they can help it; no canned goods or frozen products come into their homes. No store-bought bread has the same taste and nutritional value as *pitot* baked in the family oven at 5:00 A.M. in the morning!

The oven was generally in the basement where firewood and other equipment were stored. On the floor above it each family kept a year's supply of products—wine, dates, wheat and other grains, nuts, and so on. The family quarters were located over these storerooms, and they consisted of many rooms, because most families included several generations living together in the same house—grandparents, parents, and married and unmarried children.

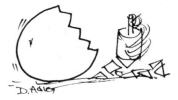

D. Adler

There was also a *succah* courtyard and a special large room used only on Shabbat, holidays, or special occasions, like these Chanukah gatherings. This room was furnished with the nicest rugs and furniture and it often contained a *livan*, a raised platform, at one end, where brides sat during the pre-wedding festivities called *henna*.

No celebration was as merry or colorful as the *henna*. The young bride sat in an upholstered chair dressed in special clothes. The embroidery was elaborate and the gold and silver coins and jewelry which were sewn into the special hairdress and gown were stunning and weighed heavily on the poor girl's head and body. On the day before the wedding, the bride's family and friends gathered around her, singing special wedding songs, sometimes accompanied by a tambourine or drum. The climax of the evening came when a reddish brown, strong-smelling mixture, called *henna,* was smeared on her palms and soles. It was then daubed on the hands of the girls and women around her, who came up to bless the bride, sitting like a queen on the *livan,* amid much yodeling and excitement. This *henna* was considered to be a *segulah* (good omen) for the new couple and their future.

This ceremony is still observed in many Yemenite households and the beautiful, valuable clothes and headdresses are carefully preserved and passed from bride to bride. Some are on display in museums. Some women are experts in caring for them and dressing the brides —it takes over an hour just to arrange the headdress!

On holidays, such as Chanukah, everyone made a special effort to dress especially nicely. "We honored the festivals with good food, pretty clothes, special songs, our best room, *divrei Torah* (words of Torah) and a merry spirit," says Rabbanit Kapach. No one could have celebrated Chanukah better.

The Ḥanukkah Flower

by Morris Epstein

On the morning after Judah Maccabee was slain in battle, lovely white flowers flecked with blood-red dots sprouted on that very spot.

Men and women, wondering at what they beheld, called the blossoms the "Blood of the Maccabees," in memory of the brave defenders of the Jewish faith.

To this day these flowers grow in the Judean hills near Jerusalem, covering the stony slopes with a colorful red and white design. When Ḥanukkah approaches each year and it is once again time to celebrate the Feast of Lights, children go out to pick the *"Dam Ha-Maccabim"* to decorate their homes. And thus does the spirit of Judah Maccabee live in the hearts of our people and in the soul of Zion.

WHY DOES MAX SLEEP WITH HIS HANUKKAH CANDLES?

HE'S A LIGHT SLEEPER

Grandfather's silver Ḥanukkah lamp was hammered and engraved by a master's hand. Two lion heads faced each other, their front paws holding the beautiful Menorah. Above the center was a majestic crown, and on either side two small cups. One was for oil to recall the tiny pitcher of oil that burned for eight days in the ancient Temple. The second cup of oil was for the Shammash.

Grandfather said that he had bought the Ḥanukkah lamp from a wanderer who had once come to the village. The Jew had added a blessing: that the lamp might beautify the Ḥanukkah holidays of my grandfather, his children, grandchildren, and great-grandchildren, from generation to generation.

I was an only grandchild. On the first night of Ḥanukkah I ran to my grandfather's house for two reasons: to see the magnificent Ḥanukkah Menorah, and to collect "Ḥanukkah gelt." Grandfather was dressed in his black silk robe, his beard carefully combed, his eyes sparkling. He hummed an old melody, gave me a hearty pinch on the cheek, and laughingly asked:

The Silver Menorah
by Moshe Dluznowsky

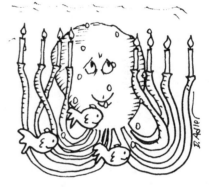

Escape by Dreidel
A Legend

Who invented the dreidel? According to an old legend, the Ḥanukkah top was dreamed up during the time of the Maccabees.

When cruel Antiochus ruled Palestine, he forbade our ancestors to study the Torah or to gather in a synagogue. To escape the king's spies, Jews would meet in small groups and study the Torah by heart. In that way, if one forgot a passage, another who remembered could teach it to him.

Teachers and pupils used to assemble secretly and study in hidden places, while one person acted as a lookout at the entrance. If soldiers were approaching, a warning was given and the group would quickly separate and hurry away through back doors and buried passages.

Among the many clever tricks that were used to avoid discovery was the dreidel game. Those who were studying kept a top on the table. If a soldier should manage to get by the lookout and accuse them of studying, someone would grab the dreidel and spin it. As far as the soldiers could tell, the Jews had only come together to play a game.

Thus the little Ḥanukkah dreidel saved the lives of many of our people.

"You came for Ḥanukkah gelt, I suppose?"

"I also want to see the lamp, Grandfather," I said, shielding my face with my hands, to keep my grandfather from pinching me on the other cheek. "I would like to hold the Shammash."

"You're trying to please me because you want a big handful of coins. But that's all right. You will hold the Shammash."

From the top shelf of his oak bookcase, Grandfather took the well-wrapped Menorah. He removed the wrappings and sat down to clean the rare treasure with a piece of velvet cloth. The lamp shone like a mirror and I saw my reflection in it better than I could in the mirror at home.

Grandfather pulled my ear and humming an old tune, he chanted: "A schoolboy should not mirror himself in a holy thing, and not in silver, you hear, not in a silver Ḥanukkah lamp. Man is created in the image of God. He should therefore be modest, not vain."

I was embarrassed. Grandfather let go of my ear, patted my burning cheek and went on humming the melody.

Done with the polishing, he hung the lamp on a nail on the wall near the window. He began to say the blessings, and he gave me the Shammash to hold. From the second pitcher he poured a little oil into the first candlestick and lit it. The wick burned brightly, lighting up the lions and all the candlesticks, and everything looked like melted gold in a silver frame.

Grandfather sang *Ma-oz Tzur* and wandered about the house in a happy frame of mind. Grandmother prepared potato pancakes and other holiday food. The Ḥanukkah lamp stood proudly, a symbol of the wonderful miracle of Ḥanukkah when a small group of fighters, struggling for their faith and for justice, had conquered a powerful enemy.

When Grandfather died, the lamp was given to his son, my father, who also cherished the valuable Ḥanukkah Menorah.

Now, more than ever, I boasted to my schoolmates about the beautiful Ḥanukkah lamp, and told how it brightened the house when we took it out for the holiday.

Bad times came, years of war and poverty. In our house there was hunger and sadness. Father often stayed home, silent and

"SHOW ME A SNEEZING CANDLE ... AND I'LL SHOW YOU A SICK WICK."

unsmiling. He tried desperately but unsuccessfully to provide a livelihood for his family.

The first day of Ḥanukkah arrived. We waited and waited for Father to open the bookcase, and take out the Menorah, and pour in the oil, and kindle the first light.

But it was almost night and Father had not opened the bookcase.

Outdoors it was bitter cold. The windows were decorated with icicles and frost-flowers. A grayness filled the house, creeping into every corner.

Father opened the pantry closet and took out two small potatoes and two wax candles. His eyes were moist. He looked at Mother and at me.

He said. "We will light the Ḥanukkah candles." Then his voice broke. "One may do that even in potatoes. One candle will be the Shammash."

"What can we do?" Mother comforted him. "Things will get better."

"This is the first time I have had to light Ḥanukkah candles in a potato. I cannot beautify the holiday. I cannot redeem the lamp from Hershel David. Perhaps, after Ḥanukkah, with God's help ..."

I knew Hershel David. Everyone in the village knew the pawnbroker. He was an honest man, to whom people would bring various possessions so that they might borrow money when the need arose.

Occasionally Father would send me to Hershel David with a slip of paper that had a few figures on it. Hershel David took the paper and inspected it with his one crossed eye that quivered a bit. Then he walked over to a big chest with iron bars over it. With a big key he opened the box, took out a few bills, gave them to me, and said:

"Guard it, boy! One has to work hard to earn it."

Now I understood that Father had pawned the precious Ḥanukkah lamp at Hershel David's shop.

I thought a minute and then went out of the house. It was almost twilight and a silver-blue snow covered the streets.

I ran to Hershel David's. I found him bent over a brass Ḥanukkah lamp, pouring oil into the cups.

He turned to me and quietly asked, "What good news do you bring, son?"

A Ḥanukkah Bummer

Being two candles short on the last day of Ḥanukkah.

"The Ḥanukkah lamp," I stammered. "Grandfather's Ḥanukkah lamp!"

He leaned on his cane. "Did you bring the money?"

"No, we do not have the money today. Maybe after Ḥanukkah. Father has to light the first Ḥanukkah candle."

"But it is pawned! Do you understand, son? I loaned your father money and he left the lamp here as security. How can I give it back to you now?"

"Lend us the lamp for eight days. Mother and Father are very upset. It has saddened their holiday." I began to cry.

The Banner of the Jew

Wake, Israel, wake! Recall today
  The glorious Maccabean rage,
The sire heroic, hoary-gray,
  His five-fold lion-lineage:
The Wise, the Elect, the Help-of-God,
The Burst-of-Spring, the Avenging Rod.

From Mizpeh's mountain-side they saw
  Jerusalem's empty streets, her shrine
Laid waste where Greeks profaned the Law,
  With idol and with pagan sign.
Mourners in tattered black were there,
With ashes sprinkled on their hair.

Then from the stony peak there rang
  A blast to ope the graves: down poured
The Maccabean clan, who sang
  Their battle-anthem to the Lord.
Five heroes lead, and following, see,
Ten thousand rush to victory!

Oh, for Jerusalem's trumpet now,
  To blow a blast of shattering
    power,
To wake the sleepers high and low,
  And rouse them to the urgent hour!
No band for vengeance—but to save,
A million naked swords should wave.

Oh, deem not dead that martial fire,
  Say not the mystic flame is spent!
With Moses' law and David's lyre,
  Your ancient strength remains unbent.
Let but an Ezra rise anew,
To lift the Banner of the Jew!

A rag, a mock at first—ere long,
  When men have bled and women wept,
To guard its precious folds from wrong,
  Even they who shrunk, even they who slept,
Shall leap to bless it and to save.
Strike! for the brave revere the brave!

Emma Lazarus

"Do you promise that you'll bring it back, the Ḥanukkah lamp, if your father cannot pay the debt?"

"I . . . I . . . I . . ." I stammered, and then the words came out clearly: "I promise. I will take good care of it."

He went to the chest, opened it, searched inside, and took out the wrapped Ḥanukkah lamp and gave it to me.

I thanked him and ran for the door.

"Wait, son!" his voice boomed. I stopped, frightened. Perhaps he had changed his mind, I thought.

His face was smiling. "Come closer," he said.

I edged toward him gingerly. He pinched my cheek the way my grandfather used to do. From the pocket of his coat he took out a few silver coins.

"Here is some Ḥanukkah gelt."

I took the coins, thanked him, and breathlessly ran home. Father had begun to say the blessings.

"We were waiting for you. Waiting to light the first candle."

Without answering, I tore off the wrappings and the beautiful Ḥanukkah lamp glistened for all to see.

"Grandfather's Ḥanukkah lamp," Mother called out. "But how? We haven't repaid our debt!"

He loaned it to me for Ḥanukkah," I said. "For all eight days."

Father took the lamp from my hands and hung it on the nail near the window, as Grandfather used to do. He poured the oil into the pitcher, and from the pitcher into the first holder. He lit the Shammash, sang the blessing, and lit the wick. The wick flickered, its light reflected in the silver.

Then he sang, *"Ma-oz tzur yeshuati."*

"A miracle. We did not shame the holiday. No, we did not put it to shame."

On the table, in the kitchen, quite lonely and deserted, were the two potatoes with the wax candles still stuck in them.

Mattathias

*He struck the traitor to the
    earth,
He raised his sword that all
    might see;
His words rang like a trumpet blast:
"All who are faithful, follow me!"*

*From near and far all Israel came;
They rallied to his battle cry;
They prayed unto God of Peace,
And for their Law went forth to die—
To die—and yet today they live:
Far down the centuries flaming see
That beacon-sword! Hear that strong cry:
"All who are faithful, follow me!"*

Hatzopheh

Ma-oz Tzur I

Sephardic melody

Lyrically

Ma - oz tzur y'-shu-a-ti___ l'-kha na-eh l'-sha-

bei - ah ti - kon beit t'-fi-la-ti___ v'-

sham___ to - dah n'-za-bei - ah l' - eit ta-khin mat-

bei - ah___ mi-tzar ham-na - bei - ah

az___ eg-mor b'-shir miz-mor___ ha-nu-kat ha-miz-bei - ah

*O God, my saving stronghold, to praise you is a
    delight.
Restore my house of prayer where I will offer you
    thanks.
When you will prepare havoc for the foe who
    maligns us,
I will gratify myself with a song at the altar.*

מָעוֹז צוּר יְשׁוּעָתִי לְךָ נָאֶה לְשַׁבֵּחַ
תִּכּוֹן בֵּית תְּפִלָּתִי וְשָׁם תּוֹדָה נְזַבֵּחַ
לְעֵת תָּכִין מַטְבֵּחַ מִצָּר הַמְנַבֵּחַ
אָז אֶגְמוֹר בְּשִׁיר מִזְמוֹר חֲנֻכַּת הַמִּזְבֵּחַ

Ma-oz Tzur II

Moderately

Ma - oz tzur y' - shu - a - ti l' - kha na - eh l' - sha - bei - aḥ

ti - kon beit t' - fi - la - ti v' - sham to - dah n' - za - bei - aḥ l' -

eit ta - khin mat - bei - aḥ mi - tzar ham' - na - bei - aḥ

az eg - mor b' - shir miz - mor ha - nu - kat ha - miz - bei - aḥ bei - aḥ

O God, my saving stronghold, to praise you is a
  delight.
*Restore my house of prayer where I will offer you
  thanks.*
When you will prepare havoc for the foe who
  maligns us,
I will gratify myself with a song at the altar.

מָעוֹז צוּר יְשׁוּעָתִי לְךָ נָאֶה לְשַׁבֵּחַ
תִּכּוֹן בֵּית תְּפִלָּתִי וְשָׁם תּוֹדָה נְזַבֵּחַ
לְעֵת תָּכִין מַטְבֵּחַ מִצָּר הַמְנַבֵּחַ
אָז אֶגְמוֹר בְּשִׁיר מִזְמוֹר חֲנֻכַּת הַמִּזְבֵּחַ

Y'Mei Haḥanukah

Moderately

Y' - mei ha - ḥa - nu - kah ḥa - nu - kat mik - da - shei - nu b' - gil u - v' - sim - ḥah m' - mal -
im et li - bei - nu lai - la va - yom s'vi - vo - nei - nu yi - sov suf - ga - ni - yot no -
khal bam la - rov ha - i - ru had - li - ku nei - rot ha - nu - kah ra -
bim al ha - ni - sim___ v' - al ha - nif - la - ot___ a - sher ḥo - l' - lu ha - ma - ka - bim

O Ḥanukah, O Ḥanukah, come light the menorah
Let's have a party we'll all dance the hora
Gather round the table we'll give you a treat
Shiny tops to play with and pancakes to eat
And while we are playing the candles are burning low
One for each night they shed a sweet light
To remind us of days long ago.

יְמֵי הַחֲנֻכָּה חֲנֻכַּת מִקְדָּשֵׁנוּ
בְּגִיל וּבְשִׂמְחָה מְמַלְאִים אֶת לִבֵּנוּ
לַיְלָה וָיוֹם סְבִיבוֹנֵנוּ יִסֹּב
סֻפְגָּנִיּוֹת נֹאכַל בָּם לָרֹב
הָאִירוּ הַדְלִיקוּ נֵרוֹת חֲנֻכָּה רַבִּים
עַל הַנִּסִּים וְעַל הַנִּפְלָאוֹת אֲשֶׁר חוֹלְלוּ הַמַּכַּבִּים

I Have a Little Dreydl

S. E. Goldfarb

I have a little dreydl I made it out of clay
And when it's dry and ready then dreydl I will play
O dreydl dreydl dreydl I made it out of clay
O dreydl dreydl dreydl now dreydl I shall play

It has a lovely body with leg so short and thin
And when it is all tired it drops and then I win
O dreydl dreydl dreydl with leg so short and thin
O dreydl dreydl dreydl it drops and then I win

My dreydl's always playful it loves to dance and spin
A happy game of dreydl come play now let's begin
O dreydl dreydl dreydl it loves to dance and spin
O dreydl dreydl dreydl come play now let's begin

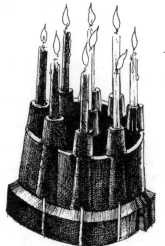

Ḥanukkah Crafts

Bottle Cap Menorah

STOP!

Some of the crafts in this chapter call for the use of a hammer, scissors, or other potentially dangerous tools. Before beginning any craft, get either help or the "go-ahead" from a responsible adult.

Most menorahs today are machine-made, but the tradition encourages making your own menorah. It can use oil or candles and should be made of a material that won't burn, like metal or clay. The candle or oil holders should be far enough apart so the flames won't touch one another and all on the same level with the exception of the shammash. *The* shammash *stands apart from the others by being set higher, lower, or farther away. The flame holders don't even have to be connected.*

An unusual Ḥanukkah menorah can be made from a distributor cap for an eight-cylinder car. Ḥanukkah candles fit perfectly into the nine holes. Maybe you can get an old one from a gas station. Another way to make a menorah from everyday objects is to use bottle caps. These menorahs are simple and can be made anywhere, by anyone, which is what the rabbis intended. They wanted everyone, no matter how poor, to light the Ḥanukkah candles.

MATERIALS

piece of wood 1 foot long and 2-1/2 inches wide
9 aluminum bottle caps
pencil
white glue
9 candles or olive oil and nine 5-inch wicks

1. Place the bottle caps on the wood in an interesting design. Then mark their locations on the wood and glue them in place with plenty of white glue.

2. Fill the caps with olive oil and 5-inch wicks, or fit candles into them.

A ḥanukkiyyah made of natural objects does two things. First, it fulfills the mitzvah of lighting the candles, and second, it unites two important parts of Ḥanukkah, the story of the Maccabees, and the winter fire festivals from which the Maccabees borrowed customs for the first Ḥanukkah. A very simple natural menorah can be made from nine halves of walnut shells containing olive oil and wicks. Iraqi Jews use a walnut menorah, but they use melted butter instead of olive oil.

Acorn Menorah

MATERIALS

thick piece of bark about 1 foot long or a fallen tree branch
9 fat acorns
alum solution
white glue
moss and lichen
9 candles to fit in the acorns

1. Take a walk in the woods to find a thick piece of bark—pine is especially good—approximately a foot long. A fallen tree branch that lies flat will also work. Then gather the caps of 9 fat acorns.

2. Soak them for 2 hours in a solution of alum (available at a hardware or drugstore) and water. This flameproofs the acorns.

3. When the acorns are dry, glue them to the flat side of the bark or branch with white glue. If there's room on the bark, glue down bits of moss and lichen for decoration. This menorah burns only candles because acorns are too small to hold enough oil to burn for a half-hour.

Although it's hard to make a fast dreidel without carpentry tools, here is an idea for a spinning dreidel that can also be used as a fancy container for chocolates, Ḥanukkah gelt, or a small gift.

Dreidel

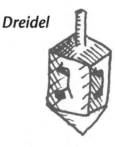

MATERIALS

1 piece of construction paper
sharpened pencil
scissors
cellophane tape
piece of candy or a coin

A Ḥanukkah Bummer

When you buy Ḥanukkah presents and the sales clerk wishes you a Merry Christmas.

1. On a piece of construction paper, draw this pattern:

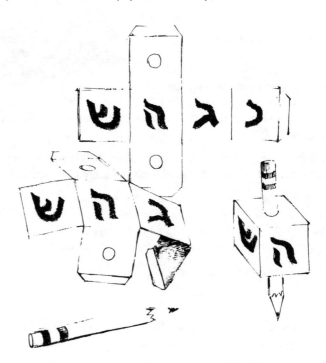

2. Cut on the outside lines, and then fold on the inside lines.

3. Tape all but one of the flaps to form a box. Put in candy or a coin before the last flap is taped.

4. Use your pencil to poke a small hole in the top and bottom of the dreidel, and then stick the pencil through it. The dreidel will spin.

These mouth-watering treats are a great way to celebrate Ḥanukkah. For extra zest, sprinkle them with cinnamon mixed with just a little nutmeg.

Ḥanukkah Recipes

Bimuelos or Loukomades (Greece)

DOUGH

2 cakes yeast (room temperature)
1-1/3 cups warm water
1 egg, beaten
1/2 teaspoon salt
1 tablespoon oil
3 cups flour, unsifted
cinnamon to sprinkle
oil to deep fry

SYRUP

1 (24-ounce) jar honey
1/4 cup water

Pour 1/2 of the warm water into a medium mixing bowl. Dissolve the yeast in the warm water.

Add beaten egg, salt, and 1 tablespoon of oil to the yeast mixture.

Put the flour in a large mixing bowl. Add the yeast mixture to the flour all at once and stir, adding remaining water gradually.

Allow the dough to rise at least 1 hour.

After the dough has risen, combine honey and water for syrup; bring to a boil. Reduce the temperature and let the syrup simmer.

Place oil for deep frying in a large pan, and heat to 375 degrees. The oil should be no deeper than half the height of the pan. Slowly and gently drop the dough from a tablespoon (which has first been dipped in oil) into the hot oil, making sure the oil doesn't splatter. Bimuelos puff up and should be turned over until evenly golden.

When the bimuelos are a golden color, remove them from the oil and drain on paper toweling.

Dip in warm syrup and sprinkle generously with cinnamon. Bimuelos are best served warm and preferably immediately, but they may be fried ahead of time and dipped in the hot syrup just before serving.

Makes about 45. Serve a minimum of 2 to 3 per person.

STOP!

A kitchen is a dangerous place. If you're not careful, you might burn yourself with splattering oil or boiling water. The recipes in this chapter are intended for older children. Before beginning, make sure an adult is available to help.

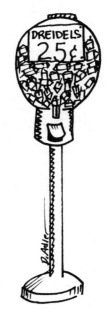

Sufganiot
(Israeli Doughnuts)

Doughnuts are fun, but burns are not. Make sure an adult is nearby to help with the frying.

1/2 package dried yeast
1 cup warm water (105–115 degrees)
2 cups flour
2 teaspoons sugar
1 teaspoon salt
1 egg
oil for frying

Place the warm water in a medium mixing bowl. Sprinkle the yeast over the warm water and let it stand until it is dissolved.

In a large mixing bowl, sift the flour with the sugar and the salt.

Beat an egg in a small bowl and add the egg to the flour mixture.

Add the yeast to the flour mixture and stir until the mixture is thoroughly blended. Cover the dough and put it in a warm place (85 degrees) to rise until it doubles in bulk.

Place oil in a frying pan to half the height of the pan and heat. When the oil is hot, slowly and gently drop the batter by spoonfuls into the oil, making sure the oil doesn't splatter. Fry on both sides until doughnuts are a golden color, then remove the sufganiot with a slotted spoon with a very long handle or a very long set of tongs. Drain them well on paper toweling. Sprinkle with granulated sugar. Serve hot.

6 servings

Potato Pancakes

When making these delicious potato pancakes, be sure to have all the ingredients ready for immediate use before grating the potatoes. (Grated potatoes that are left standing turn brown.) To keep the potatoes from turning brown, you may want to use 2 frying pans at the same time.

4 large potatoes
3 tablespoons matzah meal
3 eggs
1 teaspoon salt
1/4 teaspoon pepper
1 teaspoon onion powder
oil for frying

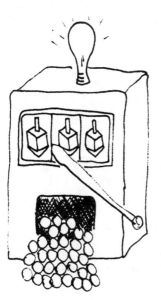

Measure the matzah meal, the salt, the pepper, and the onion powder, and mix them together in a medium mixing bowl.

In a second bowl, mix the eggs together and then add them to the matzah mixture.

Pour the frying oil into a frying pan, but do not heat it yet.

Grate the potatoes, and squeeze out as much water as possible. Add the potatoes to the matzah mixture.

Heat the oil in a frying pan. When the oil is hot, slowly and gently drop the potato mixture by tablespoons into the oil, making sure the oil doesn't splatter. Fry on both sides until brown. Remove from the oil, and drain on paper toweling.

The pancakes can be fried in advance and frozen. Before serving, lay the pancakes in one layer on a foil-lined cookie sheet and reheat in a 375-degree oven for about 20 minutes. Serve with applesauce.

6 servings

Ḥanukkah Fun

How to Play Dreidel

The most popular Ḥanukkah game is dreidel. The dreidel is a spinning top. Its name in Yiddish means "turn." The Hebrew word for dreidel is sevivon.

There are four letters on the dreidel:

נ ג ה שׁ

They stand for the words Nes gadol hayah sham, *which means "A great miracle happened there."*

Dreidels in Israel have the letters:

נ ג ה פ

They stand for the words Nes gadol hayah poh, *which means "A great miracle happened here."*

Here are the rules for playing dreidel:
Everyone starts with an equal number of pennies, nuts, raisins, or Ḥanukkah gelt. Each player puts one of these in the middle. The first player spins the dreidel. If it lands on:

נ Nun—the player does nothing;

ג Gimmel—the players takes everything in the middle;

ה Hey—the player takes half;

שׁ Shin—the player puts one in.

An easy way to remember this is:

נ N—nothing;

ג G—get;

ה H—half;

שׁ SH—share.

After each gimmel, *before the next player spins, each player puts another piece in the middle and the spinning continues.*

Dreidel Variations

See who can keep a dreidel spinning the longest.

Try spinning the dreidel upside down.

Let everyone spin a dreidel. Those whose dreidels land on the same letter get a point. The others lose. Play to a specified numbers of points.

Hebrew letters stand for numbers. Nun נ *is 50. Gimmel* ג *is 3. Hey* ה *is 5. Shin* ש *is 300. (On an Israeli dreidel, Pey* פ *is 80.) Take turns spinning the dreidel, and after each spin record each player's score. The first to get 1,000 wins.*

Try a dreidel hunt. One player leaves the room while the others hide a dreidel. The player returns to hunt for the hidden dreidel while the others sing a Ḥanukkah song. As the searcher comes closer to the hidden dreidel, the singing gets louder. As the searcher moves away, the singing gets softer.

Ḥanukkah Puzzles (Answers on page 272.)

Candle Puzzle

You have four Ḥanukkah candles. Can you add six more and just have five?

Ḥanukkah Candles

Which burns longer, the tall thin candle or the short fat one?

Ḥanukkah Gelt

For Ḥanukkah Dina got $11, all in U.S. paper bills, and none of them were $1 bills. What were they?

Ḥanukkah Anagrams

Rearrange the letters in each group, using all the letters, and form a Ḥanukkah word or name.

1. RIDDLE E

2. HERMAN O

3. AA HUNH KK

4. LAND EC

5. FIG T

CAN I MAKE SUFGANIYOT IN MY PAJAMAS?

NO. YOU NEED AN OVEN!

Ḥanukkah Riddles

1. What time is it when you sit on a burning candle?

2. How can you light a Ḥanukkah candle without a match?

3. Why did the foolish cook run out of the house when he was making latkes?

4. What has four sides, spins, and hops?

5. Why won't the candle maker make candles any longer?

6. If a candle and a half need a wick and a half, how long would it take a candle maker to make a candle using noodles and soup?

A Ḥanakkah Bummer

HAPPY HANUKKAH FROM Guess who!

When someone sends you a Ḥanukkah card and signs it "Guess who!"

Tu B'Shevat
A Celebration of Trees

About Tu B'Shevat

Happy New Year again!

It's still winter in the United States, but in Israel, by the middle of the Hebrew month of Shevat (January/February), the rainy season has ended, trees are beginning to bud, and fruits on the trees are beginning to form. The fifteenth of Shevat—in Hebrew—is celebrated as the New Year for trees, Tu B'Shevat.

In Israel it is celebrated by planting trees. Elsewhere it is a day to express our love of Israel. People eat the kind of fruits that grow in Israel, such as figs, dates, raisins, and carob. There is also a custom to eat from fifteen different fruits (because Tu B'Shevat is on the fifteenth day of the month) and to eat a new fruit, one not yet eaten during the current year, so an added blessing, she-he-ḥeyanu, can be said. Some people eat the fruits in a Tu B'Shevat seder along with four cups of wine. Each fruit is eaten after saying an appropriate verse from the Bible or Talmud. Others give a donation to the Jewish National Fund so a tree will be planted in their name in Israel. There is a custom, too, to pray on Tu B'Shevat to have a beautiful etrog for the following Sukkot.

The Date Tree
by Judah Steinberg

In ancient Israel there once lived a pious man named Micah. Micah's house stood on the highway which led to the city of Jerusalem. The house was built of stone, for Micah, who loved all growing things, refused to chop down the trees of the forest.

Once, in honor of Tu B'shevat, Micah planted a date tree beside his house. After a few years the tree grew so tall that it cast a shade all about it. Micah put a table and benches under the tree. Whenever anyone passed his house going to Jerusalem, Micah would invite him to rest under the tree and to eat and drink his fill.

Sometimes a guest would insist on paying Micah for the meal. But when the guest was not looking, the pious man would put the money back into the traveller's sack. When the guests departed, the birds would come down from the tree and eat the crumbs which were left on the table.

116

One day an old man passed Micah's house. As was his custom, Micah invited him to rest and dine. When the meal was finished, the old man left money on the table for the food. Then he noticed that his host had slipped it back into his sack when he thought he was not looking. The old man, who was a prophet, said to Micah, "Your kindness shall be repaid. No matter where you and your children may be, wherever you shall live, you shall always eat the fruit of your date tree under which the traveller enjoys your hospitality."

That moment the date tree silently gave its oath that its fruit would follow Micah and his children to all the lands of the world, so that the words of the prophet would come true.

The years passed peacefully and one bright day the date tree bore its first fruits. But no sooner did Micah and his children sit at the table to eat the dates, than the thunder of horses' hooves was heard in the distance. Micah ran out onto the highway. A foreign army was speeding on its way towards Jerusalem. Micah and his children, and thousands of other Israelites, were taken captive by the conquering king.

As the monarch was returning from Jerusalem to his land, he passed Micah's house and saw the beautiful date tree. The king dismounted from his horse, plucked one of the dates, and ate it. The pit remained stuck in his throat. The soldiers quickly bore their king to their own city, where the doctors removed the pit and threw it out-of-doors. The date pit took root and grew slowly. And it happened that the

Olive trees growing in Israel.

house where Micah's children lived was under the date tree. Each year, on Tu B'Shevat, they enjoyed the fruit of the tree, as the prophet had predicted.

But Micah's grandchildren left the land of the conquering king and went to other lands to live. Each took with him fruit of the date tree to plant beside his new home. Wherever the descendants of Micah settled, in every land of the world, they continued to eat the fruit of the date tree.

And as the Jewish children everywhere eat dates on Tu B'shevat they say, "Who knows? Perhaps, I am one of Micah's descendants."

The Apple Tree's Discovery
by Peninnah Schram and Rachayl Eckstein Davis

In a great oak forest where the trees grew tall and majestic, there was a little apple tree. It was the only apple tree in that forest and so it stood alone.

Winter came. As the snow fell to the forest floor, it covered the branches of the little apple tree. The forest was quiet and peaceful.

One night the little apple tree looked up at the sky and saw a wonderful sight. Between the branches of all the trees, the little apple tree saw the stars in the sky, which appeared to be hanging on the branches of the oak trees.

"Oh God, Oh God," whispered the little apple tree, "how lucky those oak trees are to have such beautiful stars hanging on their branches. I want more than *anything* in the world to have stars on my branches, just like the oak trees have! Then I would feel truly special."

God looked down at the little apple tree and said gently, "Have patience! Have patience, little apple tree!"

Time passed. The snows melted and spring came to the land. Tiny white and pink apple blossoms appeared on the branches of the little apple tree. Birds came to rest on its branches. People walked by the little apple tree and admired its beautiful blossoms.

All summer long, the apple tree continued to grow. The branches of the tree formed a canopy overhead as they filled with leaves and blossoms.

But night after night, the little apple tree looked up at the sky with the millions, and millions, and millions—and millions of stars and cried out, "Oh God, I want more than anything in the world to have stars in my tree and on my branches and in my leaves—just like those oak trees."

And God looked down at the little apple tree and said, "You already have gifts. Isn't it enough to have shade to offer people, and fragrant blossoms, and branches for birds to rest on so they can sing you their song?"

> **Trees**
>
> *I think that I shall never see*
> *A poem lovely as a tree;*
> *A tree that looks at God all day*
> *And lifts her leafy arms to pray;*
> *Poems are made by fools like me,*
> *But only God can make a tree.*
>
> *Joyce Kilmer*

WHAT DID THE ORANGE TREE SAY AT HARVEST TIME?

STOP PICKING ON ME!

D. Adler

The apple tree sighed and answered simply, "Dear God, I don't mean to sound ungrateful, but that is not special enough! I do appreciate how much pleasure I give to others, but what I really want more than anything in the world is to have *stars,* not blossoms, on my branches. Then I would feel truly special!"

God smiled and answered, "Be patient, little apple tree."

The seasons changed again. Soon the apple tree was filled with many beautiful apples. People walked in the forest. Whoever saw the apple tree would reach up, pick an apple and eat it.

And still, when night came to the forest, the apple tree looked at the stars

WHY DID THE PEOPLE
OF CHELM HUG
THEIR TREES?

THEY WERE
LISTENING TO
THE TREE BARK.

in the oak trees and called out, "Oh God, I want more than *anything* in the world to have stars on my branches! Then I would feel truly special."

And God asked, "But apple tree, isn't it enough that you now have such wonderful apples to offer people? Doesn't that satisfy you? Doesn't that give you enough pleasure and make you feel special?"

Without saying a word, the apple tree answered by shaking its branches from side to side.

At that moment, God caused a wind to blow. The great oak trees began to sway and the apple tree began to shake. From the top of the apple tree an apple fell. When it hit the ground, it split open.

"Look," commanded God, "look inside yourself. What do you see?"

The little apple tree looked down and saw that right in the middle of the apple—was a star. And the apple tree answered, "A star! I have a star!"

And God laughed a gentle laugh and added, "So you do have stars on your branches. They've been there all along, you just didn't know it."

Epilogue: Usually when we want to cut an apple, we cut it by holding the apple with its stem up. But in order to find its star, we must turn it on its side. If we change our direction a little bit, we too can find the spark that ignites the star inside each of us. The stars are right there within each one of us. Look carefully, look closely, and you'll find that beautiful star.

A Tu B'Shevat Bummer

Biting into wax fruit.

Hashkeidiya

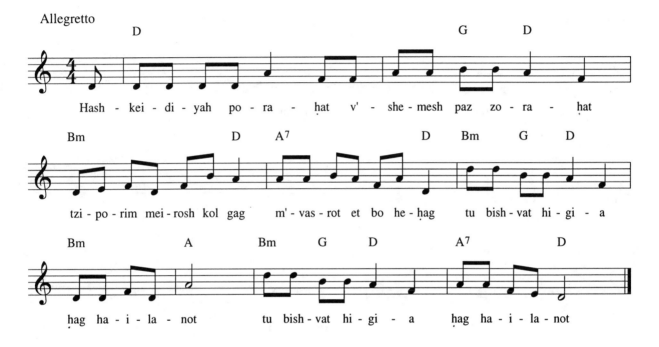

Allegretto

Hash - kei - di - yah po - ra - hat v' - she - mesh paz zo - ra - hat

tzi - po - rim mei - rosh kol gag m' - vas - rot et bo he - hag tu bish - vat hi - gi - a

hag ha - i - la - not tu bish - vat hi - gi - a hag ha - i - la - not

The almond tree is growing and a golden sun is glowing. From every rooftop the birds sing out. Tu Bishvat is here, the New Year of Trees.

הַשְׁקֵדִיָּה פּוֹרַחַת וְשֶׁמֶשׁ פָּז זוֹרַחַת
צִפֳּרִים מֵרֹאשׁ כָּל גַּג מְבַשְּׂרוֹת אֶת בֹּא הֶחָג
טוּ בִּשְׁבָט הִגִּיעַ חַג הָאִילָנוֹת

Atzei Zeitim Omdim

Olive trees stand tall.

עֲצֵי זֵיתִים עוֹמְדִים

Try this delicious vegetable instead of lettuce on sandwiches, add to salads or any vegetable dish, or enjoy simply as a healthful snack.

MATERIALS

1 tablespoon alfalfa seeds
1-quart jar
1 quart water
2 small pieces of cheese cloth

1. Place one tablespoon of alfalfa seeds (available at a health food store) in a one-quart jar. Fill the jar with water.

2. Cover the jar with 2 layers of cheesecloth and fasten with a rubber band.

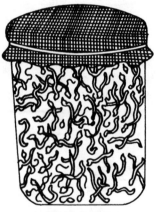

Alfalfa Sprouts

3. Turn the jar upside down over a sink and shake until all the water comes out.

4. Turn the jar right side up and tap the bottom of the jar firmly to separate the seeds. This moistens the seeds and removes the hull.

5. Place the jar where it will get light. Once in the morning, once in the afternoon, and once in the evening, fill the jar with water and shake.

6. In less than a week, you will have a jar full of alfalfa sprouts.

Planting for Tu B'Shevat

Alfalfa Sprouts You Can Eat

STOP!
Some of the crafts in this chapter call for the use of a hammer, scissors, or other potentially dangerous tools. Before beginning any craft, get either help or the "go-ahead" from a responsible adult.

STOP

You don't have to live in the tropics to grow your own orange, grapefruit, or lemon tree!

MATERIALS

grapefruit, lemon, and orange seeds
3 bowls or jars
3 pieces of paper
cellophane tape
water to cover the seeds
3 small plant pots
potting soil
several tablespoons of sand

Citrus Seed Plants

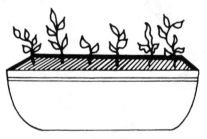

1. Collect plump grapefruit, lemon, and orange seeds. Rinse the seeds and let them dry for a few hours.

2. Put each type of seed in a separate bowl or jar. Write the name of each type on a small piece of paper and tape the paper to the container. Cover the seeds with water and let soak for two days.

3. Empty the water from the containers, keeping the different types of seeds separate.

4. Fill three small plant pots with potting soil mixed with a little sand. Push the seeds about 1/4 inch down into the soil, keeping them about 1 inch apart. Label each pot.

5. Moisten the soil with water and put the plants in a sunny spot. Continue to water only when the soil feels dry to the touch. In one to three months, plants will sprout. Trim off any leaves that don't look healthy.

Citrus Seed Plants

Some sweet potatoes are treated to prevent sprouting, so choose one that has little purple-looking buds near the top or wide end.

Sweet Potato Vine

MATERIALS
sweet potato
jar or glass
water
several toothpicks
watering can or container to hold water
plant pot 4–6 inches in diameter
potting soil

A Tu B'Shevat Bummer

Fruit flies.

1. Take a jar or glass (big enough for the potato to fit through the rim but not fall in) and fill 3/4 full of water.

2. Set the potato in the jar, budded side up, so the tapered end is in the water. You may need to insert toothpicks into the potato to hold it up.

3. Place the jar in a light spot but not in direct sunlight. Keep handy a container filled with water at room temperature and add some to the jar each day. In a few weeks, roots will start growing down and leaves will sprout up (figure A).

A

4. Wait a few more weeks for additional growth, then plant the potato in a pot filled with potting soil. Keep the soil moist and you will soon have a long vine (figure B).

B

Avocado Plant

Avocado Plant

An avocado pit will turn into a gorgeous, sun-loving plant that will brighten any room in your house.

MATERIALS
fully ripe avocado
plant pot 4–6 inches in diameter
potting soil
sand
water

1. Cut the avocado in half and remove the pit. Place the pit in a warm spot for about 24 hours or soak it in water for about 2 days, until the dark outside skin comes off.

2. Fill a plant pot with potting soil mixed with a little sand.

3. Plant the pit, pointed end up and flat end down, in the pot. Leave the tip of the pit (about 1/3 of the pointed end) exposed. Place the plant in a spot with a lot of light, but no direct sun. Water the soil well and then water every few days to keep the soil moist, but not soaking wet.

4. About 2 months later, the pit will split and a stem will sprout. When this happens, move the plant where it will get direct sunlight. If you want a broader, bushier plant, pinch off the top shoot when it grows to a height of about 6 inches.

Vegetable-Top Plant

If you don't have a vegetable garden, this is a fun way to see what some vegetables look like before they are harvested. Experiment with different vegetables and watch them grow.

MATERIALS
beet, carrot, parsnip, or turnip
cutting board
serrated knife
3 toothpicks
jar or glass
water

1. Place the vegetable on a cutting board. With your fingers safely behind the serrated knife, carefully cut off the top of the vegetable, cutting down about 1-1/2 inches.

2. Insert 3 toothpicks into the top part of the vegetable, so the top half is kept out of the water. Put the vegetable in a dish or drinking glass and add water until it covers the bottom half of the vegetable.

3. Change the water every few days, keeping it at the same level. After a few weeks, fern-like leaves will start to grow.

Vegetable-Top Plant

Ask your parents to help with this nifty upside-down garden.

Upside-Down Garden

MATERIALS

1 beet
1 carrot
1 parsnip
1 turnip
grapefruit knife
melon ball scoop
skewer or other thin, pointed object
fishing line
water

1. Cut each vegetable in half. With a grapefruit knife and melon ball scoop, carefully make a hollow in the cut side of the top half of each vegetable. Leave the walls around the cavity intact.

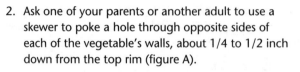

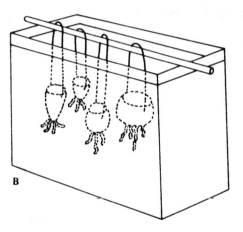

2. Ask one of your parents or another adult to use a skewer to poke a hole through opposite sides of each of the vegetable's walls, about 1/4 to 1/2 inch down from the top rim (figure A).

3. Thread a length of fishing line through both holes and hang the string of vegetables from a tension rod between the sides of a window, tie to the bottom of a coat hanger, or hang from a dowel resting on a large plastic or glass container, such as an aquarium (figure B).

4. Fill the hollows with water. Replace with fresh water every other day. Keep the garden in bright sunlight and soon leaves will start growing from the bottom of each plant.

Pineapple-Top Plant

Pineapples can be very hard to cut, so ask an adult to cut the pineapple for you.

MATERIALS

1 pineapple
serrated knife
gloves (optional)
container large enough to hold pineapple top
plant pot
potting soil

1. With a serrated knife, cut off the leafy top of a pineapple, including about one-half inch of the fruit (figure A). Break off any growths around the base of the pineapple top. Cut down at an angle toward the bottom center (figure B). Continue around the pineapple top until you have a pointed base (figure C). You may want to protect your hands with gloves.

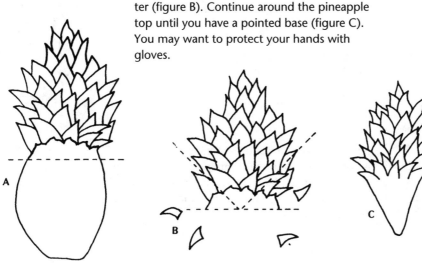

2. Place the pineapple top in a container of water small enough for the pineapple to rest on top. Make sure the pointed base of the pineapple is under the water. If you use a clear container you will be able to see the root growth.

3. Change the water every 3 or 4 days. After a few weeks, a full root system will develop (figure D).

4. Plant the pineapple in potting soil. Put in a sunny place and keep the soil moist by watering the top center of the foliage instead of watering the soil itself. Unless grown in a controlled hothouse environment, the pineapple will not flower or bear fruit. However, in a few months, you will have a hardy plant with beautiful foliage (figure E).

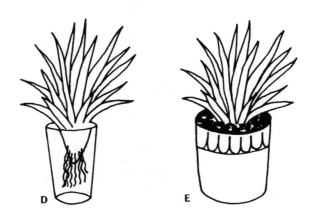

SHOW ME A ROLLING BOWL OF FRUIT... AND I'LL SHOW YOU AN APPLE TURNOVER.

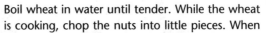

Tu B'Shevat Recipe

Kofyas (Turkey)
Wheat Pudding

This traditional treat for "Las Frutas" was also made to celebrate the occasion of a baby cutting its first tooth. The honor of preparing kofyas went to the person who first discovered that the tooth was through the baby's gum.

1 cup whole grain wheat
water to cover the wheat
sugar or honey to taste
cinnamon to taste
nuts to taste

Boil wheat in water until tender. While the wheat is cooking, chop the nuts into little pieces. When the wheat is tender, add sugar or honey to taste and cook a few minutes longer. Turn off the burner and remove the pot of wheat. Top with cinnamon and nuts. Serve.

Serves 4

STOP!
A kitchen is a dangerous place. If you're not careful, you might burn yourself with splattering oil or boiling water. The recipe in this chapter is intended for older children. Before beginning, make sure an adult is available to help.

STOP

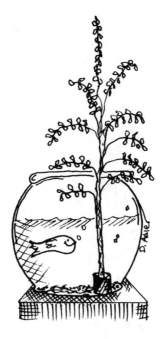

Tu B'Shevat Fun

Tu B'Shevat Puzzles (Answers on page 272.)

Unscramble the letters in each box and find the names of the fruits in the basket.

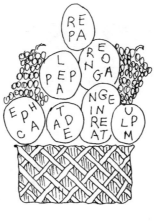

Mixed-Up Fruit Basket

How can you divide 7 apples equally among 5 people?

Apples

In all, there are 100 almonds, raisins, and dates in a dish. There are twice as many almonds as raisins and just as many raisins as dates. How many almonds, raisins, and dates are in the dish?

Almonds, Raisins, and Dates

Place an almond on a table and cover it with a hat. Then tell a friend that you can remove the almond without touching the hat. Reach under the table and then close your hand into a fist. Tell your friend, "See, I told you I could get the almond without touching the hat." Your friend, of course, will not believe that you have the almond and will lift the hat to check. That's when you take the almond without touching the hat.

Almost Magic

Purim

Be Happy!

About Purim

Be happy!
It's Purim!

The fourteenth day of the Hebrew month of Adar (March/April) is Purim, a joyous celebration of a great Jewish victory. The day before Purim is the Fast of Esther, recalling Queen Esther's three-day fast before she pleaded for the Jewish people. On the night and following morning of Purim, Jews gather at synagogues and temples to hear the reading of the Megillah, the Book of Esther. It tells how the wicked Haman plotted to destroy the Jewish people. Many people, especially children, come to the reading dressed in outlandish costumes, a custom which originated in Italy some five hundred years ago.

Many hundreds of years ago people would write Haman's name on pieces of stone and then rub the stones together until his name was erased. This evolved into the custom we have today. During the reading of the Megillah, people drown out Haman's name with Purim noisemakers.

In many congregations half dollars are collected in remembrance of the half shekels collected in Biblical times. The money collected is given to charity.

On Purim gifts of food, shelakh manot, are exchanged between families and gifts of charity are given to the poor. During the afternoon there is a Purim seudah, a feast, with wine and hamantaschen, which are Purim pastries filled with jelly, poppy seeds, or cheese, and shaped like Haman's three-cornered hat. It is a custom, too, to eat vegetables and recall that Queen Esther, unwilling to eat non-kosher food, only ate vegetables in the palace of the king.

Throughout our history many communities have had interesting Purim customs.

During the eighteenth century in Frankfurt-am-Main, Germany wax figures of Haman and his wife Zeresh were made with a wick inside. They were lit just as the reading of the Megillah began. As the reading progressed, the congregation could listen to and watch the downfall, the "melting," of Haman and Zeresh.

In the Caucasus region of Russia, there was a custom for each family to burn a wooden effigy (statue or dummy) of Haman. In Tunisia, effigies of Haman were thrown into a bonfire. In Syria, a cloth effigy was hung up outside the synagogue and then attacked with sticks and swords.

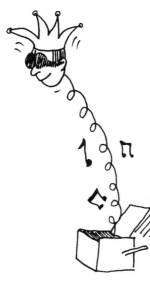

Before the Megillah reading in many communities, there was a custom for Jews to write Haman's name on the soles of their shoes. Then, during the reading, they stomped their feet every time Haman's name was read. By the end of the reading Haman's name was wiped out.

DAY SCHOOL DAZE   by Shepsil Scheinberg

*Y*ou have heard, of course, of anti-semitism. It is a modern name for a very old, evil thing. Anti-semitism is prejudice against, and sometimes even hatred of, the Jews. It is so old that we find it in the pages of the Bible. It is described in the Book of Esther.

After the Babylonians had captured Jerusalem, they exiled the leaders, nobles, priests, and a large part of the people of Judah to Babylonia. The people settled down in Babylonia, determined to be good citizens and loyal subjects of the king. Indeed, they received a letter from their great prophet Jeremiah advising them to do this. They followed his wise counsel. They organized their little community and became law-abiding citizens. When Persia later conquered Babylonia, and the Jews became subjects of the new Empire, they gave their allegiance to their new king, the king of the Persians.

Years passed. The Jews of Persia lived in peace. But that peace came to an end in the reign of King Ahasuerus (Xerxes, 485–465 B.C.E.).

The Story of Esther
adapted by Mortimer J. Cohen

133

Purim

Be Happy!

An enemy named Haman, the Agagite, arose who hated the Jews and plotted to destroy them.

The Book of Esther tells of this plot, and how the Jews were saved from cruel destruction by the courage and loyalty of a beautiful Jewish maiden, Esther. Thankful to God for their deliverance, the Jewish people established the Feast of Purim. And on Purim the Book of Esther is read in synagogues. This book is also called the Megillah, *or "The Scroll of Esther."*

In later times, when similar enemies plotted to destroy them, the Jews remembered their deliverance in the days of Esther and Mordecai; they placed their faith in God's help, and took new courage and hope.

While anti-semitism is prejudice against Jews, the Jews have not been the only victims of misunderstanding and hatred. Unfortunately, many men and women of different religions, races, or nationalities at various times have been the innocent victims of these evils, but only partly because they happened to be different from the people about them. More often power-mad or money-hungry people have used hatred against the Jews and people of other groups to hide their own evil ambitions and schemes. The Book of Esther, therefore, has a message for all people as well as for Jews. It warns mankind against the terrible evil of prejudice which brings so much persecution, suffering, and unhappiness into the world.

The King's Banquet

In the third year of his reign, Ahasuerus, king of Persia, gave a feast for all his princes and servants. For one hundred and eighty days he showed them the riches of his glorious kingdom.

When these days were completed, the king made a seven-days' feast in the enclosed garden of the royal palace at Shushan. Vashti, the queen, also gave a feast for the women in the royal palace which belonged to King Ahasuerus.

On the seventh day, when King Ahasuerus had been drinking wine, he commanded his seven court attendants to bring Vashti, the queen, before him with the royal crown on her head, to show the people and the princes her beauty, but Queen Vashti refused to come. Therefore, the king was very angry.

In his anger the king said to his counselors:

"According to law what shall we do to Queen Vashti?"

Memuchan, one of his high officials, said before the king and his officers:

"Vashti, the queen, has done wrong not only to the king but also to all the nobles and to all the people in all the king's provinces. For the refusal of the queen will be reported to all the women so that they will disobey their husbands. If it seems best to the king, let him send out a royal command, and let it be written

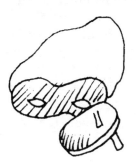

among the laws of Persia and Media, in order that it may not be changed, that Vashti may never again come before King Ahasuerus; and let the king give her place as queen to another who is better than she."

This plan pleased the king, and the king did as Memuchan advised.

Shortly after this, the king's pages who waited upon him said:

"Let beautiful young maidens be sought for the king, and let them be gathered in the palace at Shushan. And let the maiden who pleases the king be queen instead of Vashti."

The plan pleased the king.

Now there was in the royal palace at Shushan a certain Jew named Mordecai, whose ancestors had been exiled from Jerusalem with the captives by Nebuchadnezzar, the king of Babylonia. He had adopted Esther, his uncle's daughter, for she had neither father nor mother.

When the king's command was made known, among the many maidens brought to the royal palace at Shushan, Esther also was taken. Esther had not revealed who her people were or her family, for Mordecai had told her not to tell. Every day Mordecai used to walk in front of the court of the women's quarters to ask after Esther's welfare and what had been done with her.

When Esther's turn came to go in to the king, Ahasuerus loved her more than all the other women. She became his favorite and won his love, so that he placed the royal crown on her head and made her queen instead of Vashti. Then the king gave a great feast to all his princes and servants in honor of Esther.

In those days, while Mordecai was sitting in the king's gate, two of the king's servants, who guarded the entrance of the palace, plotted to kill King Ahasuerus. Mordecai learned of the

plot and told it to Queen Esther; and she told the king in Mordecai's name. When the truth was known, the men who plotted against the king were both hanged. The incident was written down in the daily record of events that was kept before the king.

Haman Schemes Revenge

Now, King Ahasuerus promoted Haman, the Agagite, and gave him a place above all the princes who were with him. All the king's servants who were in the king's gate bowed down before Haman, for so the king had commanded. But Mordecai did not bow down before Haman.

When Haman saw that Mordecai did not bow down before him, he was very angry. But, as he had been told that Mordecai was a Jew, he decided not to lay hands on him alone but to plot to destroy all the Jews in the kingdom of Ahasuerus.

Haman told King Ahasuerus:

"There is a certain people scattered among the peoples in all the provinces of your kingdom; and their laws differ from those of every other people; and they do not keep the king's laws. Therefore it is not right for the king to leave them alone. If it seems best to the king, let an order be given to destroy them, and I will pay ten thousand talents of silver into the royal treasury."

The king took off his ring and gave it to Haman, and said:

"The money is yours and the people also, to do with them as you wish."

Messages then were sent by men on horses to all the king's provinces, to destroy, to kill, and to put to an end all the Jews, young and old, little children and women, on the thirteenth day of the twelfth month, and to rob them of all that they had. Meanwhile the king and Haman sat down to drink, but the people of Shushan were troubled.

When Mordecai learned all that had been done, he tore his clothes and put on sackcloth, and he put ashes on his head (as a sign of mourning), and went out into the city and raised a loud and bitter cry of sorrow. He went as far as the king's gate, for no one could enter the gate clothed in sackcloth. In every province, wherever the king's command came, there was great mourning, fasting, weeping, and wailing among the Jews. And many of them sat in sackcloth and ashes.

When Esther's maids and servants told her about it, she was greatly troubled. She sent garments for Mordecai to put on, that he might take off his sackcloth. But he would not accept them. Esther then called Hatach, one of the king's servants whom he had appointed to wait on her. She ordered him to go to Mordecai to learn what this meant and how it had happened.

Hatach went to Mordecai at the city square in front of the king's gate. Mordecai told him all that had happened to him and the exact sum of money that Haman had promised to pay into the king's treasury. He also gave him a copy of the order to destroy the Jews, that had been given out in Shushan, to show to Esther that she might know about it. He also urged her to go to the king and ask his mercy and plead with him for her people.

When Hatach came and told Esther what Mordecai had said, she commanded Hatach to go and say to Mordecai:

"All the king's servants and the people of the king's provinces know that death is the punishment for any man or woman who goes to the king into the inner court without being called, except for the one to whom the king may hold out the golden scepter, which means that he may live. Now for thirty days I have not been called to go in to the king."

When Mordecai was told what Esther had said, he sent back this answer to Esther "Do not think that you alone of all the Jews will escape because you belong to the king's household. If you keep silent at this time, help will come to the Jews from somewhere else, but you and your family will perish. Who knows but that you have been raised to the throne for a time like this?"

Then Esther sent this message to Mordecai "Go, gather all the Jews in Shushan and fast for me. Do not eat or drink anything for three days and nights. I and my maids will fast also, and I will go in to the king, although it is against the law. And if I perish, I perish."

Mordecai did as Esther directed.

On the third day, Esther put on her royal robes and stood in the inner court of the royal palace opposite the king's house. The king was sitting on his throne in the palace, opposite the entrance. When he saw Queen Esther standing in the court, she won his favor, and he held out to her the golden scepter that was in his

A Purim Bummer

When you dress up as Queen Esther and so does everyone else.

Queen Esther Before the King

WHAT DID HUMPTY
DUMPTY DO ON PURIM?
HE CRACKED UP!

Purim
Disguises

Seymour
Glass

Wise
Guy

Lotta
Hats

Snow
Man

No
Man

hand. Esther went up and touched the tip of the scepter. Then the king said to her, "Whatever you wish, Queen Esther, and whatever you ask, it shall be granted, even to the half of my kingdom."

Esther replied, "If it seems best to the king, let the king and Haman come today to the feast that I have prepared for him."

The king said, "Bring Haman quickly, that Esther's wish may be granted."

So the king and Haman went to the feast that Esther had prepared. While they were drinking wine, the king said to Esther, "Whatever you ask shall be granted, even to the half of my kingdom."

Esther answered, "If I have won the king's favor and if it seems best to the king to grant what I ask, let the king and Haman come to the feast which I shall prepare for them. Tomorrow I will do as the king wishes." Haman went out that day joyful and happy, but when he saw Mordecai in the king's gate and noticed that he neither stood up nor moved for him, he was furiously angry with Mordecai. But Haman controlled his temper and went home. He called together his friends and Zeresh, his wife, and told them, "Queen Esther brought no one with the king to the feast which she had prepared but me, and tomorrow also I am invited by her along with the king. Yet all this does not satisfy me as long as I see Mordecai, the Jew, sitting at the king's gate."

Then Zeresh, his wife, and all his friends said to him, "Let a gallows seventy-five feet high be built and in the morning speak to the king and let Mordecai be hanged on it. Then go merrily with the king to the feast."

This advice pleased Haman, and he had the gallows built. That night the king was unable to sleep. He gave orders to bring him the books that told of great deeds and they were read before the king. In them was written how Mordecai had told about the two servants of the king who had tried to kill King Ahasuerus. Then the king said, "How has Mordecai been honored and rewarded for this?"

The king's courtiers replied, "Nothing has been done for him."

The king demanded, "Who is in the court?"

Now Haman had just entered the outer court of the king's house to speak to the king about hanging Mordecai on the gallows that he had prepared for him. So the king's courtiers said to him, "Haman is standing there in the court."

The king commanded, "Let him enter."

Haman entered, and the king asked him, "What shall be done to the man whom the king delights to honor?"

Haman thought to himself, "Whom besides me does the king delight to honor?"

So Haman said to the king, "To the man whom the king delights to honor, let a royal garment be brought, which the king has worn, and the horse on which the king has ridden and on whose head a royal crown has been placed. Then let the garment and the horse be placed in charge of one of the king's noble princes and let him clothe the man whom the king delights to honor and make him ride on the horse through the city square and proclaim before him: `This is what is done to the man whom the king delights to honor.'"

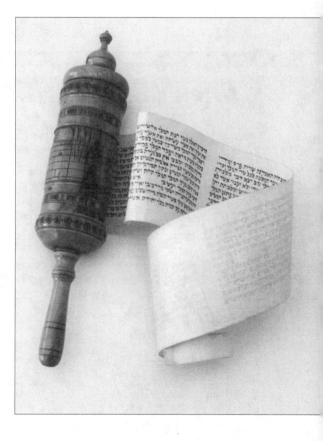

Then the king said to Haman, "Make haste and take the garment and the horse, as you have said, and do thus to Mordecai, the Jew, who sits in the king's gate. Do not fail to do all you have said."

So Haman took the garment and the horse and clothed Mordecai, and made him ride through the city square and proclaimed before him:

"This is what is done to the man whom the king delights to honor." Mordecai returned to the king's gate, but Haman hurried to his house, mourning, with his head covered. Haman told Zeresh, his wife, and all his friends everything that had happened to him. Then his friends and Zeresh, his wife, said to him, "If Mordecai before whom you have already been disgraced is a Jew, you can do nothing against him, but you will surely fall before him."

While they were still talking with him, the king's servants came and escorted Haman to the feast that Esther had prepared. The king and Haman went to drink with Queen Esther. And the king said to Esther, "Whatever you ask, Queen Esther, it shall be granted you, even to the half of my kingdom."

Queen Esther answered, "If I have won favor, O king, and if it seems best to the king, let my life and my people be given me at my request. For I and my people have been sold to be destroyed, to be killed, and to perish!"

King Ahasuerus said to Queen Esther, "Who is he and where is he who dares to do this?" Esther answered, "A foe, an enemy, this wicked Haman."

There Have Been Other Purims

"Anyone to whom a miracle has happened may make that day Purim." So says the Midrash. And looking back at our long history reveals at least 30 special "Purims." It's really amazing to see the basic features of the Megillah story repeated over and over: the flare-up of anti-Semitism, danger threatening a community, and—at the last possible minute—sudden rescue. Here are a few of the special Purims recorded in the chronicles of the Jewish past.

The Cairo Purim

In the 16th century, Selim I of Turkey ruled over Egypt, Syria, and Palestine. He was kind to his Jewish citizens, and gave them high government positions. Abraham de Castro was appointed director of the Egyptian Mint. One day, Abraham was approached by a rebel named Ahmad Shaytan, who suggested that Ahmad Shaytan's name be stamped on all new coins instead of the name of the Sultan. This meant treason, and when the order came in writing, Abraham fled to Constantinople. The Jews of Cairo were at the mercy of Ahmad, who ordered them slaughtered and robbed. But Ahmad's inferiors rose against him, wounded him as he came from the baths, attacked his palace and, by nightfall, beheaded him. This happened on the 27th day of Adar, 1524. A special Megillah was written in which these events were recorded and it was read every year.

The Curtain Purim

In the absence of the Governor of Prague in 1623, rare curtains were stolen from his palace. An announcement ordering the return of the curtains was made in all public places, including houses of worship. Suddenly, the curtains appeared, brought to Hanokh Altshul, shammash of the Meisel Synagogue, by a Jew named Joseph Thein, who said he had bought them from two soldiers. Altshul refused to name the man who had brought the curtains, so he was thrown into prison and ordered to be hanged the next day. The congregation commanded Altshul to reveal Thein's name, and Thein him-

Haman shrank in terror before the king and the queen. Harbonah, one of those who waited on the king, said, "There, standing in the courtyard of Haman's house, are the gallows, seventy-five feet high, which Haman built for Mordecai."

The king said, "Hang him on them."

So they hanged Haman on the gallows that he had prepared for Mordecai. And the wrath of the king was quieted.

self was released only when the synagogue paid 10,000 florins, carried in linen bags by ten prominent Jews escorted by soldiers to the City Hall. The story was inscribed in a Megillah and read every year in Prague.

The Fettmilch Purim
On August 22, 1614, a baker of Frankfort named Vincent Fettmilch led an attack against the Jewish quarter. Forewarned, the Jews barricaded their street, prayed, fasted. The enraged mob broke through the barricade, overcame all resistance and began to pillage and to kill. Suddenly a band of armed citizens appeared and drove them out. The Town Council advised all Jews to leave the city, and they stayed away one year and a half. Meanwhile, Fettmilch was beheaded and the Jews invited to return. This they did, on February 28, 1616. Music played as a new law was read to them: Since the council could not protect them, they now were once again the private property of the Emperor. A large shield was placed on the gate to their

street. On it was painted the imperial eagle and the words: "Under the Protection of His Roman Imperial Majesty." Moreover, the Christian community had to pay the Jews 175,919 florins in damages. From that day on, Frankfort Jews celebrated two events: Adar 19 as a fast day in memory of their exodus, and Adar 20—"Purim Fettmilch"—to celebrate their return.

Baker-Woman's Purim
In 1820, the Greek city of Chios, then under the rule of the Turks, was attacked by Greek rebels. The Jewish community was in desperate danger when suddenly, a Jewish baker-woman accidentally shot off a cannon with a spark that flew out of her oven. The Turks were aroused, the city was saved, and the Jews celebrated yet another Purim.

Shiraz Purim
In the 13th century, Abu el Hassan, a converted Jew, accused the Jews of cursing the Moslem faith. When he suddenly died, a confession was found and the Jews were declared innocent.

The Jews' Triumph

King Ahasuerus then gave the property of Haman, the Jews' enemy, to Queen Esther. And Mordecai was made one of the king's advisers, for Esther had told of his relationship to her. The king also drew off his signet-ring, which he had taken from Haman, and gave it to Mordecai; and Esther placed Mordecai in charge of Haman's property.

Mordecai went out from the presence of the king in royal garments of violet and white and with a great crown of gold and with a robe of fine linen and purple. The people of Shushan shouted and were glad. To the Jews there came light and gladness, joy and honor. And in every city and country, where the king's command came, there was gladness and joy among the Jews, and a holiday. On the fourteenth day of the month Adar, the Jews rested and made it a day of feasting and rejoicing. Therefore the Jews who live in the country villages keep the fourteenth day of the month Adar as the day of rejoicing and feasting and a holiday, and as a day on which they send gifts to one another. But the Jews in Shushan rested on the fifteenth day of the same month and made it a day of feasting and rejoicing.

The Jews made it a custom for them, and for their children, and for all who should join them, so that it might not be changed, that they should observe these two days as feasts each year. For Haman had plotted to destroy the Jews completely, and he cast *Pur,* that is, lots, to destroy them. For this reason these days are called Purim.

An Orange for All Seasons

by Zalman Schneour

A box of oranges is going across the blue ocean. Its destination is a little village somewhere in Lithuania. God knows into what hands the oranges will fall. Was it worth drinking in the warmth of the African sun, the cool dew of the Algerian nights? Wait and see!

At last the box of oranges arrives at the village of Shklov. It is dragged along in a little peasant wagon, and jolted in a Jewish cart.

The wife of the spice-merchant of Shklov calls to her husband: "Open the oranges for the Purim presents."

Eli, the spice-merchant, is an expert at unpacking. His wife stands beside him giving advice. At last the box is opened, and out of the bits of blue tissue paper gleam the golden cheeks of the oranges.

In a little while, the oranges are set out in the little shop window, peeping out on the muddy market place, the gray, cloudy sky, the little heaps of snow in the gutters.

Aunt Feiga arrives with her woolen shawl about her head, and a basket in her hand. She sees the fresh fruit, and goes in to buy Purim gifts. And here begins the immortality of the orange.

Aunt Feiga selects the best, the heaviest orange, wraps it up, and drops it carefully into the basket, between eggs, onions, goodies for Purim of all sorts. She comes home, and the little ones clamor around her, for they have all been given a Purim holiday from school. They immediately start turning their mother's basket inside out.

"Oh, how beautiful!" cries the youngest child. "Oh, how it smells!"

"It grows in Palestine," puts in the Talmud student, and somehow feels proud and grave.

When the Purim feast begins, the orange sits at the head of the table, among a host of little tarts and jellies and figs and sweets, and shines like a golden gem in a multi-colored mosaic.

Aunt Feiga covers it with a cloth, and gives it to the Shalahmanot bearer to take away. The children follow him on his travels with longing eyes. They know that it will have to pass through many changes until it is brought back to them by the shammash.

And so it is. One aunt exchanges the orange for a lemon, and sends it to another relative. And Aunt Feiga has the lemon. So she sends the lemon to another relative, and there it again meets the orange, and they exchange places. And Aunt Feiga gets her precious orange back again.

When Purim is over, the orange lies in the drawer, still whole and happy. If relatives call, and Sabbath dainties are served up, the orange has the place of honor on the table. The apples and the nuts disappear one by one, but the orange always escapes from the hands of the relatives, and remains whole. Relatives in Shklov know what good manners are.

About ten days after Purim, Aunt Feiga's eldest daughter becomes engaged to a respectable young man. And again the orange is displayed. True, one cheek is a bit withered by now, but

Early American Purim Disguises

George Washing machine

Lolly Madison

Patrick Hen

Nathan Pail

it still looks majestic. The youngsters have already hinted repeatedly to their parents that it is high time they had a taste of the orange. But Aunt Feiga replies,"When the time comes, we shall notify you. Your father and mother won't eat it up themselves. You needn't be afraid of that."

The youngsters are all atremble at the engagement party. Will the bridegroom eat the orange?

But he belongs to Shklov. He knows that an orange has not been made for a bridegroom to eat at his betrothal party, but only to decorate the table. So he holds it in his hand just for a minute, and his Adam's apple bobs up and down, and the orange again is left intact.

But at last the longed-for moment arrives. The orange is no longer as round as it has been, nor so fragrant. But it does not matter. It is still an orange.

Aunt Feiga turns to Uncle Uri:

"Uri, divide the orange among the children. How long is it to lie here?"

Uncle Uri, an experienced orange-eater who has probably eaten half a dozen oranges in the course of his life, opens up the big blade of his pocket-knife and starts the operation. Carefully and calmly he cuts straight lines across the fruit, from "pole" to "pole." And then he begins to peel the orange. At last, the orange rolls out of its yellowish-white wrapping and is artistically divided up into equal pieces.

"Children," cries the newly-engaged girl, placing a big glass on the table, "don't forget the pits. Throw them in here. They will be soaked and planted."

The first blessing is the privilege of Uncle Uri himself. He chews one bite, and swallows it with enthusiasm.

"A tasty orange! Children, come over here . . ."

The youngest goes first. This is his right. Whenever there is anything nice to be had, he is always first after his father. He says the blessing at the top of his voice, with a little squeak, flings the half-moon into his mouth, and gulps it down.

"Don't gulp!..." says Uncle Uri very patiently. "No one is going to take it away from you."

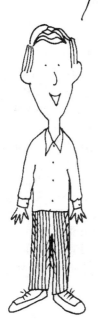

SHOW ME QUEEN ESTHER'S TEACHER ... AND I'LL SHOW YOU AN <u>ESTHER TESTER</u>

"And where is the seed?" asks his engaged sister, pushing forward the glass.

"Swallowed it . . ." says the youngster, frightened, and flushes to his ears.

Then the remaining portions of the orange are given to the family.

Afterward they all sit round the table in silence for a while, gazing at the moist seeds which the betrothed girl has collected. Next week she will plant them in the flowerpots; and after her wedding, she will take them with her to her own home, place them in her window and let them grow under upside-down glasses.

You no doubt think that this is the end. Well, you have forgotten that an orange also has a peel . . .

One of the youngsters makes a discovery—when you squeeze a bit of orange peel near the lamp, a fine shower of fragrant drops squirts out, and when you squirt these into the eyes of your brother, he starts to squint. But before he has time to develop his discovery, he gets a smack on his hand. And all the bits of peel vanish into Aunt Feiga's apron.

She places the peel overnight into the warm stove to dry. Then with her sharp kitchen-knife, she cuts the peel into long strips and small oblongs. She puts them into a bottle, pours brandy on them, sprinkles them with soft sugar, and puts the bottle away to stand. The bits of orange peel swell out, take on their one-time bloom. You pour out a tiny glassful, sip it, and taste the genuine flavor of orange peel.

Relatives come to pay you a visit, take a sip, and feel refreshed, and the women ask Aunt Feiga how she came to think of such a clever thing.

"Look," says Uncle Zaydel to Miriam his wife, "you let everything go to waste. You also had an orange for Purim! Where is the peel? Thrown away."

The bottle is tied up again with a piece of white cloth about the cork, in order not to evaporate. It is put away in the cupboard and stands there, all alone.

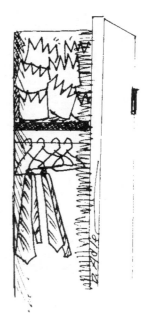

Sometimes a bottle like that stands for years. From time to time you add fresh brandy, and it is tasted very rarely, until the bits of orange peel at the bottom of the bottle begin to lose their strength. Then Uncle Uri knocks them out on a plate.

This is always done on a Saturday night, after Havdalah, when Uncle Uri gives everyone a faded, sugared bit of peel.

But at the very moment that the last speck of the famous orange is disappearing from Uncle Uri's house, the heirs of the orange—the swollen little seeds—have long since shot up in the flowerpots at the home of Uncle Uri's married daughter. They are sprouting slowly, and the young wife looks after them, watering them daily. And God knows what may grow out of them one day.

Even More Purim Disguises

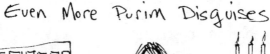

Jack 'N Jail   Little 'O' Peep   Patty Cake   Jack B. Thimble

A Wicked Man

O once there was a wicked, wicked man
And Haman was his name sir
He would have murdered all the Jews
though they were not to blame sir
O today we'll merry merry be (3)
And nash some hamentashen

And Esther was the lovely queen
Of King Ahashverosh
When Haman said he'd kill us all
O my how he did scare us
O today we'll.............................

But Mordechai her cousin bold
Said: "What a dreadful chutzpa!

If guns were but invented now
This Haman I would shoot sir."
O today we'll.............................

The guest of honor he shall be
This clever Mr. Smarty
And high above us he shall swing
At a little hanging party
O today we'll.............................

Of all his cruel and unkind ways
This little joke did cure him
And don't forget we owe him thanks
For this jolly feast of Purim
O today we'll.............................

148

Purim

Be Happy!

Ḥag Purim

Joyously

Ḥag Pu – rim   ḥag Pu – rim   ḥag ga – dol hu   la – y'hu – dim

ma – sei – khot   ra – a – sha – nim   z'mi – rot   ri – ku – dim

ha – va nar – i – sha   rash rash rash   ha – va nar – i – sha   rash rash rash

ha – vah nar – i – shah   rash rash rash   ba – ra – a – sha – nim

The holiday of Purim is a great day for the Jews.
There are masks, groggers, songs and dances.
Come, let's make noise with our groggers.

חַג פּוּרִים חַג גָּדוֹל הוּא לַיְהוּדִים
מַסֵכוֹת רַעֲשָׁנִים זְמִירוֹת רִיקוּדִים
הָבָה נָרְעִישָׁה רַשׁ רַשׁ רַשׁ בָּרַעֲשָׁנִים

Ani Purim

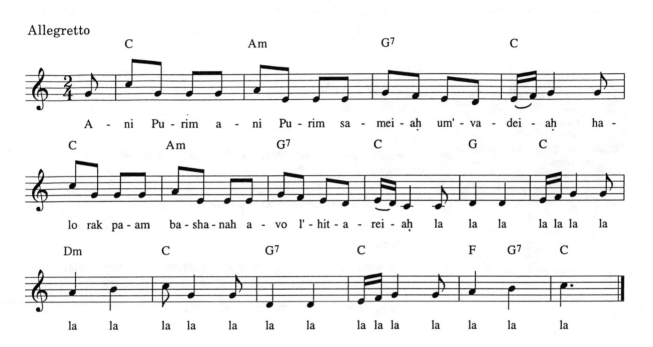

A - ni Pu - rim a - ni Pu - rim sa - mei - ah um' - va - dei - ah ha -
lo rak pa - am ba - sha - nah a - vo l'-hit - a - rei - ah la la la la la la la
la la la la la la la la la la la la la la

How sad that Purim festivities come but once a year.
Wouldn't it be fun if Purim came every month or,
better yet, twice a week!

אֲנִי פוּרִים שָׂמֵחַ וּמְבַדֵּחַ
הֲלֹא רַק פַּעַם בַּשָּׁנָה אָבוֹא לְהִתְאָרֵחַ. לַ לַ לַ
הֵידָד פוּרִים הַכּוּ תֹף וּמְצִלְתַּיִם
הוֹי מִי יִתֵּן וּבָא פוּרִים לְחֹדֶשׁ לֶחֳדָשַׁיִם. לַ לַ לַ
רַבִּי פוּרִים אֱמֹר נָא לִי מַדּוּעַ
מַדּוּעַ לֹא יָחוּל פוּרִים פַּעֲמַיִם בַּשָּׁבוּעַ

Purim Crafts

Bag or Box Costumes

A large paper bag makes a simple and attractive costume, and is easy to cut out. A large cardboard box makes a more durable costume.

Start with a bag or box long enough to cover half of your body and wide enough to go over your shoulders. If you are using a box, remove the cover.

STOP!
Some of the crafts in this chapter call for the use of a hammer, scissors, or other potentially dangerous tools. Before beginning any craft, get either help or the "go-ahead" from a responsible adult.

MATERIALS

large paper bag or cardboard box
scissors
newspapers
gesso
fingerpaints, acrylic paints, or decorative paper or material
white glue

1. Spread newspapers on your work surface.

2. Turn the bag or box upside down and cut out holes for your head and arms.

3. Paint on a base coat of gesso (plaster available from paint or craft stores) and let it dry. Be sure to read the directions that come with the gesso.

4. Now follow the directions below to create one of four special Purim costumes.

Queen Esther

MATERIALS

wide crepe paper and narrow crepe paper
scissors
white glue
small stones, costume jewelry, or glitter
thin cardboard or construction paper
crayons or felt-tip pens
stapler and staples (optional)

1. Gather together the wide crepe paper until you have enough to go around the bag or box.

2. Cut a long piece of narrow crepe, enough to fit around the bag or box and still have enough left over to tie a bow.

3. Glue the crepe skirt to the belt, the narrow piece of crepe paper.

4. Glue the gathered skirt around the bottom of the bag or box and tie a big bow on the belt.

5. Decorate the costume with glued-on jewelry or glitter. You can also paint small stones in pretty colors and glue them to the costume.

6. Follow the directions later in this chapter to make a crown from thin cardboard or construction paper.

Mordecai

MATERIALS

drapable fabric
white glue
cord belt
pins (optional)

1. Drape the fabric around the top of the bag or box, letting the folds fall down the front and back.

2. Glue the folds in place.

3. Tie a cord belt around the "waist" of the bag or box.

4. To make a turban, wind fabric around your head and tie the ends or pin them together.

King Ahasuerus

MATERIALS
drapable fabric
white glue
cord belt
costume jewelry
thin cardboard or construction paper

1. Make the king's costume the same way as Mordecai's.

2. Glue fabric trim and jewelry onto the material.

3. Instead of a turban, make a crown of thin cardboard or construction paper following the instructions later in this chapter.

Three-Cornered Hat →

Beard →

Cotton and Wire Beard

Material Skirt →

Haman

MATERIALS

fabric, enough to make a skirt
thin wire
cotton
white glue

1. Glue a short skirt of material around the inside bottom of the bag or box.

2. To make the beard, bend a piece of thin wire into a U shape. Bend the ends of the wire to fit comfortably over your ears. Glue cotton to the wire.

3. To make Haman's three-cornered hat, see the directions on p. 153.

4. When you are ready to wear the Haman costume, wear a shirt with full sleeves and long pants gathered at the bottom and tied with string or ribbon. Put on the prepared bag or box. Add the beard and hat.

Costume Hats

Make these hats to provide the finishing touch on your Purim costumes!

Paper Crown

MATERIALS

newspapers
paper or thin cardboard
scissors
paint, crayons, or felt-tip pens
white glue
stapler and staples (optional)
glitter or colored glass "jewels"

1. Cover your work surface with newspapers.

2. Cut a length of thin cardboard or construction paper, long enough to go around your head and overlap slightly.

3. Cut a jagged or scalloped design around the top edge and decorate the crown with paint, crayons, or felt-tip pens.

4. Staple or glue the overlapping paper together.

5. Glue on glitter, jewelry, or painted stones.

MATERIALS

paper bag
scissors
crayons, felt-tip pens, or paint
white glue (optional)
fabric or colored paper (optional)

Paper Bag Headdress

1. Decide on the style of the headdress and cut out the opening from a paper bag.

2. Decorate with crayons, felt-tip pens, or paint.

3. To add a hat, glue on fabric or colored paper.

MATERIALS

15-inch circle of fabric
15-inch circle of cardboard
scissors

Three-Cornered Hat

1. Glue fabric onto the circle of cardboard.

2. Cut out an inner circle from the material-lined cardboard, large enough to fit on the top of your head (figure A).

3. To form the three corners, fold up the sides of the circle (figure B), keeping the material on the outside (figure C).

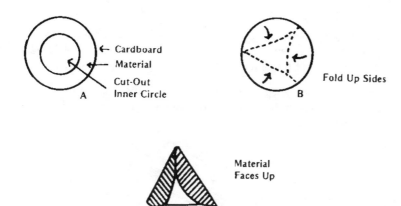

154
Purim
Be Happy!

Noisemakers

Fill these noisemakers with dried beans, rice, candies, and other goodies and shake them loudly every time Haman's name is mentioned.

A Purim Bummer

When you dress up for Purim as a monster and everyone knows it's you.

Foil Pie Plate Noisemaker

MATERIALS

handful of dried beans or rice
2 aluminum foil pie plates
stapler and staples
several felt tip pens in different colors

1. Place a handful of dried beans or rice in an aluminum foil pie plate. Cover with another pie plate and staple together.

2. With felt-tip pens, draw Haman's face. At the sound of Haman's name, drum the noisemaker with your fingers or hit it with a spoon.

Salt Box Noisemaker

MATERIALS

empty cardboard salt container
handful of dried beans or rice
cellophane tape
pen
wooden dowel
acrylic paint
paintbrush

1. Open the little metal flap in the salt box, fill with dried beans or rice, and tape closed. Use a pen or another slightly pointed object to poke a hole in the top and bottom of the container. Insert a wooden dowel.

2. Spread newspapers on your work surface, place the *grager* on the newspaper and paint the *grager* with bright acrylic paints. Let it dry before using.

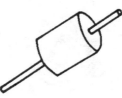

Three-Cornered Cardboard Noisemaker

MATERIALS

poster board
dinner plate or other circular object
pencil
handful of dried beans, rice, or wrapped candies
white glue or staples and stapler
acrylic paints, crayons, or felt-tip pens

1. Place the poster board on a flat surface. Place a circular object like a dinner plate on top of the poster board. Use a pencil to trace around the dinner plate.

2. Cut out the poster board in the shape of the circle.

3. Fold up the edges of poster board into the shape of a three-cornered hat. Fill with a handful of dried beans, rice, or wrapped candies.

4. Glue or staple the top of the poster board closed. Let dry.

5. Decorate with paint, crayons, or felt-tip pens.

Purim Recipe

Hamantaschen (Eastern Europe)

Hamantaschen are traditionally filled with prunes, but you can also fill these favorite Purim cookies with poppy seeds and honey, or cheese and jam and nuts.

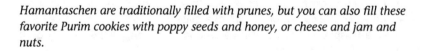

STOP!
A kitchen is a dangerous place. If you're not careful, you might burn yourself with splattering oil or boiling water. The recipe in this chapter is intended for older children. Before beginning, make sure an adult is available to help.

FILLING

1 pound uncooked pitted prunes
1 small apple
2 teaspoons honey

Put the prunes in a medium saucepan. Add enough water to cover the prunes. Bring to the water to a boil, then lower the temperature and cook at medium heat for 20 minutes.

After 20 minutes, remove from heat and turn off the burner. Let the prunes cool. Chop or grind the prunes by hand or in a food processor and put them in a medium-size mixing bowl.

Wash and grate the apple and add it to the prunes. Add the honey and mix well. Set the filling aside.

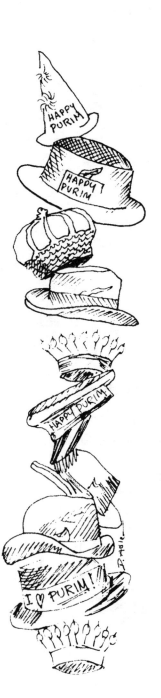

WHAT'S THE BEST THING TO PUT IN A HAMANTASCHEN?

YOUR TEETH!

DOUGH

3/4 cup sugar
2 cups flour
2 teaspoons baking powder
1/4 teaspoon salt
1/3 cup margarine
1 egg
2–3 tablespoons water
bowl of filling
extra flour for coating board and
    rolling pin

Preheat the oven to 350 degrees.

Grease 2 cookie sheets and set aside.

Put the sugar, flour, baking powder, and salt into a large mixing bowl. Mix well, counting 35 to 40 strokes, to blend thoroughly.

Cut the margarine into little pieces and add to the bowl. Mix with a fork or with your hands until you have an evenly crumbly mixture. Be patient—it'll take a few minutes.

Add the egg and water. Mix until the dough sticks together in a ball.

Wash your hands if they are sticky. Sprinkle flour on the board, the rolling pin, and your hands. Leave a little extra flour on the back corner of the board.

Pinch off a piece of dough. Roll it between your hands into a 1-1/2-inch round ball. Dip the ball in the extra flour. Roll it flat with the rolling pin to about 1/8-inch thickness. If you like, you may roll out all the dough and cut circles with a cookie cutter, or the rim of a glass.

Take a teaspoon of filling. With a second teaspoon, scrape the filling off into the middle of the dough.

Fold up 3 edges of the dough and pinch them together to make a triangle. Put it on the cookie sheet. Repeat steps 5, 6, and 7 until you have used up all the dough.

Put the cookie sheets in the oven and bake for 20 minutes.

Here are 2 other mixtures you can use to fill your hamantaschen.

Soak 1 cup of poppy seeds overnight. Drain them. Grind in a food grinder. Add 4 tablespoons of honey and mix.

Mix 3 ounces of cream cheese or farmer cheese, 2 teaspoons jam, and 1/4 cup chopped nuts.

20 small pastries

Purim Fun

Purim Puzzles   (Answers on page 272.)

If it takes 15 minutes to bake 3, how long would it take to bake 5?   *Hamantaschen*

Rearrange the letters in each group, using all the letters, and form a Purim   *Purim Anagrams*
word or name.

    1. THESE R

    2. THIS AV

    3. TRAP Y

    4. CHAIR ODE M

    5. READ P A

What is the weight of a *shelakh manot* plate if it weighs 2 pounds plus   *How Heavy?*
half its weight?

Tell a friend to think of something related to Purim and you will read his   *Almost Magic*
mind and before he even thinks it you will write "what you're thinking."
And that's what you do. You write, "What you're thinking."

Unscramble each set of letters to form four Purim words or names. Write   *Purim Scramble*
each unscrambled word in the squares and circles, one letter to each. Then
unscramble the circled letters to form the answer to the riddle.

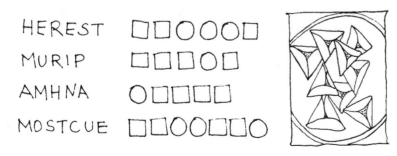

    ***Riddle:* What did the baker like to put in his hamantaschen?**

        Answer: _ _ _   _ _ _ _ _

Purim, Purim, Purim

by Barbara Spector

1. What was Esther's Hebrew name?

2. Who was queen before Esther?

3. In which city was King Ahasuerus's palace?

4. How did Haman determine the day the Jews were to be abolished?

   (a) He read the stars; (b) He had a dream; (c) He drew lots.

5. The Fast of Esther is observed for one day, the day before Purim. How many days did Esther actually fast?

6. Does the Fast of Esther begin at sunrise or sunset?

7. On Purim it is customary to get so silly that you can't tell the difference between which two people in the Purim story?

8. Is it permissible to decorate the Megillah with pictures?

9. When the Megillah is read on Purim, the verses listing the ten sons of Haman are read _____.

   (a) very slowly; (b) in one breath; (c) under one's breath.

10. What does the word *Purim* mean?

11. From which language does the name *Mordecai* come?

    (a) Hebrew; (b) Babylonian; (c) Greek; (d) Yiddish.

12. What is a *Purim seudah?*

13. What is a *Purim shpiel?*

    (a) the reading of the Megillah; (b) another name for hamantaschen; (c) a Purim play; (d) Yiddish term for the custom of giving *shalach manot.*

A Purim Bummer

When you're told to eat the burnt hamantaschen. The good ones are for the guests.

14. *Ozen Haman* is the Hebrew term for _____.

15. Besides hamantaschen, what other food is traditionally eaten at Purim?

    (a) *kreplach;* (b) knishes; (c) *knaidlach;* (d) kasha.

16. What is the minimum number of food items you must give on Purim in order to fulfill the *mitzvah* of *mishloach manot?*

17. True or false: The Scroll of Esther is not the only Megillah.

18. Which country has a tomb where, according to tradition, Mordecai and Esther are buried?

19. Who was Zeresh?

20. What is known as *orrechi d'Aman* in Italy?

Pesaḥ/Passover
Why Is This Night Different?

About Pesaḥ

In many homes the end of Purim marks the beginning of a month-long period of preparation for Pesaḥ—Passover, the spring holiday beginning on the fifteenth of Nisan celebrating the Jews' escape from slavery in Egypt. The preparation includes buying Pesaḥ foods and ridding the home of all bread, cakes, and other chametz—leaven.

In Israel and among Reform and Reconstructionist Jews, Pesaḥ is celebrated for seven days with the first and last days as full-festival, no-work days. The middle five days are called ḥol hamoed and are semi-holidays. Outside Israel, among traditional Jews, Pesaḥ is celebrated for eight days. The first two and last two are full festival, no-work days. The middle four days are ḥol hamoed.

In Ashkenazi households, kitniyot—corn, rice, beans, and other legumes—are not eaten because they are sometimes ground into flour and used to make bread.

Matzah is essentially bread that has not risen, and we eat it on Pesaḥ to remind ourselves of the Jews' great rush to leave Egypt. They didn't wait for the bread they were baking to rise. There is a custom not to eat any matzah from Purim until Pesaḥ to create a craving for it.

Central to the celebration of Pesaḥ is the seder, the ceremonial meal on the first two nights of the holiday. (In Israel and among Reform and Reconstructionist Jews there is only one, on the first night.) The word "seder" means "order" and there is a definite order to the seder rituals.

At the seder each participant should celebrate as if he or she just became free. At the seder we recline while we eat the matzah and drink the wine. Reclining is a symbol of freedom and this is how royalty ate and at the seder each of us is a king or queen. It is also a custom to pour wine for others but not for ourselves because members of the royal family do not serve themselves.

On the seder plate in the middle of the table are karpas (a vegetable), ḥaroset (an edible mortar-like mixture), maror (bitter herbs), beitzah (a roasted egg), and zeroah (a roasted shank bone).

The vegetable used for karpas is usually parsley, celery, or a baked

potato. During the seder the karpas *is dipped into salt water or vinegar, symbolic of the tears the slaves shed.*

Ḥaroset, *the mortar-like mixture, reminds us of the bricks the slaves were forced to make. Several of the many traditional* ḥaroset *recipes can be found later in this chapter.*

Eating maror, *the bitter herbs, reminds us of the bitter taste of slavery. Romaine lettuce and freshly ground horseradish are used.*

The beitzah, *roasted egg, reminds us of the Temple sacrifice offered on holidays, and the* zeroah, *the roasted bone, of the special Pesaḥ sacrifice.*

We drink four cups of wine or grape juice at the seder symbolizing the four promises of redemption in the Book of Exodus (6:6-7). A fifth cup of wine, Elijah's cup, is on the table, too, for the prophet who, according to legend, visits every Jewish home on Pesaḥ.

Many people use only red wine at the seder, a reminder of the blood the Jews spread on their doorposts before the last of the ten plagues, the death of the first-born sons. The sons of the Egyptians died, but God spared the sons of the Jews with blood on their doorposts. Red wine is also a reminder that Pharaoh killed Jewish children and bathed in their blood, a supposed cure for leprosy.

For Moroccan Jews the Pesaḥ celebration is one day longer. On the day after the holiday they have a festive meal, the maimuna. *Traditionally the day of the* maimuna *is a good day to arrange a marriage!*

DAY SCHOOL DAZE

by Bayla S. Jacobs & Shepsil Scheinberg

A Very Special Passover
A True Story About a Man, a Prison, and a Rabbi

by Sheila Gruner

It was the eve of Passover, 1947. A pale thread of afternoon light slipped through the bars of the death cell in the Central Jail in Jerusalem. It reached across the gray, barren walls and fell on the prisoner wearing the red cloth of the condemned. Dov Bela Gruner, a member of the underground movement, Irgun Zvai Leumi, and in jail awaiting his execution, had just learned that the British commandant would not permit the six condemned men to celebrate the Passover seder with the other Jewish inmates.

"This is outrageous!" the young Hungarian-born freedom fighter said. "The British are playing a devilish game. They've tried everything to make me sign the appeal . . . and now this! Not to allow a religious man his seder."

Suddenly there was a rapping on the bars. Dov raised himself up to the small window. The young boy who had climbed up the huge blocks of the outer wall whispered, "Chief Rabbi Dr. Herzog is trying to find a rabbi to conduct the seder in your cell," then he scrambled back down the wall.

"This will have to be a very special man," Dov said to the other condemned men.

"Yes," agreed one of the other prisoners. "He'll have to be acceptable to the British, and that's a hard chore in these times."

"Which rabbi would be willing to sacrifice the celebration with his own family in order to spend Passover night in this unhappy death cell?" asked another prisoner.

"Don't worry," said Dov Gruner kindly. "If Dr. Herzog is looking for a special rabbi, he'll find one."

News of Dr. Herzog's rabbi spread fast through the prison. Dov learned that it was to be a Rabbi Goldman who would come to Dov's cell. The news also carried a sad note . . . there would be no wine or matzot, nor any of the other necessities for Dov's seder unless he personally begged the commandant for them.

"Never," Dov cried upon hearing the news. "I refuse to ask even the smallest favor of the prison officials."

"But how can we celebrate a seder without wine and matzot?" his baffled cellmates asked.

HOW MANY MATZAHS WOULD IT TAKE TO FEED A FAMILY OF 6?

ONLY ONE . . . A REAL BIG ONE.

A Passover Bummer

When you open your lunch bag and instead of a matzah sandwich all you have are matzah crumbs.

"We shall sacrifice," Dov said softly, "as Rabbi Goldman will do." Already Dov Gruner's stubbornness and selfless idealism were legendary. All over Eretz Israel the Jews were moved by this young man's courage and devotion to his principles.

Dov would not budge from his position for the mere granting of a few pleasures. He remembered the reason for being in this jail. He had been sentenced to hang for his part in a raid on a Ramat Gan police station. It was one of 80 fortresses which the unwelcome British built all over Palestine in the late 1930s. All alike, they were known as the Tegart Forts. They were painted light brown like the color of the soil. Each was a low concrete structure with towers and machine-gun turrets. On top were a searchlight and a radio mast. The fort was in the middle of an open field and was surrounded by a double wire fence.

Dov had covered the retreat of his group which had penetrated the fort and had taken a number of arms. When he turned to leave, he became entangled in the barbed wire and a British bullet found its mark in his jaw. Just then British reinforcements arrived and he was taken prisoner. When Dov regained consciousness in the prison hospital, he asked if anyone had been injured. He was pleased to learn there was only one man who was slightly injured. The Irgun soldiers had desperately wanted to spare all lives, so one of the officers held up traffic to prevent anyone from getting hurt by the explosion.

For weeks after the raid, Dov lay seriously wounded and was able to take nourishment only through a straw. Although he was very weak, his eyes were like burning candles glowing in the darkness. He was brought to trial by the British military court that told him all he had to do was to appeal, and he would not be executed. Dov refused to recognize the legality of the court, and so would neither testify nor appeal.

"The League of Nations invited the British court to come to Eretz Israel," he said, "for the revival of the Jewish state in the country of our forefathers. Instead, you blocked entrance to Israel

MATZAH GINGERBREAD MEN

D. Adler

and not one homeless Jew could enter. You have no right to be here. That is why I cannot recognize your competence to try me."

Dov Gruner became known throughout the world. There were those who disagreed with his principles, but there were many more who agreed. Even many Britons understood Dov's valiant fight for his ideals, but things had gone too far. If Dov was executed, the British feared all the countries would be against them and they would lose world prestige. If Dov was not hanged, Britain thought the terrorists would take over Palestine.

The dispute between Israel and Britain had continued for almost a year, with the prizes being Gruner's life and British prestige. The Irgun kidnaped two British citizens in Palestine to force the British military court to free Dov, and terrorists threatened to strike if he died, so Dov's execution had been put off several times. Finally a severe curfew was called on all people in Palestine, including British civilians. Dov remained steadfast despite all the requests and trickery used to get him to sign his appeal and get Britain off the hook.

That Pesaḥ, as Dov awaited the word on his execution once again, Rabbi Goldman prepared to go to the desolate Central Prison for the seder. He knew it was up to him to make Dov's last seder a joyful one. Silently he promised himself that he would not mention a word to Dov about signing the appeal that would commute his death sentence.

Rabbi Goldman entered the cell and greeted the men with "Shalom! Gut Yom Tov." He was surprised to see a makeshift table set up. The Jewish prisoners who were housed in another part of the jail had arranged for the necessities of the seder to be brought to Dov's cell. There were the matzot and the wine, the parsley, the bitter herbs and salt water, the ḥaroset and the roasted shankbone. There was even an extra goblet for the Prophet Elijah.

Then, in the gray gloom of the death cell, the story of our exodus from Egypt began, and a soft, warm glow spread across the men. Soon everyone felt as comfortable as he had when he was a child in his father's home and waited impatiently to hide the

WHAT CAN YOU PUT IN A BOX OF MATZAH MEAL TO MAKE IT WEIGH LESS?

A HOLE!

afikomen—the piece of matzah which was a symbol of the Passover lamb—and claim the prize for returning it. Deep into the night the rabbi and the condemned soldiers read and discussed the Haggadah, ignoring the tragedy of the present. Only once did Dov refer to his fate and that was when he asked Rabbi Goldman, "Please see to it that we are no longer bothered by those people who mean well and try to get us to sign the appeal. We cannot ask favors of an authority we do not recognize as legal in our country."

He turned to the five men who stood beside him in his fight to liberate Israel once again from a powerful nation, and said, "Let us go to the gallows with a clear conscience and an unspoiled record." Then he cried out to the semi-darkness, "What pains me now with the end so near is the awareness that I have not done enough for my country."

And Dov Gruner was removed to the Akko Prison. While efforts were still being made to save his life, the British executed him. He died on April 16, 1947, and witnesses say that a smile of triumph was on his lips.

The sun shone down brightly on Seville. It was spring, and the proud capital of Andalusia was filled with a hum of excitement. Easter was coming, and the people of Spain loved holidays.

In the marketplace, a man slowly walked past the stands of the country merchants and turned into one of the side streets leading off the square. His eyes scanned the old building that stood well back from the street. He dipped down into a little bag he was carrying and checked a description. Good. This was the house. So far Providence had not failed him. He quickened his step. Now he was at the large, oaken door. He tapped sharply. The door opened an inch, and a pair of dark eyes peeped out.

"Yes?" It was a little boy's voice.

"Is this the home of Diego de Susa?"

"Y-yes."

"And you are his son, Fernando. Is that not so?"

A Passover in Spain
by Curtis Lubinski

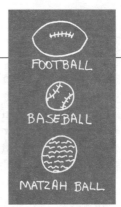

The boy's eyes widened in surprise.

"Tell your father that I bring greetings from—Antwerp."

"Oh, come in!" The door swung open and the stranger slid in swiftly. "We have been waiting for you for so long. We thought you'd never come."

"I thank the Almighty," said Fernando's father, a tall, bearded Spanish grandee, who had been right behind his son. "You have arrived safely. You must be very tired. Come inside. Fernando! Bring us some wine."

The two men retired to the study. Fernando burned with curiosity, but there was nothing he could do about it, so he rushed into the kitchen to get the wine. When he returned, his father changed the subject of conversation. But at least the stranger had a name now. It was Abraham Mendes, and Fernando's father was telling him what it meant to be a Jew in Spain in 1510.

"It has been this way for eighteen years, you know. Little Fernando does not remember, of course, but we remember too well that second day of August in 1492 when we were exiled from Spanish territory by royal decree. Every Jew discovered on Spanish soil after that day was to be burned alive. But there is no need to tell you all this. You know it—else you would not be here."

Abraham Mendes put his arm around Fernando's shoulder. "Soon it will be different, young man." Fernando hungered to know more, but his father broke in.

"Is everything prepared, Mendes? There are many of us, you know."

"The arrangements are complete to the last detail. And it will be most fitting, since tonight is the Eve of Passover." He paused.

The Guest

by Sholom Aleichem

Adapted from the translation by Chaya M. Burstein

We had such a guest for Passover. When it is time to say *kiddush* over the wine, my father and the guest hold a Hebrew conversation.

I am proud to find that I understand nearly every word.

My father: *Nu?* (That means, "Won't you make the *kiddush?*")

The guest: *Nu, nu.* ("Please, *you* make it.")

My father: *Nu-ah?* ("Why not you?")

The guest: *Ah-nu?* ("Why not *you?*")

My father: *Ee-ah.* ("You first.")

The guest: *Ah-ee* ("*You* first.")

My father: *Eh-ah-ee* ("I beg you to make it.")

The guest: *Ee-ah-eh* ("I beg *you* to make it.")

My father: *Ee-eh-ah-nu?* ("Why shouldn't *you* make it?")

The guest: *Eh-ah-eh-nu-nu?* ("Well, if you really want me to, I'll do it.")

"Tell me, Señor de Susa, how did you know the date of Passover? I know that you Marranos keep your faith alive within you, but I also know you dare not keep a Hebrew calendar, nor any Hebrew books."

DO GRAPES MAKE WINE?

NO. YOU HAVE TO SQUEEZE IT OUT OF THEM.

Diego de Susa sighed. "That is true. But we have learned to watch for other signs, much like a blind man who develops his sense of hearing. This is March and tonight will be the full moon. Thus the heavens tell us that Passover has come."

"Truly amazing," Mendes said, almost to himself. "And thus you keep all our Jewish customs?"

"As many as we humanly can," de Susa replied. "Wait. I have an idea. Why don't you walk with us? You will observe how we Jews prepare for the Passover. And you will meet—at a distance, it is true— some of those whom you will get to know much better—in a little while." Fernando's father ended in a whisper, as though he were afraid the walls might have ears.

"May I go, too, Father?" Fernando spoke up bravely.

The two men looked at each other. "There will be no harm in that," said de Susa. "Fernando has known how to fool the king's guards almost since birth. Come along, my son."

They left the house and walked to the gardens which flanked the river Guadalquivir. In their broad berets and wide-sleeved velvet jackets they looked like any good citizens of Seville. Nobody paid any attention to them when they climbed down to the river bank. De Susa nodded to an old friend who stood at the water's edge. "It's all right," he whispered. "My companion is one of us." Abraham Mendes watched the old man cut a few willow branches and start to beat the waters of the river. A royal soldier passing by laughed loudly. "Ho, there," he shouted. "You won't catch any fish *that* way."

The soldier moved on. "You see," Fernando's father said, "the soldiers never even suspected our fellow-Jew. As you know, he wasn't fishing. Now he has observed our old Spanish custom of beating the waters to remind us of how the waters of the Red Sea gave way to Moses and his people when they left Egypt. And no one is the wiser. But it is hard. Very hard."

Together they moved through the winding streets. At last they reached the marketplace.

"Here we have to be most careful," Fernando said to the visitor. "You see, there are signs up all over the city telling people how to identify Jews. The posters are on all the public buildings. And one certain way is to catch them buying food for Passover."

"And yet," the elder de Susa interrupted, "if you look sharply, you will see what Fernando and I see. But please pretend you are glancing about casually."

Abraham Mendes let his eyes rove over the crowd that thronged the merchants' stalls. People were buying food; a little parsley here, some nuts there, a head of lettuce, an apple or two. Never more than one fruit or vegetable at one stall, and always in tiny quantities.

"In that way no one suspects us," he said softly. "And this has been going on for eighteen years. Thank God that for many of us in Seville this awful secrecy will end—tonight."

Nearly a hundred people had assembled in the patio of the de Susa home when they returned there. Careful not to make any noise, they greeted each other with silent gestures. The only source of light in the patio was the pale glow of the full moon. The guests could barely be seen by its light. They wore heavy traveling shoes, held staves in their hands, and had a bundle thrown over their shoulders. They were observing another Spanish-Jewish custom, a custom that required that people dress for the Seder the way the Jews dressed when they left Egypt.

"Go ahead, Fernando," said Diego de Susa. The boy bent down and opened a trap door. One by one the visitors walked down a dozen stone steps. The basement had no window to give the Jews away. Many small tables were set with brightly burning candles, and in the center was a long table. Everyone took his seat. The master of the house sat in the big armchair at the head

WHAT DID THE
MATZAH DO WHEN
IT HEARD AN
ELEPHANT JOKE?

IT CRACKED UP.

of the long table, with Fernando on his right and Mendes on his left.

A deep silence hung over the assembly. Was it as if they were all waiting for another deliverance?

Diego de Susa began the Seder: "Blessed art Thou, O Lord our God, King of the Universe, Creator of the fruit of the vine . . ."

A dish of water passed from guest to guest. Each washed his left hand and passed the dish on. Then they dipped a bit of the lettuce in the tart sauce and twice in the spices. Before the roast lamb was brought in, Diego de Susa raised his voice: "Let us all say Grace," and they all answered, "Blessed be He and blessed be His name."

Only once did Diego de Susa do something unusual. When his son Fernando stood up to ask the question, "Mah Nishtanah—why is this night different from all other nights of the year?" Diego de Susa smiled and his eyes filled with tears. The entire gathering began to cry and laugh at once.

"Why did they?" asked Fernando to himself. "Why?"

He knew the answer four hours later when the de Susas and a hundred other Jewish families from Seville were on their way to the port of Cadiz. They still wore the same heavy traveling shoes, and these were put to good use. In the port of Cadiz, the full Passover moon shone down upon a Dutch schooner that was ready to sail. She was loaded with spices for the Netherlands, and it was not until it was too late that the Spanish government learned that the ship had been brought by Señor Mendes from Antwerp to carry his fellow Jews to the safety of friendly shores.

The Seder Dish

Bring us in the Seder dish,
Long before the meat and fish!
Come Charoses, Morror, too
We shall taste of both of you!
Little bone that means a lamb,
Egg that just like Isaac's ram
Takes the place of sacrifice,
Come and make our Seder nice!
Isn't Pesaḥ simply fine,
With the matzahs and the wine?
Here's a seat for you and me,
All sit down in company!

Sulamith Ish-Kishor

A Passover Bummer

Behind the bookcase?
In the shoebox?
In the kitchen
Under the table?
Under my bed?
In my closet!

When you can't remember where you hid the afikomen.

Kadeish Urhatz

This is the order of the Passover Seder.

קַדֵּשׁ וּרְחַץ כַּרְפַּס יַחַץ
מַגִּיד רָחְצָה מוֹצִיא מַצָּה
מָרוֹר כּוֹרֵךְ שֻׁלְחָן עוֹרֵךְ
צָפוּן בָּרֵךְ הַלֵּל נִרְצָה

Mah Nishtanah

Freely, in recitative style

Traditional

Mah nish-ta-nah ha-lai-lah ha- ze___ mi-kol ha-lei-lot___ sheb'- khol ha-lei-lot a-nu okh-

lin ha-meitz u-ma-tzah___ ha- lai lah ha-ze___ ku- lo___ ma-tzah___

Repeat in similar fashion
for additional verses

Why is this night different from all other nights?
On this night why do we eat matza and bitter herbs;
dip parsley in salt water and horseradish in charoset;
and why do we recline at the table when we eat?

מַה נִּשְׁתַּנָּה הַלַּיְלָה הַזֶּה מִכָּל הַלֵּילוֹת.
שֶׁבְּכָל הַלֵּילוֹת אָנוּ אוֹכְלִין חָמֵץ וּמַצָּה
הַלַּיְלָה הַזֶּה כֻּלּוֹ מַצָּה.

Az Yashir Moshe

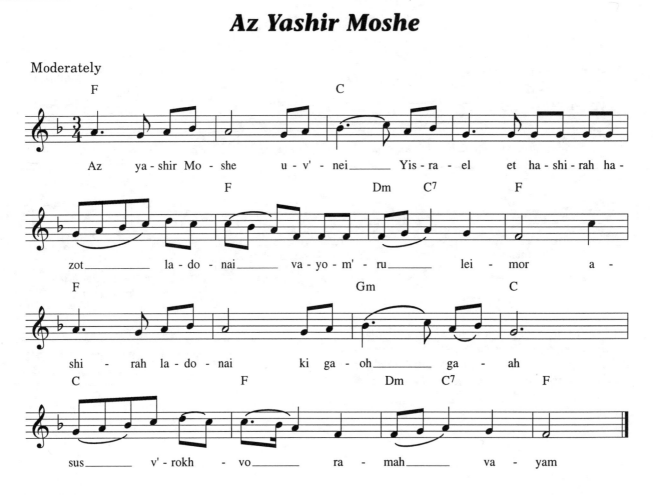

Then Moses and the children of Israel sang this song
to the Lord; they said: I will sing to the Lord for He
has triumphed; the horse and its rider He has hurled
into the sea.

אָז יָשִׁיר מֹשֶׁה וּבְנֵי יִשְׂרָאֵל
אֶת הַשִּׁירָה הַזֹּאת לַיְיָ
וַיֹּאמְרוּ לֵאמֹר.
אָשִׁירָה לַיְיָ כִּי גָאֹה גָּאָה
סוּס וְרֹכְבוֹ רָמָה בַיָּם

Dayeinu

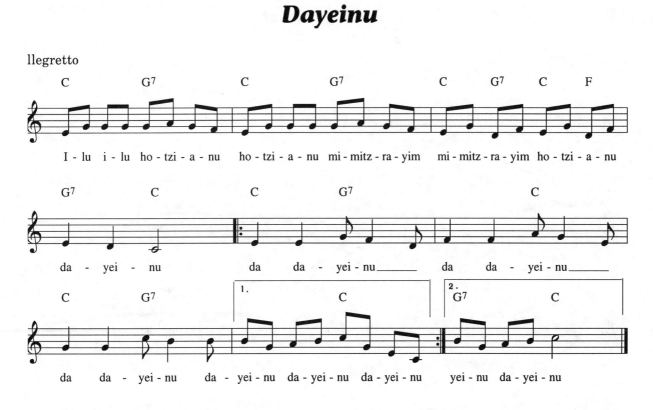

Had He only brought us out of Egypt it would have been enough for us!

אִלּוּ הוֹצִיאָנוּ מִמִּצְרַיִם דַּיֵּנוּ.

Ḥad Gadya

Allegretto

Had gad - ya_____ ḥad gad - ya ḥad gad -
ya_____ ḥad gad - ya d' - za - bin a - ba bit - rei_ zu - zei ḥad gad -
ya_____ ḥad gad - ya v' - a - ta shun - rah v' - akh - lah l' - gad - ya d' -
za - bin a - ba bit - rei_ zu - zei ḥad gad - ya_____ ḥad gad - ya

One little goat, my father bought for two coins.
Then came a cat and ate the goat my father bought
for two coins. Then came a dog and bit the cat that
ate the goat my father bought for two coins........

חַד גַּדְיָא חַד גַּדְיָא
דְּזַבִּין אַבָּא בִּתְרֵי זוּזֵי
חַד גַּדְיָא חַד גַּדְיָא

וְאָתָא שׁוּנְרָא וְאָכְלָה לְגַדְיָא
דְּזַבִּין אַבָּא בִּתְרֵי זוּזֵי
חַד גַּדְיָא חַד גַּדְיָא

Eḥad Mi Yodei-a

Who knows one? I know one.
One is our God, in heaven and on earth.

Who knows two? I know two.
Two are the tablets of the covenant;
One is our God, in heaven and on earth.

אֶחָד מִי יוֹדֵעַ אֶחָד אֲנִי יוֹדֵעַ
אֶחָד אֱלֹהֵינוּ שֶׁבַּשָּׁמַיִם וּבָאָרֶץ

שְׁנַיִם מִי יוֹדֵעַ שְׁנַיִם אֲנִי יוֹדֵעַ
שְׁנֵי לֻחוֹת הַבְּרִית
אֶחָד אֱלֹהֵינוּ שֶׁבַּשָּׁמַיִם וּבָאָרֶץ

Quen Supiese

Allegretto

Ladino folktune

Who would know and understand, praising and believing in God?

What is one alone? One is the Creator, Blessed be He, blessed be His name.

What are two? Two are Moses and Aaron; One is the Creator, Blessed be He, blessed be His name.

What are three? Three are our fathers: Abraham, Isaac, Jacob; Two Moses and Aaron, One is the Creator, etc...

What are four? Four are our mother: Sarah, Rivka, Leah, Rachel, Three are our fathers, etc...

What are five? Five books of the Law, etc...

What are six? Six days of the week, etc...

What are seven? Seven days with the Sabbath, etc...

What are eight? Eight days for the circumcision, etc...

What are nine? Nine months of pregnancy, etc...

What are ten? Ten commandments of the Law, etc...

What are eleven? Eleven tribes without Joseph, etc...

What are twelve? Twelve tribes with Joseph, etc...

Quen supiese y entendiese, alavar al Dio creense cualo es el uno:

Uno es el Criador, Baruch hu, baruch sh'mo

Quen supiese y entendiese alavar al Dio creense

Cualos son los dos: Dos Moshe y Aron, Uno es el Criador, Baruch hu baruch sh'mo

Cualos son los tres: tres padres muestros son: Avram Yitzchak, Yaakov, Dos Moshe.........

Cualos son los cuatro: Cuatro madres muestras son:, Sara, Rivka, Leah, Rachel, Tres muestros padres.....,

Cualos son los cinco-cinco livros de la Ley etc.....,

Cualos son los seij-seij dias de la semana, cinco etc.....,

Cualos son los siete-siete dias con Shabbat, seij etc....,

Cualos son los ocho-ocho dias de la mila, siete etc..,

Cualos son mueve-mueve mezes de la prenada, etc.,

Cualos son los diez-diez mandamientos de la Ley, etc,

Cualos son los onze-onze trivos sin Yosef, diez, etc...,

Cualos son los doze-doze trivos con Yosef, onze, etc..

The rabbis discouraged showing off wealth but, on Passover, the home should shine with beauty. Just as spring adorns the earth, so this is a perfect time to adorn the house with splendid ritual objects.

Elijah's cup should look different from the other cups on the table. Here is an idea for an Elijah's cup that will make a colorful addition to the seder table. Use a clear plastic wine glass that can be found in party supply stores. You may have to buy several at a time, but they are inexpensive and can be used as gifts.

MATERIALS

clear plastic wine glass
old newspapers
permanent felt-tip markers in several colors
spray can of lacquer

1. Place old newspapers on your work surface.

2. Color the entire outside surface of the glass, stem included, with permanent felt-tip markers—you can draw figures also.

3. When the cup is dry, spray the outside with a light coat of lacquer. Be sure to follow the painting instructions on the can. Spray cans of lacquer can be found in hobby or hardware stores. When the lacquer dries, the plastic will be dull and look like delicate blown glass.

4. Wash the cup by hand before using it. The inside should be clean and shiny.

Pesaḥ/Passover Crafts

Elijah's Cup

STOP!
Some of the crafts in this chapter call for the use of a hammer, scissors, or other potentially dangerous tools. Before beginning any craft, get either help or the "go-ahead" from a responsible adult.

Seder Plate

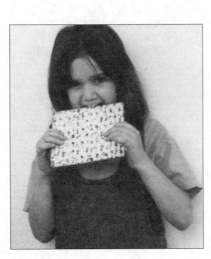

Another Pesaḥ necessity is the seder plate. Even if your family already has one, a few plates are helpful to allow everyone at the table to be near a plate. If you want to use the plate for more than one seder, use nut cups to hold the food so it doesn't soil the plate.

MATERIALS

heavy 10-1/2 inch paper plate
pencil
wool yarn
white glue
aluminum foil
permanent felt-tip markers in several colors

1. On a heavy 10-1/2 inch paper plate, use a pencil to draw 5 circles, 2 inches in diameter, around the inside edge of the plate. You may draw the circles by hand or trace around the base of a cup or another object 2 inches in diameter. You may also use a compass. These circles, which will hold the 5 symbolic foods, should be the same distance apart.

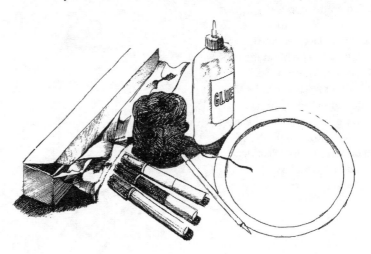

2. Cut the wool yarn into 5 pieces, each the size of the 5 drawn circles.

3. Dip the pieces of wool yarn in white glue and paste them around the rims of the circles.

4. Draw a design around the outside rim of the plate and glue more yarn to it.

5. When the glue is dry, cover the plate, including the bottom, with aluminum foil. Press the foil down, so that the yarn underneath makes a pattern.

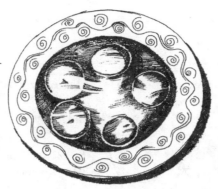

6. Color the center of the circles and the outside rim design with permanent felt-tip markers to make a sparkling seder plate.

Now you have made a wine cup for Elijah and a seder plate for holding parsley, a roasted egg, a shankbone, bitter herbs, and ḥaroset. But how about something for the matzah? Here is an idea for a fancy matzah cover that allows you to make your own design.

Matzah Cover

MATERIALS

piece of fabric 1 foot square
iron-on patches

1. Cut a piece of fabric 1 foot square. It can be white, colored, or have a pattern, but the pattern should be small.

2. Hem or sew a fringe to all 4 sides.

3. Write the word matzah, in English or Hebrew, on an iron-on patch. The Hebrew letters should be 2 inches high, the English letters 1 inch high. You may need 2 patches.

4. Cut out the letters and iron them onto the center of the fabric.

5. Then create your own designs or repeat the designs you made for Elijah's Cup and the Seder Plate. Draw them on more iron-on patches, cut them out, and iron them onto the fabric.

Passover Pillowcase

The pillowcase upon which the leader reclines can also be decorated.

MATERIALS

white or solid-colored pillowcase
8 1/2" x 11" piece of paper
permanent felt-tip markers in several colors

1. Put the piece of paper inside the pillowcase.

2. Draw pictures on the case with felt-tip markers. The paper inside the case will keep the ink from soaking through to the inside of the material. Since the *afikoman* is often hidden in the pillowcase, don't forget to draw an *afikoman*.

Pesaḥ /Passover Recipes

Five Ḥaroset Recipes for Pesaḥ/Passover

Ḥaroset is made in many different ways and there are so many good recipes that we have included several.

STOP!
A kitchen is a dangerous place. If you're not careful, you might burn yourself with splattering oil or boiling water. The recipes in this chapter are intended for older children. Before beginning, make sure an adult is available to help.

STOP

First Turkish Recipe

2 cups apples
1/2 cup pitted dates
1/2 cup dried apricots
water
1/2 cup chopped walnuts

Cut the apples into slices and then peel them. Place them in a medium saucepan along with the pitted dates and the dried apricots.

Add enough water to cover the fruits and cook at medium heat until apricots and dates are tender enough to mash with a fork.

Stir the fruit until it is blended. Chop the nuts and add them to the mixture.

About 3 cups

Second Turkish Recipe

3/4 cup dark Muscat raisins (soak to puff)
1 orange
1 apple
1 pound pitted dates
sweet wine to moisten

Polly wants
a matzah!

Soak the raisins in water until they are puffy.

While the raisins are soaking, peel and section the orange and place it in a blender or food processor.

Peel and core the apple and add it to the orange. Add the pitted dates and the puffy raisins.

Grind all of the fruits together; moisten with wine and mix to combine.

About 3 cups

Third Turkish Recipe

2 apples
8 ounces pitted dates
8 ounces raisins, either dark or golden variety
1/2 cup nuts
orange juice (or wine) to moisten

Peel and grate the apples and place them in a blender or food processor.

Add the pitted dates and the raisins.

Ask an adult to grind all the fruits together; moisten with juice.

Chop the nuts until they are in fine pieces and add to the fruit mixture.

About 2 cups

Fourth Turkish Recipe

1 orange
1 pound raisins
1 cup sugar

Grind whole orange and raisins; add sugar. Cook until thickened.

About 2 cups

Ḥaroset (Eastern Europe)

1/2 cup nuts
3 apples
1 teaspoon cinnamon
2 tablespoons sweet red wine

Chop the nuts and set them aside.

Slice the apples, peel them and remove their cores. Place the slices in a bowl.

Add nuts and cinnamon and chop until fine.

Add wine and mix.

Serves 6–8

Babanatza (Sephardic)
Passover raisin pudding

Babanatza is usually served lukewarm or cold, but in our house we love it hot out of the oven.

1 teaspoon vegetable oil for greasing pan
3 matzahs
3/4 cup raisins
1/4 teaspoon salt
3 eggs
1 apple
1/2 cup chopped walnuts
1/4 cup oil
1/3 cup honey

Preheat the oven to 350 degrees. Grease an 8-inch round cake pan.

Break up the matzah. Soak it in water in a medium-size bowl for a few minutes until it gets soft, then drain off the water. Add the raisins and salt to the matzah.

Beat the eggs slightly in a separate bowl and add them to the matzah mixture. Mix well.

Peel and core the apple. Dice it coarsely into 1/4- to 1/2-inch cubes and add it to the matzah mixture.

Add the nuts, oil, and honey to the matzah mixture. Mix well.

Pour into the pan and bake for 40–45 minutes.

Take out the pan of babanatza and cover it tightly with foil. It will be hot, so ask an adult to help.

Serves 4–5

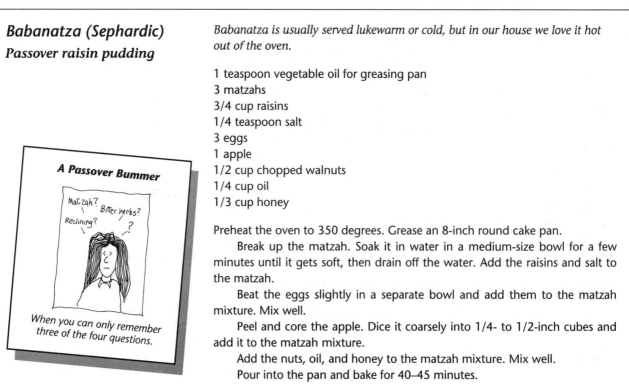

A Passover Bummer

Matzah? Bitter herbs?
Reclining? ?

When you can only remember three of the four questions.

Albondigas de Matzah (Greece)
Sephardic Matzah Ball Soup

In Greece, this dish is traditional for the Passover Seder. These albondigas do not puff up in size and this recipe is not to be confused with the traditional Ashkenazi matzah ball soup.

4 eggs
3/4 cup water
salt and pepper
3 cups matzah meal
6 cups strong chicken broth
6 cups water (approximately)
chopped walnuts (optional)

Beat eggs and 3/4 cup water together in a bowl; add salt, pepper, and matzah meal and knead into dough. Cover and let stand at room temperature for 1 hour.

After 1 hour, grease your hands and shape the albondigas into tiny marble size balls. Place them carefully on a large, flat pan to keep them from sticking together.

Pour the chicken broth and the 6 cups of water into a large pot and bring the liquid to a boil. Salt the liquid to taste.

Carefully drop the albondigas into the boiling liquid, a few at a time, and cook for 1 hour in the partially covered pot. After boiling, allow to stand 1/2 hour before serving. Sprinkle with chopped walnuts at the table, if desired.

The albondigas can be made the night before and left to dry at room temperature.

Serves 10

Bimuelos de Matzah (Turkey)
Fried Matzah Pancakes

Simple to prepare, these bimuelos are traditionally served for breakfast during Passover.

4 matzahs
2 eggs
1/2 teaspoon salt
oil to deep fry

Soak matzahs in warm water in a bowl until very soft, at least 15 minutes. Squeeze out as much water as possible.

Add eggs and salt; mix well.

In a frying pan, pour oil to 1 inch deep. With a tablespoon, form matzah mixture into round shapes. Slowly and gently drop the matzah mixture into the oil and brown on both sides. Make sure the oil doesn't splatter. Drain on a paper towel.

Serve with syrup for breakfast or brunch. Excellent served with preserves.

Serves 3–4

Quick Macaroons

These macaroons taste great with almonds. You may even want to set a whole almond on top of each cookie before you bake them.

5 cups flaked coconut
1 can (14 oz.) sweetened condensed milk
1 teaspoon vanilla
1/2 cup chopped nuts
Margarine (to grease cookie sheet)

Preheat oven to 350 degrees.

Mix ingredients together in bowl. Make sure they are mixed well.

Drop by teaspoonfuls onto lightly greased cookie sheet.

Bake for about 15 minutes or until lightly browned.

Makes 3 dozen

Matzah Brei (Eastern Europe)

Top this traditional fried matzah dish with jelly or cinnamon and sugar.

4 matzahs
3 eggs
1/2 cup milk
3 tablespoon oil or margarine

Crumble matzahs into a bowl.

In a separate bowl, beat the eggs.

Add eggs and milk to the matzah and mix well. Let stand for 5 minutes to soften the matzah.

Heat oil in a frying pan. Put matzah mixture into pan and fry on both sides until crisp.

Serves 4

Hawaiian Matzah Fry (North America)

There are lots of different ways to eat matzah, and this is one of the tastiest.

5 matzahs
1 cup crushed pineapple
1/4 cup shredded coconut
3 eggs
2–3 tablespoons margarine
2 tablespoons sugar
1/4 teaspoons cinnamon

Crumble matzah into bowl and add pineapple with juice.

Beat the eggs in a separate bowl and then add the eggs to the matzah.

Stir in coconut.

Heat butter or margarine in a frying pan. Pour in matzah mixture and brown on both sides. Sprinkle with cinnamon sugar.

Serves 4–6

Pesaḥ/Passover Fun

Pesaḥ/Passover Puzzles (Answers on page 273.)

The Effect: You balance a wine cup, empty, of course, on the edge of a plate.

Turn to page 273 to see how this trick is done.

Pesaḥ/Passover Magic

Can you measure exactly 4 cups of wine (or grape juice) using just these 3 pitchers?

Four Cups of Wine

Danny was making matzah balls to put in soup. One ball rolled off the kitchen counter, out the door, into the yard and into a deep, deep, narrow hole. Danny tried to reach the matzah ball but couldn't. How can Danny retrieve the matzah ball?

The Matzah Ball Problem

The Adlers have 4 boxes of matzah in the pantry, twice as many on top of the refrigerator, and half as many on the kitchen table. Mrs. Adler empties all the matzah into a large box in the dining room. How many boxes of matzah do the Adlers have?

Matzah, Matzah, Matzah

How could you drop a matzah from a 50-foot ladder without having the matzah break?

The Unbroken Matzah

Yom Hashoah
Remember the Six Million

About Yom Hashoah

The State of Israel has established the twenty-seventh of Nisan as Yom Hashoah, Holocaust Remembrance Day, to remember the six million Jews murdered by the Nazis. In many temples and synagogues there are special memorial services on Yom Hashoah with psalms and/or appropriate Holocaust readings.

The twenty-seventh of Nisan was chosen perhaps because it comes shortly before Yom ha-Azma'ut, Israel's Independence Day, and for some the two events are historically and emotionally linked. Some people believe that one reason the world endorsed the establishment of Israel was because of its collective guilt following the Holocaust. And for the Jewish people, the Holocaust made clear the need for a Jewish state as a safe haven for Jews. Nonetheless, the date selected is controversial, with many people preferring to remember the tragedy on either the

Ghetto children.

Jews being arrested.

186

11

Victims of the Holocaust.

Forced labor.

Tenth of Tevet or Tisha b'Av, fast days already observed, or on the six-teenth of Ḥeshvan, the Hebrew date of Kristallnacht—The Night of Broken Glass. But whatever the date, there is no controversy about the need to remember the Holocaust.

Important Dates in the History of the Holocaust, 1933–1945

1933

January 30	Adolf Hitler appointed Chancellor of Germany.
February 27–28	Fire destroys the *Reichstag*. All one hundred Communists elected to the *Reichstag* are arrested.
March 23	The first concentration camp opens in Dachau, a German town near Munich.
March 27	In response to a planned boycott of Jewish-owned stores and businesses in Germany, 55,000 protest at a rally in New York City's Madison Square Garden and those present threaten to boycott all German goods. Nazis

The Sywalki Strelecki family, victims of the Holocaust.

change their plans and limit their boycott to one day.

April 1	Boycott in Germany of Jewish-owned stores and businesses.
April 7	Jewish government workers are ordered to retire.
April 26	The Gestapo, German secret police, is established.
May 10	Books written by Jews and opponents of Nazism are burned.

Books considered harmful to Germany being burned in Berlin, May 10, 1933.

June 27	Mass Jewish rally in London to protest Nazi anti-Semitism.
July 14	Nazi party declared the only legal party in Germany.
October 19	Germany withdraws from the League of Nations.

October 27	Arabs in Palestine riot to protest Jewish immigration there.	
April 7	Several thousand attend a pro-Nazi rally in Queens, New York.	*1934*
May 17	More than twenty thousand attend a pro-Nazi rally at Madison Square Garden in New York City.	
June 30–July 2	"Night of the Long Knives." Leaders of the SA (Brown Shirts), once among Hitler's closest friends and allies, are killed by the SS (Black Shirts) on Hitler's orders.	
August 2	Paul von Hindenburg, president of Germany, dies. Hitler becomes president and commander-in-chief of the armed forces.	
March 16	Hitler rejects the Treaty of Versailles and begins to draft Germans into military service.	*1935*

Boys in the Warsaw Ghetto.

A brother and sister share their small ration of food in the Lodz ghetto.

	May 31	Jews may no longer serve in the German army.
	June	Anti-Jewish riots in Poland.
	September 15	The Nuremberg Laws are passed. Among them are laws denying Jews citizenship in Germany.
		The Nazi symbol, a black swastika, within a round white field on red cloth becomes the official German flag.
	November 15	German law defines a Jew as anyone who considers himself a Jew and has two Jewish grandparents, and anyone with three or more Jewish grandparents, whether he considers himself a Jew or not.
1936	February 4	Swiss Nazi leader Wilhelm Gustloff is assassinated to protest Nazi anti-Semitism in Germany.
	March 3	Jewish doctors no longer allowed to work in German government hospitals.
	March 7	German troops march into Rhineland in violation of the Treaty of Versailles.
	April 21	Arabs riot in Tel Aviv-Jaffa to protest Jewish immigration to Palestine.
	June 30	Polish Jews strike to protest anti-Semitism.
	October 25	Hitler and Mussolini sign treaty forming Rome-Berlin Axis.
1937	March 15	Large anti-Nazi rally in New York City.
	July 16	Buchenwald concentration camp opens.
	September 5	In Nuremberg Hitler views parade of 600,000 German soldiers.
	November 25	Germany and Japan sign military agreement.
1938	January 21	Jews in Romania lose their rights as citizens.
	March 13	The *Anschluss*—the German army marches into Austria. German anti-Semitic decrees now apply to the Jews in Austria.

April 26	All Jewish property must be registered with the Nazis.
May 29	Anti-Jewish laws passed in Hungary.
July 5	Evian Conference on German refugees opens.
July 23	Identification cards stamped with a large "J" are issued to all Jews.
August 17	Jewish women must add "Sara" to their names. Men must add "Israel."
September 29–30	At the Munich Conference the leaders of England and France agree that Germany may annex the Sudetenland.
October 5	All Jews must have their passports marked with a large red "J".
October 28	Polish Jews living in Germany are expelled.
November 7	In Paris, Herschel Grynszpan shoots Ernst von Rath, a German embassy employee.
November 9	*Kristallnacht,* the "Night of the Broken Glass." Many thousands of Jewish-owned stores and business are broken into and robbed. Synagogues are burned. Jews are arrested and degraded. Some are killed.
November 15	Jewish children may no longer attend German schools.

A synagogue burns on Kristallnacht.

1939

January 30	In a speech before the German Parliament, Hitler declares that if there is war, the Jews of Europe will be destroyed.
February 9	Anti-Jewish laws passed in Italy.

Yom Hashoah

Remember the Six Million

Nazi soldiers guarding a ghetto entrance.

Jews were forced to wear identifying stars of David on their clothes.

March 15	Germans occupy Bohemia and Moravia (part of Czechoslovakia)
March 25	In New York, 20,000 march in huge public "Stop Hitler" protest while an estimated 500,000 line the streets and watch.
August 23	Germany and Russia sign the Molotov-Ribbentrop Pact, agreeing not to attack one another.
September 1	The German army invades Poland.
September 3	France and England declare war on Germany.
September 21	German orders are issued to establish ghettos in Poland.
October 24	Jews in Wloclawek, Poland, required to wear a large yellow triangle.
October 30	British government publishes report of Nazi brutality in concentration camps.
November 23	Polish Jews are ordered to wear in public at all times armbands with yellow stars of David.
November 28	Ghetto set up in Piotrkow, the first in Poland.

1940

February 8	Orders issued to set up a ghetto in Lodz, Poland.
April 9	German army invades Denmark and Norway.
April 27	Orders are issued to set up a concentration camp at Auschwitz, Poland.
May 1	Lodz ghetto is established.
May 10	German army invades Holland, Belgium, and France.

A Jewish child selling armbands in the Warsaw ghetto.

June 4	French and British troops evacuated from Dunkirk.
June 22	France surrenders.
September 27	Japan signs a treaty with Germany and Italy forming the Rome-Berlin-Tokyo Axis.
November 15	Walls surrounding the Warsaw ghetto are completed and closed.

1941

June 22	German army invades Russia. Einsatzgruppen (Nazi murder squads) begin mass killings of Jews in Russia.
June 28	"Red Friday." Nazis burn the Jewish section in Bialystok, Poland. More than one thousand Jews, forced into the synagogue, are killed.
July 31	Heydrich is appointed to carry out the "Final Solution".

Ghetto streets were crowded.

Electrified wires surrounding Auschwitz.

Hungry children living in the streets of the Lodz ghetto.

September 1	Jews in Germany are required to wear a yellow star on their clothing.
September 28	Murder of Jews at Babi Yar (near Kiev, Russia) begins. More than 30,000 will be killed within two days.
October 15	Orders issued that any Jew in Poland found outside a ghetto will be shot.
December 7	The Japanese attack Pearl Harbor, Hawaii. United States declares war on Japan.
December 8	Chelmno death camp begins mass killings.
December 11	Germany and Italy declare war on the United States.

1942

January 20	At Wannsee Conference plans are formed for the total destruction of the Jews in Europe, the "Final Solution."

Building the walls of a ghetto.

| February 24 | *SS Struma*, a small boat with 769 Romanian Jewish refugees on board, sinks in the Black Sea. |
| March | Trains begin to arrive at Auschwitz. |

Jews arriving at Auschwitz.

Inside the Warsaw ghetto.

March 1	Gas chambers begin operations at Sobibor.
March 17	Killings begin in Belzec (Poland) death camp.
June 1	Treblinka death camp opens.
June 30	Jewish schools in Germany are closed.
July 12	Deportations from the Warsaw ghetto to Treblinka begin.
July 28	The Jewish Fighting Organization (ZOB) is established in the Warsaw ghetto.
December 22	Jewish resistance fighters in Cracow, Poland, attack German troops.

| January 18 | Jewish resistance begins in the Warsaw ghetto. | **1943** |
| February 5 | Jewish resistance begins in the Bialystok ghetto. | |

Warsaw ghetto fighters caught.

April 19	The Warsaw ghetto revolt begins.
	At the Bermuda Conference, American and British representatives discuss resettlement of refugees of Nazi persecution. No action is taken.
June 11	Himmler orders all Jews in Polish ghettos to be sent to camps.
June 21	Himmler orders all Jews in Russian ghettos to be sent to camps.
August 2	Rebellion of inmates in Treblinka.
August 16	Revolt begins in the Bialystok (Poland) ghetto.
October 2	The Danish underground helps 8,000 Jews escape to Sweden.
October 14	Prisoners revolt at the Sobibor death camp.

1944

May & June	An estimated 400,000 Hungarian Jews are killed at Auschwitz.
June 6	D-Day, the Allied invasion of Nazi-held Europe.
July 20	German army officers attempt to assassinate Hitler, but fail.
July 24	Russian forces discover abandoned Maidanek death camp.

October 7	Revolt in Auschwitz.
November 8	Death march of Jews from Budapest to Austria begins.

January 17	Death march from Auschwitz begins.	***1945***
	Raoul Wallenberg is arrested by Russian police in Budapest. His fate remains unknown.	
April 15	Bergen-Belsen liberated by the British.	
April 25	Invading American forces from the west and Soviet forces from the east meet in Torgau, Germany.	
April 29	Dachau is liberated by American troops.	
April 30	Hitler commits suicide.	
May 8	Germany surrenders.	
November 22	Nuremberg Trials of Nazis begin.	

Aaron Tibor Katz, of Romania, victim of the Holocaust.

Memorial to victims of the Holocaust at Yad Vashem, Jerusalem.

Ani Ma'amin

I believe with perfect faith in the coming of the Messiah; and although he may tarry, I will wait daily for his coming.

אֲנִי מַאֲמִין בֶּאֱמוּנָה שְׁלֵמָה
בְּבִיאַת הַמָּשִׁיחַ
וְאַף עַל פִּי שֶׁיִּתְמַהְמֵהַּ
עִם כָּל זֶה
אֲחַכֶּה לּוֹ בְּכָל יוֹם שֶׁיָּבוֹא

Suggested Reading

Nonfiction

Here is a sampling of the many good books about the Holocaust for young readers.

Abells, Chana Byers. *The Children We Remember*. New York: Greenwillow, 1987.

Adler, David A. *Child of the Warsaw Ghetto*. New York: Holiday House, 1995.

Adler, David A. *Hilde and Eli: Children of the Holocaust*. New York: Holiday House, 1994.

Adler, David A. *The Number on My Grandfather's Arm*. New York: UAHC Press, 1987. Photo essay.

Adler, David A. *A Picture Book of Anne Frank*. New York: Holiday House, 1993.

Adler, David A. *We Remember the Holocaust*. New York: Henry Holt, 1989.

Appleman-Jurman, Alicia. *Alicia, My Story*. New York: Bantam Books, 1988.

Atkinson, Linda. *In Kindling Flame: The Story of Hannah Senesh, 1921-1944*. New York: Lothrop, Lee & Shepard, 1985.

Auerbacher, Inge. *I Am A Star: Child of the Holocaust*. New York: Prentice Hall, 1985.

Bacharach, Susan D. *Tell Them We Remember: The Story of the Holocaust*. Boston: Little, Brown and the U.S. Holocaust Memorial Museum, 1994.

Baer, Edith. *A Frost in the Night: A Girlhood on the Eve of the Third Reich*. New York: Pantheon, 1980.

Berenbaum, Michael. *The World Must Know: The History of the Holocaust as Told in the United States Holocaust Memorial Museum*. Boston: Little, Brown, 1993.

Bernheim, Mark. *Father of the Orphans: The Story of Janusz Korczak*. New York: Lodestar Books, 1989.

Block, Gay and Malka Drucker. *Rescuers: Portraits of Moral Courage in the Holocaust*. Holmes and Meier, 1992.

Brown, Gene. *Anne Frank: Child of the Holocaust*. New York: Rosen, 1992.

Chaikin, Miriam. *A Nightmare in History: The Holocaust 1933-1945*. New York: Clarion, 1987.

Drucker, Malka and Michael Halperin. *Jacob's Rescue: A Holocaust Story*. New York: Bantam, 1993.

Drucker, Olga Levy. *Kindertransport*. New York: Henry Holt, 1992.

Dwork, Deborah. *Children with a Star: Jewish Youth in Nazi Europe*. New Haven: Yale University Press, 1991.

Finkelstein, Norman H. *Remember Not to Forget: A Memory of the Holocaust*. New York: Franklin Watts, 1985.

Frank, Anne. *The Diary of a Young Girl*. New York: Doubleday, 1995.

Friedrich, Otto. *The Kingdom of Auschwitz*. New York: HarperCollins, 1982.

Greene, Carol. *Elie Wiesel: Messenger from the Holocaust*. New York: Ticknor & Fields, 1993.

Greenfeld, Howard. *The Hidden Children*. New York: Ticknor & Fields, 1993.

Hautzig, Esther. *The Endless Steppe*. New York: Thomas Y. Crowell, 1968.

Herman, Erwin and Agnes Herman. *The Yanov Torah*. Rockville, Maryland: Kar Ben Copies, 1985.

Hurwitz, Johanna. *Anne Frank: Life in Hiding.* Philadelphia: Jewish Publication Society, 1988.

Isaacman, Clara. *Clara's Story.* Philadelphia: Jewish Publication Society, 1984.

Katz, William Loren. *An Album of Nazism.* New York: Franklin Watts, 1979.

Koehn, Ilse. *Mischling, Second Degree: My Childhood in Nazi Germany.* New York: Greenwillow Books, 1977, and New York: Puffin Books, 1990.

Landau, Elaine. *We Survived the Holocaust.* New York: Franklin Watts, 1991.

Leitner, Isabella with Irving Leitner. *The Big Lie: A True Story.* New York: Scholastic, 1992.

Levi, Primo. *Survival in Auschwitz: The Nazi Assault on Humanity.* New York: Collier Books, 1986.

Linnea, Sharon. *Raoul Wallenberg: The Man Who Stopped Death.* Philadelphia: The Jewish Publication Society, 1993.

Meltzer, Milton. *Never to Forget: The Jews of the Holocaust.* New York: HarperCollins, 1976.

Meltzer, Milton. *Rescue: The Story of How Gentiles Saved Jews in the Holocaust.* New York: HarperCollins, 1988.

Nir, Yehuda. *The Lost Childhood: A Memoir.* San Diego: Harcourt Brace Jovanovich, 1989.

Pettit, Jayne. *A Place to Hide: True Stories of Holocaust Rescues.* New York: Scholastic, 1993.

Ransom, Candice F. *So Young to Die: The Story of Hannah Senesh.* New York: Scholastic, 1993.

Reiss, Johanna. *The Upstairs Room.* New York: Thomas Y. Crowell, 1972.

Rogansky, Barbara. *Smoke and Ashes: The Story of the Holocaust.* New York: Holiday House, 1988.

Rosenberg, Maxine B. *Hiding to Survive: Stories of Jewish Children Rescued from the Holocaust.* New York: Clarion, 1994.

Rossel, Seymour. *The Holocaust: The World and the Jews, 1933-1945.* New Jersey: Behrman, 1993.

Roth Hano, Renee. *Touch Wood: A Girlhood in Occupied France.* New York: Puffin Books, 1988.

Schur, Maxine. *Hannah Szenes: A Song of Light.* Philadelphia: Jewish Publication Society, 1986.

Siegel, Aranka. *Upon the Head of a Goat: A Childhood in Hungary 1939–44.* New York: Farrar, Straus and Giroux, 1981, and New York: Puffin Books, 1994.

Spiegelman, Art. *Maus, A Survivor's Tale.* New York: Pantheon Books, 1986 and 1991 (2 volumes).

Stadtler, Bea. *The Holocaust: A History of Courage and Resistance.* New York: Behrman House, 1975.

Toll, Nelly S. *Behind the Secret Window: A Memoir of Hidden Childhood.* New York: Dial, 1993.

van der Rol, Ruud and Rian Verhoeven. *Anne Frank, Beyond the Diary: A Photographic Remembrance.* New York: Viking Press, 1993.

Wiesel, Elie. *Night.* New York: Hill and Wang, 1969, and New York: Bantam Books, 1982.

Zar, Rose. *In the Mouth of the Wolf.* Philadelphia: Jewish Publication Society, 1984.

Zeinhert, Karen. *The Warsaw Ghetto Uprising.* Connecticut: Millbrook, 1993.
Zyskind, Sara. *Struggle.* Minneapolis: Lerner, 1989.

Ackerman, Karen. *The Night Crossing.* New York: Knopf, 1994.
Adler, David A. *One Yellow Daffodil.* New York: Harcourt Brace, 1995.
Baylis White, Mary. *Sheltering Rebecca.* New York: Lodestar Books, 1991, and New York: Puffin Books, 1993.
Bishop, Claire Huchet. *Twenty and Ten.* New York: Viking, 1952.
Bunting, Eve. *Terrible Things.* Philadelphia: Jewish Publication Society, 1989.
Cormier, Robert. *Tunes for Bears to Dance To.* New York: Delacorte, 1992.
Dillon, Eilis. *Children of Bach.* New York: Scribners, 1992.
Herman, Erwin and Agnes. *The Yanov Torah.* Rockville, Maryland: Kar-Ben Copies, 1985.
Innocenti, Roberto. *Rose Blanche.* Mankato, Minnesota: Creative Education, 1985.
Kerr, Judith. *When Hitler Stole Pink Rabbit.* New York: Coward, McCann & Geoghegan, 1972.
Laird, Christa. *Shadow of the Wall.* New York: Greenwillow, 1990.
Levitin, Sonia. *Journey to America.* New York: Atheneum, 1970.
Levoy, Myron. *Alan and Naomi.* New York: Harper & Row, 1977.
Lowry, Lois. *Number the Stars.* Boston: Houghton Mifflin, 1989, and New York: Dell, 1990.
Marvin, Isabel R. *Bridge to Freedom.* Philadelphia: Jewish Publication Society, 1991.
Matas, Carol. *Daniel's Story.* New York: Scholastic, 1993, and Washington D.C.: U.S. Holocaust Museum, 1993.
Morpurgo, Michael. *Waiting for Anya.* New York: Scholastic, 1990.
Oppenheim, Levey. *The Lily Cupboard.* New York: HarperCollins, 1992.
Orgel, Doris. *The Devil in Vienna.* New York: Dial, 1978.
Orlev, Uri. *The Man from the Other Side.* Boston: Houghton Mifflin, 1991, and New York: Puffin, 1995.
Provost, Gary and Gail Levine Provost. *David and Max.* Philadelphia: Jewish Publication Society, 1988.
Richter, Hans Peter. *Friedrich.* New York: Henry Holt, 1970.
Sachs, Marilyn. *A Pocketful of Seeds.* New York: Doubleday, 1973, and New York: Puffin, 1994.
Sender, Ruth Minsky. *The Cage.* New York: Macmillan, 1986.
Sender, Ruth Minsky. *The Holocaust Lady.* New York: Macmillan, 1992.
Suhl, Yuri. *Uncle Misha's Partisans.* New York: Franklin Watts, 1975.
Treseder, Terry Walton. *Hear O Israel: A Story of the Warsaw Ghetto.* New York: Atheneum, 1990.
Volavkova, Hana, ed. *I Never Saw Another Butterfly: Children's Drawings and Poems from Terezin Concentration Camp.* New York: Schocken, 1978.
Yolen, Jane. *The Devil's Arithmetic.* New York: Viking, 1988, and New York: Puffin, 1990.

Fiction

Yom ha-Azma'ut and Yom Yerushalayim

Happy Birthday, Israel/Jerusalem Reunited

About Yom ha-Azma'ut and Yom Yerushalayim

Happy Birthday Israel!

On the fifth day of the Hebrew month of Iyar 5708 (May 14, 1948), the Jewish State of Israel was founded. Today the fifth of Iyar is celebrated as Yom ha-Azma'ut, Israel's Independence Day, with parties and parades.

In Israel the preceding day, the fourth of Iyar, is Yom Ha-Zikaron, Remembrance Day, in memory of the thousands who have been killed defending the Jewish State. People light candles and visit cemeteries. In the late afternoon sirens are sounded, and the entire state observes a few moments of silence in memory of the dead.

The twenty-eighth of Iyar is Yom Yerushalayim (Jerusalem Day), celebrating the reunification of Jerusalem during the 1967 Six-Day War.

Long Is the Way to Jerusalem

by Miriam Bligh-Grotto

In the office of the Eilat police station in Israel stood an annoyed, black-eyed boy. From his Yemenite Arabic, the police officers could only make out that he had come thirteen hundred miles on foot, all alone. Finally a Yemenite fisherman was called in and he began to interpret:

"They used to call me Dawood, but my real name is David Ben-Ezra Damari," said the boy. "*Damari* because I come from the City of Damar; and *Ben-Ezra* because Shafika said that my father's name was Ezra." When the pieces were put together, his history went somewhat like this:

It was a cool, quiet night; even the jackals did not feel like howling. Suddenly a harsh grip had shaken David out of his sleep and he faced Shafika. He followed her into the courtyard and they sat down on the huge grindstone.

On Shafika's palm—glittering in the moonlight like the blade of a knife—lay a peculiar, six-pointed star on a leather band. She explained that this was the star of the Jews and was called a Magen David.

"I am not your mother, Dawood," she said. "You are a Jew. Your parents died in the Great Sickness which struck that region when you were still a baby." She fastened the Magen David round

12

Jews immigrating to Israel in the 1950s.

his neck. "Your real mother—her name was Rachel—left this for you. Her last wish was that on the thirteenth spring of your life you shall be in the land of the Jews; in the Holy City of Jerusalem."

"*Ya-Allah!* The Holy City? But how do I get there?"

"It's a long, long way to the north," Shafika said, pressing a few coins into his hand. "To be there in time you must go now. Go, and Allah be with you . . ."

A last embrace and—on went David, leaving behind the slumbering city of Damar.

At daybreak he reached a village in the mountains. The dreary song of women who were grinding corn echoed through the fresh morning. He approached several of them, asking for the way to Jerusalem. Their shrewd eyes glared at him from behind the black veils, but they only shrugged and continued singing.

In the last clay hut of the village, an old woman pointed with her bony hand: "There, son, go north and Allah be with you."

Exhausted and thirsty, David reached Tuah, a town at the foothills of the A-Sarat mountains, which he intended to cross. After he quenched his thirst from the water of the public rain-barrel, he bought dry lamb, pittah-bread and a huge skin bottle: the equipment for his journey.

In Tuah he learned of something he had never thought about before: borders. And what was the usual penalty for smuggling across a border? It was—"chopping off." Of what? A hand, an ear, a head—no one cared in particular.

The most disturbing fact of all, though, was that he had to smuggle across many borders in order to reach Jerusalem. And the first one had to be braved that very night!

But he was caught.

Nothing helped. Neither the Magen David to which he prayed nor the tears which he shed in an attempt to soften the guard's heart and grip. So he was being carried off to be chopped. Chopped! David summoned all his courage and strength, tore his hand from the guard's grip, and plunged into the nearby wheatfield.

The bullets swished by. A sudden slap and pull . . . and a warm liquid began to flow down his left thigh and ankle.

David did not remember how long he lay there on the soft, warm earth. Only when his heart beat normally again, did he realize that the bullet had hit only his skin bottle; that not blood but water had wet his ankle. So after all, perhaps the Magen David had saved him.

In the morning David bought a new skin bottle from a passerby and continued his journey over the A-Sarat mountains.

The nights he spent in caves and kept a fire alight, to keep the mountain beasts away. During the day he climbed. The higher he went, the steeper the path became, the barer the mountains, and the lonelier the way. The huge eagles and ugly vultures in the clear sky frightened him. But he continued; it was his mother's last wish—he must fulfill it!

After almost a month of walking, he saw that the barren path began to wind downward. The mountains turned gentler, the

Faces of a People, the People of Israel

slopes greener, inhabited. How happy David was to see human beings again. He had almost forgotten what they looked like.

Arriving in the city of Akhroum, in Saudi Arabia, he again inquired about the way to Jerusalem. "North," was the answer. The passersby gazed curiously at the boy who would not tell why he wanted to get to Jerusalem. Stubbornly David continued on the main road towards the kingdom of Hejaz.

But after nearly three months, David's strength began to fail him. His clothes were in rags, his shoes torn, his feet sore and bleeding. Yet he continued. But he reached only the gates of the city of Taif. There a kind passerby found him, lying in the dust and weeping.

Fed and wrapped in a comfortable blanket, David told the stranger his story.

His host was a Jew—the first Jew David had ever spoken to. He listened patiently and then said, "I have an idea."

It was the season of the annual pilgrimage to the Holy City of Mecca. Why not go to Mecca, mix with the crowd and join a group whose way home (northward through the Arabian peninsula) would lead David into the kingdom of Jordan—only one border-smuggle from Jerusalem!

Mecca was crowded with pilgrims from every country in the Arab world. Soon David made friends with a Syrian group. They let him sleep under their blankets. After the completion of their religious services in Mecca, they set out on their way back north.

A monotonous month of plodding through the towns and villages parallel to the shores of the Red Sea passed as if in a dream. Then the pilgrims crossed the border of the kingdom of Jordan, into the city of Qualat al-Maudawara. The same night David slid from under the heavy blankets and out of the encampment.

Three weeks later he was in the town of Aqaba.

Eilat was just at the opposite side of the Gulf of Aqaba. At night its lights flickered and twinkled invitingly; they seemed so close, as if only within an arm's length. David waited until the last lights disappeared in Aqaba and in Eilat. Then he started off, towards the last and best-guarded border.

The sand and gravel crackled and whispered under his feet. The sweat of fear wet his forehead. His hand clutched the Magen David. ". . . Not now, at the last border . . ." he pleaded in a whisper, "please . . ."

A Yom ha-Azma'ut Bummer

"You don't mind taking your brother, do you?"

When you have to take your brother to the parade.

Suddenly a harsh hand grasped David's shoulder. Another hand pressed on his mouth and the cold steel of a weapon tickled his spine. He had run straight into a cordon of rifle barrels. Then, quietly, he was put on a truck among dark, silent figures which smelled of grass and gunpowder.

"And that's how I got here," David finished his story. "But they wouldn't believe me!" He unbuttoned his shirt. On his bony chest hung a small, rusty Magen David: "I *am* a Jew . . . honestly I am . . ."

K'tonton, the tiny hero of this story, is a Jewish boy no taller than your middle finger. Stories of his adventures have delighted children since their first appearance in print in 1930.

Size Isn't Everything
by Sadie Rose Weilerstein

K'tonton was in Haifa. Below him were the blue waters of the harbor. Big ships lay at anchor. He looked up. The city had climbed a mountain. White houses, sparkling in the sun, peeked from between cool pine trees and bright gardens.

K'tonton's heart beat fast. This was Mount Carmel. At the top of the mountain was the Technion, the school with the wonderful machine K'tonton had heard about. One of the many people K'tonton had met in Israel told him that the Technion had a microscope that made small things big.

A student was standing at the curbstone, trying to hitch a ride up the Carmel. He had set down a package he was carrying. K'tonton slipped into the wrappings—where the paper folded over—just as a small compact car came to a stop. The student picked up the package and hopped in, not knowing that he was taking with him another hitchhiker, a thumb-sized one.

So it was that K'tonton arrived at the Technion, and was left in a package on a desk in a sunny office.

A sign on the desk read:

A. CARL

K'tonton heard a door shut with a bang, then open again. He looked for a moment. Then he slipped out of the wrappings of the package and looked up—into a man's startled eyes. The startled look quickly changed to a smile of welcome.

"Is there anything I can do for you?" Mr. Carl asked.

Yom ha-Azma'ut
and Yom Yerushalayim

Happy Birthday, Israel/
Jerusalem Reunited

"My name is K'tonton. I'm from America. If you please, could you take me to the machine that makes little things big?" K'tonton glanced at the slip of paper in his jacket. "You call it . . . mic . . . microscope. It *is* here, isn't it?"

"We have many microscopes here," said Mr. Carl. "What do you want a microscope for?"

"So I can get big," K'tonton answered, surprised that Mr. Carl should ask. "I've heard that if you put something very small on the big glass shelf and look through a kind of tube, the small thing gets big. Please, sir," K'tonton said eagerly, "will you put *me* on the glass so I can grow big?"

Mr. Carl picked up K'tonton in his hand. "K'tonton," he said gently, "I'm afraid you don't quite understand what a microscope does. The little thing on the slide—slide is what we call the glass shelf—the little thing doesn't really get big. It just *looks* big. When you take it off the glass, it's as small as before. Besides, you're too big to fit on the glass. The things we look at through a microscope are so tiny we couldn't even see them without the microscope."

Disappointment choked K'tonton's throat, looked out of his eyes.

"Why do you want to be big?" Mr. Carl asked. "I like you as you are."

K'tonton blinked back a tear. "Because if I were big I would be able to do big things."

"I know some *little* things that can do big things," said Mr. Carl. "Come! Let me introduce you to them."

So K'tonton began what Mr. Carl called his "special course at the Technion."

"Lesson One," said Mr. Carl, as he carried K'tonton into a big room he called a biology lab. It was after school hours, and the students had all left.

"There's the microscope you're so interested in," Mr. Carl said, and he set K'tonton down on a table near something with a stand, a long tube, and a little glass shelf. K'tonton saw at once that he could not have fitted on the glass. It was comforting to know that he was too *big* for something, but not comforting enough to make up for his dreadful disappointment. He had so wanted to be big.

"Look at this slide, K'tonton." Mr. Carl pointed to the oblong glass.

K'tonton looked. All he saw was a drop of water.

"Now look at it through the microscope."

Mr. Carl held K'tonton up to the lens and K'tonton pressed an eye against it. The drop of water turned into a pond with tiny wriggling creatures swimming around.

"Do you know what these tiny creatures can do?" said Mr. Carl. "They can make a strong man sick. And these"—he pointed to another slide—"can make a sick man well."

K'tonton hardly heard him. He was too busy being sorry for himself because the microscope couldn't help *him.*

"Maybe Lesson Two will go better," said Mr. Carl. "We'll try the Mining Engineering Department."

He carried K'tonton into another building. Specimens of rocks and metals of every kind and color were arranged on shelves.

"Which do you think is the most precious?" Mr. Carl asked.

K'tonton didn't answer.

"That one is." Mr. Carl pointed to the smallest stone of all. "It's a diamond."

"I know," said K'tonton. "You put diamonds in rings."

"And in watches to make them go and in machines to drill and to grind. These tiny stones can cut the hardest rock."

K'tonton was no longer listening.

"Well, there's still Lesson Three," said Mr. Carl hopefully.

This time he carried K'tonton across the campus to a lecture hall in a fine new building.

K'tonton saw rows and rows of seats. Up front was desk with a blackboard behind it. A chalk diagram with big and little circles and pointing lines was drawn on the blackboard.

"That's a drawing of something we call an atom," Mr. Carl said, "but a million, billion times bigger than it really is. You know the size of a toy balloon?"

K'tonton nodded.

"Well, you could put a hundred million billion atoms in one toy balloon. That's how tiny they are. And do you know what those tiny atoms will do for us when our students learn how to put them to work? They'll make electricity for our homes and our factories. They'll run our ships. They'll help doctors make people well. They'll even move mountains, if we want them to!"

This time K'tonton's eyes were sparkling with excitement.

"That's what atoms can do," Mr. Carl went on. "And they're so tiny you can't see them even with a microscope—not even with

an electronic microscope. That's the most powerful kind of all. Do you still think little things can't do big important work?"

It would have been better if Mr. Carl had not mentioned the microscope. The word set K'tonton thinking again about his mistake. The sparkle left his eyes.

Mr. Carl looked discouraged for a moment. Then a gleam came into his eyes. Back across the campus he went, K'tonton tucked into his pocket. Students nodded to him as he passed. A tall professor stopped to ask if he could spare a few minutes. There was something he wanted to discuss. Mr. Carl asked him if it could wait until the next day. He had an important visitor from America.

Back in his office, Mr. Carl took a map out of a drawer and spread it wide on his desk. It was a map of the world.

"K'tonton," Mr. Carl said, setting him down on the map, "can you find America for me?"

K'tonton found it.

"Europe? Asia? Africa?"

K'tonton found them all.

"Now the Mediterranean Sea," said Mr. Carl.

K'tonton found the Mediterranean Sea, and many countries on the shores of the sea: Italy shaped like a boot, Greece, Turkey, Egypt.

"Where is Israel?" Mr. Carl asked.

Israel was harder to find. It was so tiny. When K'tonton tried to point to it, his finger touched its neighbors Lebanon, Syria, and Jordan.

"Hm," said Mr. Carl. "Israel can't be very important. It's just a speck on the map."

"But, Mr. Carl, Israel is *very* important!" K'tonton sprang to Israel's defense. "It's the land God promised to Abraham. The whole Bible came from Israel. And now . . ."

A twinkle in Mr. Carl's eyes made K'tonton stop in the middle of his sentence. Now he knew what Mr. Carl had been trying to teach him.

"I guess size isn't everything," he admitted. And he grinned up at Mr. Carl.

The disappointment in K'tonton's heart had melted away. He and the State of Israel were both K'tontons.

A Yom ha-Azma'ut Bummer

THE END

Missing the parade.

Hatikvah

As long as a Jewish heart beats, and as long as Jewish eyes look eastward, then our two thousand year hope to be a free nation in Zion is not dead.

כָּל עוֹד בַּלֵּבָב פְּנִימָה
נֶפֶשׁ יְהוּדִי הוֹמִיָּה
וּלְפַאֲתֵי מִזְרָח קָדִימָה
עַיִן לְצִיּוֹן צוֹפִיָּה
עוֹד לֹא אָבְדָה תִּקְוָתֵנוּ
הַתִּקְוָה בַּת שְׁנוֹת אַלְפַּיִם
לִהְיוֹת עַם חָפְשִׁי בְּאַרְצֵנוּ
בְּאֶרֶץ צִיּוֹן וִירוּשָׁלַיִם

**Yom ha-Azma'ut
and Yom Yerushalayim**

*Happy Birthday, Israel/
Jerusalem Reunited*

Am Yisrael Ḥai

The Jewish people lives! Our Father yet lives!

עַם יִשְׂרָאֵל חַי
עוֹד אָבִינוּ חַי

Hinei Mah Tov

In easy fashion

*Behold how good and pleasant it is for brothers to
dwell together in unity.*

הִנֵּה מַה טּוֹב וּמַה נָּעִים
שֶׁבֶת אַחִים גַּם יָחַד

Yom ha-Azma'ut
and Yom Yerushalayim

Happy Birthday, Israel/
Jerusalem Reunited

Havah Nagilah

With great joy

Hasidic melody
Lyrics: M. Nathanson

Ha - vah na - gi - lah ha - vah na - gi - lah ha - vah na - gi - lah

v' - nis - m' - ḥa   v' - nis - m' - ḥa   ha - vah n' - ra - n' - nah

ha - vah n' - ra - n' - nah   ha - vah n' - ra - n' - na   v' - nis - m' - ḥa

v' - nis - m' - ḥa   u - ru   u - ru a - ḥim

u - ru a - ḥim b' - leiv sa - mei - aḥ   u - ru a - ḥim b' - leiv sa - mei - aḥ   u - ru a - ḥim b' - leiv sa - mei - aḥ

u - ru a - ḥim b' - leiv sa - mei - aḥ   u - ru a - ḥim   u - ru a - ḥim b' - leiv sa - mei - aḥ

Come let us be glad and rejoice, Arise, brethren,
with a joyful heart.

הָבָה נָגִילָה וְנִשְׂמְחָה
עוּרוּ אַחִים בְּלֵב שָׂמֵחַ

Everything you need to make this doll for a younger brother or sister is readily available except perhaps the Israeli flag picks—and these you may find at a party goods store or synagogue gift shop. You can also make your own with paper, felt-tip pens and toothpicks.

Yom ha-Azma'ut Crafts

Doll That Waves the Israeli Flag

MATERIALS

1 sheet of 8-1/2" x 11" white paper
8-1/2" x 11" piece of lightweight cardboard
pencil
scissors
1 paper fastener
felt-tip pens in several colors
1 piece of 18" yarn in any color
2 Israeli flag picks
white glue

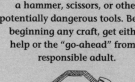

STOP!
Some of the crafts in this chapter call for the use of a hammer, scissors, or other potentially dangerous tools. Before beginning any craft, get either help or the "go-ahead" from a responsible adult.

1. Place the sheet of white paper over the body pattern (figure A) and the arm pattern (figure B) and trace the patterns.

2. Cut out the patterns from the sheet of white paper, place them on the cardboard, and trace around them with a pencil. Poke a hole in the body and in each arm, as shown in figures A and B.

3. To assemble, put a paper fastener through the hole in the body and, placing the arms behind the body, through the hole in each arm. Close the fastener loosely, so the arms can move up and down. Enlarge each hole slightly if the arms do not move easily.

4. Draw facial features and a costume on the doll with the pens.

5. Poke a hole in each hand. Thread one end of the yarn through each hole, making a knot behind it.

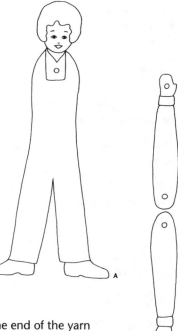

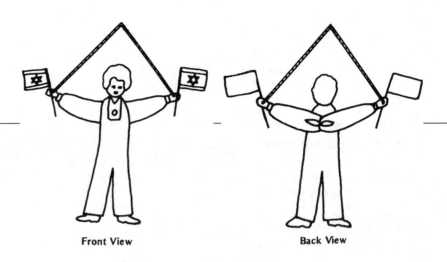

Front View   **Back View**

6. Glue a flag in each hand (figure C). Let dry.

7. To move the doll, simply pull the yarn up and down above the doll's head.

Israeli Stamp Key Chain

Key Chain

You can collect Israeli stamps by corresponding with someone in Israel, or you can buy stamps in a variety store or hobby shop. You'll also need to buy a small plastic sample with a hole punched in it at a home supply center. Some stores will supply samples of discontinued samples free of charge.

MATERIALS

small plastic sample
rubbing alcohol
Israeli stamp
white glue
metal key chain

1. Remove any printing from the sample by pouring a little rubbing alcohol on a paper towel and gently rubbing the plastic.

2. Attach an Israeli stamp to the plastic with white glue. Be sure all the edges of the stamp are glued down.

3. Thread a metal key chain (available at a craft or hobby shop) through the hole in the plastic.

Israeli Stamp Bookmark

These bookmarks make great gifts. Use them as party favors or give them to your favorite reader.

MATERIALS

2 pieces of clear adhesive-backed 2" x 6" paper
1 piece of decorative material or paper, about 1-3/4" x 5-1/2"
3 or 4 Israeli stamps
pinking shears or regular scissors

Bookmark

1. Peel the backing off 1 piece of clear adhesive-backed paper and place it sticky side up.

2. Center the piece of decorative material or paper face up on the sticky surface. Arrange 3 or 4 Israeli stamps on the material.

3. Peel the backing off another piece of clear adhesive-backed paper. Center it, sticky side down, on the stamp-covered material. Pressing firmly with your fingers, rub the back and front of the bookmark to help the layers stick together.

4. With pinking shears or regular scissors, slightly trim the edges of the adhesive-backed paper.

Yom ha-Azma'ut Recipes

Pita Sandwiches (Middle East)

Pita is a flat bread that opens like an envelope. It is usually filled with felafel, which are deep-fried balls of mashed chickpeas, and salad. Teḥina, a sauce made of sesame seeds, is poured on top. You can make felafel from a packaged mix or use the felafel recipe in this chapter. The pita, felafel mix, and teḥina can be bought at a kosher butcher store, supermarket, or a store that sells foods from other countries. The Israelis learned to make these spicy sandwiches from their Arab neighbors. They eat them on the run, just as we eat hot dogs.

1/2 onion	4 pita breads
1 cucumber	16 felafel balls
1 green pepper	teḥina sauce
2 tomatoes	

Peel the onion and the cucumber.

Cut the green pepper in half. Scoop out the seeds and white ribs and throw away.

Slice the tomatoes.

Cut all the vegetables into narrow strips. Then cut the strips into little pieces. Put them in the bowl and mix.

Slit the top edge of each pita. Pull the sides apart to make an open "pocket." Fill each pocket with 1/4 of the vegetables. Add 4 felafel balls.

Pour teḥina sauce over the filling in each pocket.

Serves 4

STOP!
A kitchen is a dangerous place. If you're not careful, you might burn yourself with splattering oil or boiling water. The recipes in this chapter are intended for older children. Before beginning, make sure an adult is available to help.

STOP

Felafel

If you want to mix your own felafel, here is a recipe to use. Whether you buy a mix or make your own, be sure to ask an adult to help with the deep frying. Splattering oil can burn you.

1 cup cooked or canned chickpeas (garbanzo beans)
1 clove garlic
1/2 teaspoon salt
1/8 teaspoon pepper
2/3 cup fine bread crumbs
2 eggs
2 tablespoons oil
oil for deep frying, enough to fill the pot about 3 inches

If you are using canned chickpeas, be sure to drain them. Mash the chickpeas in a large bowl.

Cut the garlic into tiny pieces. Add the garlic, salt, pepper, and bread crumbs to the chickpeas and mix them together.

Add the eggs and oil. Mix thoroughly.

Heat the oil in a pot to 375 degrees, or until little bubbles rise to the surface.

Shape the mixture into balls about 1 inch in diameter. Gently place the balls in the pot with the mixing spoon—don't drop them in because the hot oil may splash. Fry a few at a time until golden brown, about 5 minutes.

Remove the felafel with the slotted spoon. Drain on a plate covered with paper towels.

Makes 16 balls

Teḥina Sauce

Teḥina is a paste made from sesame seeds. You can buy a can of teḥina in stores that sell felafel or pita and turn it into teḥina sauce.

3/4 cup teḥina
1/3 cup lemon juice
1/8 teaspoon garlic powder
1/3 cup water

Put the teḥina, lemon juice, and garlic powder in a small mixing bowl. Mix until you have a smooth sauce.

Add the water, one teaspoon at a time, until the sauce is thin enough to pour.

Pour teḥina over pita sandwiches or use as a dip for raw vegetables.

Makes about 1 cup

Yom ha-Azma'ut Fun

Yom ha-Azma'ut Puzzles (Answers on page 274.)

Two mothers and two daughters go to the Yom ha-Azma'ut parade. Each waves her own Israeli flag but together they only wave 3 flags. Can you explain?

Parade Puzzle

Amy made 53 flags for Yom ha-Azma'ut. She gave away all but 4 of the flags. How many flags did she have left?

Flags

Two drummers were marching in the Yom ha-Azma'ut parade. The young drummer was the old drummer's son but the old drummer was not the young drummer's father. Who was the old drummer?

The Drummers

For Yom ha-Azma'ut, a shopkeeper was selling what he called "a rare old Israeli coin." It was a 1-shekel coin with the words "State of Israel" in both Hebrew and English and the date 1934. He was selling the coin for $100. Would you buy it?

The Valuable Coin

A Yom ha-Azma'ut Bummer

"LOOK AT THE GOODY, GOODY!"

"HA HA!"

When you're the only one who remembered to wear blue and white.

All-about-Israel Quiz

by Barbara Spector

1. Israel is located between which two continents?

2. Who gave Eretz Yisrael the name Palestine?

   (a) the Israelites; (b) the Philistines; (c) the Romans; (d) the British.

3. Which one of the following Israeli cities is the largest?

   (a) Jerusalem; (b) Tel Aviv-Jaffa; (c) Haifa.

4. About how long does it take to cross the State of Israel from west to east, traveling by car (Mediterranean coast to Jordan valley)?

   (a) seven hours; (b) five hours; (c) one and a half hours; (d) twenty minutes.

5. True or false: The majority of Israeli Jews were born in Israel.

6. In general, do Arabs serve in the Israeli army?

7. When Menachem Begin was in the Irgun, the underground movement that fought for Palestine's independence against the British Mandatory government, he often was disguised as _____.

   (a) an old woman; (b) an Arab; (c) a bearded rabbi; (d) a camel.

8. Theodor Herzl suggested a different Zionist flag from the one now used by the State of Israel. What did Herzl's suggested flag look like?

   (a) a gold Magen David on a red background; (b) a white flag with a blue menorah in the center; (c) seven blue stripes with six white stars; (d) seven gold stars against a white background.

9. Which city in Israel is not mentioned in the Bible?

   (a) Hebron; (b) Beersheba; (c) Tel Aviv; (d) Jerusalem.

10. When did Moshe Dayan lose his eye?

    (a) 1941; (b) 1948; (c) 1956; (d) 1967.

11. Has a Miss Israel ever won the Miss Universe pageant?

12. Which city in Israel is named after philanthropist Nathan Straus?

13. Israel has not one, but two, chief rabbis. Which two communities do they represent?

14. The giant menorah that stands outside the Knesset building in Jerusalem was a gift to the people of Israel from the parliament of which country?

15. Approximately what percentage of Israel's population lives on kibbutzim today?

    (a) 48.2 per cent; (b) 23.9 per cent; (c) 12.5 per cent; (d) 2.7 per cent.

16. Kibbutz Yad Mordecai in Israel is named after _____.

    (a) Mordecai of the Purim story; (b) Mordecai Anilewicz, leader of the Warsaw Ghetto Uprising; (c) Mordecai Kaplan, founder of Reconstructionism.

17. Which building in Israel houses the famous "Chagall windows"?

18. What picture was on the first stamps issued by the State of Israel on May 16, 1948?

    (a) a Magen David; (b) a portrait of Theodor Herzl; (c) ancient Jewish coins; (d) a menorah.

19. Which of the following people was born in Israel?

    (a) Menachem Begin, former Israeli prime minister; (b) David Ben-Gurion, first prime minister of Israel; (c) Gene Simmons, bass guitarist of the rock group Kiss.

20. Mapai, Likud, and Mapam are names of Israeli _____.

Lag B'omer
Picnics and Hikes

About Lag B'omer

Forty-nine days of the "omer" are counted beginning on the second night of Pesaḥ, the day during ancient times that the omer, a measure of barley, was offered in the Temple.

The seven-week omer period is one of semi-mourning. It is a time to remember the suffering during the Roman rule over Israel and the atrocities of the Crusades during the Middle Ages. During talmudic times thousands of the students of Rabbi Akiva died from disease. On the thirty-third day of the omer, Lag B'omer, the plague either ended or no one died that day. Customs vary, but generally during the Omer there are no weddings or other public celebrations until after Lag B'omer and for some, until Rosh Ḥodesh Sivan.

In Israel on Lag B'omer, thousands of people mark the day with a trip to Meron, to the tomb of Rabbi Simeon bar Yoḥai who died on this day. He was a student of Rabbi Akiva and author of the Zohar, a classic text of mystical Jewish teachings. Picnics and other outdoor activities are also commonly held on Lag B'omer. There is a tradition that children play with toy bows and arrows on Lag B'omer, a reminder of a victory of Bar Kokhba in his revolt against the Romans. It is also a reminder of how Rabbi Akiba's students fooled the Romans. The students carried bows and arrows, pretending to be hunters. Then they snuck off into the woods to study Torah.

Immediately following the forty-ninth day of the Omer, we celebrate the holiday of Shavuot. The counting connects Pesaḥ, which commemorates the Exodus, with Shavuot, which commemorates receiving the Torah on Mount Sinai.

13

DAY SCHOOL DAZE

by Bayla S. Jacobs & Shepsil Scheinberg

The friendship of Shlomo and Avrahom was stronger than the sturdiest rope. They enjoyed the same things and shared their joys and woes. When they had arguments, they succeeded in settling them peacefully. "If you ever have a complaint against me," Avrahom told Shlomo, "make sure to tell me so we can settle it." Shlomo wholeheartedly agreed, and made Avrahom promise to do the same.

Unfortunately, the rest of the world was not as peace-loving as these two. Avrahom and Shlomo lived in separate provinces. Their princes quarreled and went to war instead of discussing and solving their problems. Suddenly, thousands of people were in battle, hating and killing each other. Property was destroyed and lives—of men, women, and innocent children—were lost daily. Said each prince, "I must win, no matter how much blood must be spilled."

Caught up in this madness, to their great sorrow, were Avrahom and Shlomo, who were forced to join opposing armies.

Shlomo was assigned to spy for his side. He found out the enemy's location and strength, and began his return to report back, but he was stopped by a sentry.

"Halt! Who are you? What are you doing here?"

"Why, I had just lost my way, and ..."

The Sefirah Days

adapted from the Midrash by Rabbi Eliezer Gevirtz

Me'am Loez, Vayikroh 19:18

But the guard could not be fooled. He took Shlomo to the prince who looked at him with bitter hatred. "So you wanted to supply secrets to the enemy? Tomorrow at dawn you'll be taken out and executed!"

Shlomo was stunned. "Your Majesty," he pleaded, "I have no fear of death. But I have a wife and young child who are innocent. They do not even know that I am a spy. Why should they become victims of the war? If you kill me tomorrow, they will die, for I have left them very little. I beg you, Your Majesty, let me return home for three weeks, to collect all debts due me, and make sure my family doesn't starve. Then I will gladly return here to face my fate."

The prince broke into laughter. "Do you take me for a total fool? How could I for a moment believe that you would ever return? No—the execution will take place tomorrow."

Yet, before the prince could order Shlomo taken away, a soldier spoke up. "Would Your Majesty agree to the prisoner's request if someone agreed to take his place, and to die for him if he fails to return?"

Shlomo immediately recognized him: "Avrahom!"

"And who," asked the prince, "will take his place?"

Avrahom smiled, "I will."

"You realize," said the prince, "that if the prisoner does not return within three weeks, you will die."

Avrahom nodded.

"In that case," the prince decided, "the prisoner will be released, and this man will be held in his place."

A week passed. Two weeks. Avrahom languished in jail, but he seemed calm and unfrightened. Then the third week began, and there was still no sign of Shlomo. Still, the prince did not relent. "Get that foolish man ready for execution," he ordered as the third week neared its end.

Avrahom was led to the executioner's block, and was prepared for beheading. The executioner raised his axe, counted one, two, and . . .

Just then there came the sound of running footsteps as a man ran straight to Avrahom, pushed him out of the way, and placed himself in the path of the axe instead. Shlomo had returned!

A Lag B'omer Bummer

Ants in your picnic basket.

But Avrahom fought back. He pushed Shlomo away, yelling, "No, I shall die and you will live."

"I won't let you!" replied Shlomo. "I was caught, not you."

The two began a mighty struggle to see who would die in place of the other.

The prince watched in amazement, and then shouted, "Stop!" Silence fell. The prince announced: "I have never before seen such unselfish caring for someone else. I have, therefore, reached this conclusion—*neither one will die.* For such friendship, they both deserve to live, so that they can be an example to others."

During the Sefirah days we should try and remember this wonderful story, for during these sad days, 24,000 students of Rabbi Akiva died. Why? Because they did not show enough respect for one another. God expects us to love and honor one another. Every year during these sad days, we should remember the story of the thousands who died because they did not think of others, and of the two friends who lived because they did not care about themselves.

Manager Jones Plays A Hunch
by M. Levin

When the game had started, the gang had been feeling pretty swell. What a break that the big game should come out right on Lag B'Omer and they could go to a big league ball game instead of going to Hebrew School. And Joey Benson had fixed it with his brother, Lou, who was on the team and the boys of the Hebrew School had the best seats you could get. And maybe their idol, Joey's brother, Lou, would get his chance today. He was new on the team and wasn't a regular yet. He hadn't played much but all the boys knew he would show them when he got his opportunity. They could see him on the bench with his back toward them, no. 33, between no. 27, Jeff Owen, and old Doc Martin. They were all very proud of Lou Benson. He had been a pupil of their school and now he was a real big league ball player.

Everything had gone along fine. Right in the first inning, the home team had scored a run. A sizzling grounder past first had

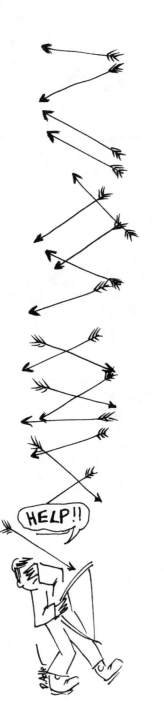

HELP!!

sent a run in. From then, both pitchers were holding firm. The home team was holding its lead, and it looked like the game would end 1-0 in their favor. And then in the 8th inning, things began to happen. Barger, the first baseman of the visiting team, had started a rally which ended with the visitors in the lead 3-1.

And now it was the last half of the 9th. The score still stood at 3-1 and things looked pretty bad. The gang was pretty glum.

"Why don't they do something?" said Pee-wee to the other boys. "Bet if they put Lou Benson in now, he could fix everything."

"They'll never put him in now," Joe Benson said bitterly.

"Maybe not, but I've got on idea," said Pee-wee decidedly. He got up and began working his way to the aisle.

"Where do you think you're going?" the boys asked.

"I'm going to talk to Jones, the manager," he said simply.

"You're crazy! You can't go down there!" they all said.

"Who do you think you are, a coach?" Joe Benson said sharply. Pee-wee ran down the aisle and disappeared around the stairway. A minute later, they saw him come out on the field. One of the guards started toward him but Pee-wee had reached the dug-out. Manager Jones came out. Pee-wee said something to him. Jones listened and smiled. He patted Pee-wee on the head, then shook his hand. Pee-wee started back to the stands.

The first man at bat struck out. Then Jenkins, the short-stop, was hit by a pitched ball and took a base. Lefty Fuller was up. The first ball was high. On the next ball, Fuller bunted and tore down toward first base. Jenkins headed out for second with everything he had. The catcher had thrown off his mask and was chasing after the ball down the base line. He picked it up and threw quickly to second to catch Jenkins. But the throw was wide and the second baseman was drawn off the base. Jenkins was safe and there was a man on first and second.

The crowd was on its feet, calling for a rally. Freeman, the left fielder, was at bat. The catcher was talking to the pitcher. The crowd was getting more excited every minute. The pitcher was taking it very slow, watching the batter and keeping an eye on the men on base. He threw a fast one. Freeman let it pass him. "Strike 1" called the umpire behind the plate. Freeman started to say something to the umpire but changed his mind. He hit the next ball pitched. It popped up very high over the infield. The short-stop dashed out and grabbed it. The crowd groaned. Two men out.

Manager Jones came out of the dug-out. He walked over to the bench and said something to the players. The boys saw Lou Benson hop up. He picked up a bat and took a few trial swings with it. "Attention, please!" came from the microphones. "Benson, no. 33, batting for Harvey, Benson!"

The crowd was up again. A pinch-hitter. The boys were dancing about madly. "It's Lou," they shouted. "Lou's up! Lou's up!"

Lou Benson was pawing the ground with his left foot, watching the pitcher. The first ball came over. It was low and wide. "Ball 1" called the umpire.

Benson hit the next ball furiously. It popped into the stands, a foul. "We want a hit, we want a hit!" the crowd was shouting. The next pitch came across the plate like a bullet. Benson struck at it and missed.

"Atta boy, Jim!" called the catcher to the pitcher. "One more like that and it's all over.

The pitcher looked about him at the men on base. Then he looked long at Benson. The batter was standing quite still now, watching the pitcher carefully. He was winding up. And there it was. Benson hit the ball with everything in him. The crack was like a shot. A tremendous roar went up from the crowd. The ball headed straight out, way over the head of the short-stop, over the outfielder who was running frantically toward the fence of the ball-park. Benson was tearing around the bases after his two teammates who were crossing the plate. Nobody ever saw the ball again.

"A home run! Three in!" the crowd was screaming and shouting with joy. "What a man, Benson. What a ball-player! What a ball game!" Benson crossed the plate and was surrounded by his team-mates. The crowd poured over the stands into the field to congratulate him.

Benson's brother and his friends from Hebrew School waited outside the dressing room until Lou came out, dressed just like an ordinary person. "Come here, you kids," he said smiling. He put his arm around Pee-wee. "What did you tell Jones? He said he was putting me in on a hunch he got from a kid."

Pee-wee was embarrassed. "Well, I told him today was Lag B'Omer, 33rd day in the Omer and it might be a good idea to put in player no. 33. That's all."

It rained Katz and dogs at the Lag B'Omer picnic.

D. Adler

Lag B'omer Craft

Woven Picnic Basket

STOP!
Some of the crafts in
this chapter call for the use of
a hammer, scissors, or other
potentially dangerous tools. Before
beginning any craft, get either
help or the "go-ahead" from a
responsible adult.

This handy basket will hold your tasty Lag B'omer picnic treats!

MATERIALS

1 large square piece of cardboard
pencil
ruler
scissors
heavy cord, plastic lacing, jute cord, or raffia
cloth tape, any color (craft or variety store)

1. To make the basket base, draw a small square in the center of the large piece of cardboard (figure A).

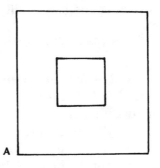

A

2. Draw wide strips on the cardboard, starting nearest the drawn square and proceeding to the outer edge. Cut out every other strip, as shown in figure B.

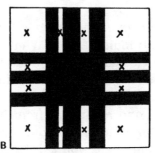

B

3. Fold the strips along the lines of the small square.

4. Tape one end of the cord to the bottom of one of the strips. Wind the cord in and out of the strips until you are about 3/4 of the way up. Reverse the direction of the winding until you reach the top. Cut the cord and tuck it under one of the woven strips (figure C).

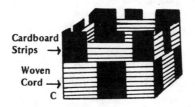

Cardboard Strips →

Woven Cord →

C

5. Cut a strip of tape long enough to go around the top edge of the basket. Center the tape, sticky side down, on top of the basket. Press down one side of the tape on each side of the basket. This keeps the woven strips from sliding off.

6. To make the handle, cut 2 long pieces of cord and insert through the strips of weaving (figure D). Tie the ends together.

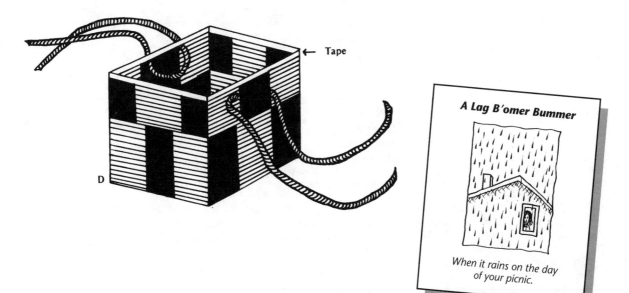

← Tape

D

A Lag B'omer Bummer

When it rains on the day of your picnic.

Lag B'omer Recipes

Invite your family and friends on a picnic to honor Lag B'omer. The recipes included below are especially suited to picnicking because they are easily portable and can be served at room temperature. If the weather is nice, take your picnic to a beautiful site—the woods, a lake, even the ocean! But even if the weather isn't nice, you can still have a picnic right at home. Set your table with a festive red and white checked table cloth. Use paper plates and cups and plastic spoons and knives to create that "picnicky" feeling.

Baked Salmon

This baked salmon can be served hot or cold. Even better, it tastes great on a bagel—although you might want to leave off the egg sauce if you are making a bagel sandwich.

SALMON

4-pound piece of salmon
1 medium onion
1 lemon
1/2 cup Italian or French dressing

EGG SAUCE

3 hard-cooked eggs
1 cup mayonnaise
1 tablespoon lemon juice

GARNISH

small beets
black olives
cherry tomatoes
white horseradish

STOP!

A kitchen is a dangerous place. If you're not careful, you might burn yourself with splattering oil or boiling water. The recipes in this chapter are intended for older children. Before beginning, make sure an adult is available to help.

Preheat the oven to 375 degrees.

Slice the onion and the lemon and set aside.

Place the salmon on a large piece of foil. Place half the onion slices and half the lemon slices in the cavity of the salmon, and top with half the dressing.

Put the rest of the onion and lemon slices on top of the fish, and cover with the rest of the dressing.

Fold the foil over the fish, and crimp the edges together tightly.

Place the fish on a flat baking sheet, and bake for 1 hour or for 15 minutes per pound.

While the fish is baking, make the egg sauce. Chop the eggs and mix them with the mayonnaise and the lemon juice. Chill.

A Lag B'omer Bummer

When you shoot an arrow and it doesn't go anywhere.

If you like horseradish, scoop out the beets with a melon baller and fill them with white horseradish. Set aside.

Remove the fish from the oven and open the foil, being careful to keep away from the opening in case there is steam.

Put the salmon back in the oven and bake for 15 more minutes. Do not over-bake.

Serve hot or cold with the egg sauce. You can either pour the sauce over the fish before you serve it, or you can serve the sauce separately in its own bowl.

Garnish the fish with the small beets, black olives, and cherry tomatoes or serve them as a separate dish.

8 to 10 servings as a main dish

Coleslaw

No picnic would be complete without coleslaw. For best results, make the coleslaw the night before and chill it.

5 cups cabbage, shredded (1 small head)
1 carrot
1 green pepper
1 red pepper
1 cup celery, sliced thin
2 scallions
1/2 cup white wine vinegar
1/2 cup water
1/2 cup mayonnaise
1/4 cup sugar
salt to taste
parsley

Wash the cabbage, and cut it in half. Put the cabbage in salted cold water to soak for 30 minutes.

While the cabbage is soaking, grate the carrot. Slice the green and red peppers and thinly slice the celery and the scallions.

Grate or shred the cabbage and put it in a bowl. Add the carrot, green and red peppers, celery, and scallions, and mix.

In a separate bowl, mix the vinegar, water, mayonnaise, sugar, and salt. Pour it over the cabbage mixture and mix it well.

Season the coleslaw to taste, adding more sugar if desired.

Refrigerate for a few hours or overnight.

Chop up a few sprigs of parsley and scatter them on top before serving.

8 servings

Apricot Bars

This delicious dessert is easy to make. Use any type of nuts—walnuts, pecans, peanuts, and cashews are favorites. Or feel free to omit the nuts altogether—the apricot bars will still taste great.

1 orange
1 cup dried apricots
2 eggs
1 cup sugar
1/3 cup oil
1 cup flour
1/4 teaspoon baking powder
1/4 teaspoon salt
1 cup nuts, chopped

Preheat the oven to 350 degrees.

Cut the orange in quarters, and remove the seeds but not the peel. Ask an adult to put the apricots and orange through a blender or food processor.

Beat the eggs with the sugar, and add the oil.

Sift the flour into a separate bowl. Fold the flour, the baking powder, and the salt into the egg mixture.

Add the apricot and orange mixture into the egg and flour mixture. Add the nuts and mix well.

Spread the mixture into a greased, shallow 9" x 13" pan and sprinkle with sugar. Bake for 25 minutes. While warm, cut into 32 bars.

32 bars

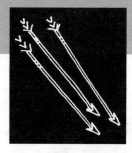

Lag B'omer Fun

Lag B'omer Puzzles (Answers on page 275.)

What comes after every Lag B'omer? If you start with the right letter in this box of letters and go around the box twice reading every other letter, you'll find the answer. If you can't find the answer, see page 275.

The Letter Box

This strange target was at the Lag B'omer picnic. Can you find a way to score exactly 100?

On Target

Shavuot
The Day God Gave the Torah

About Shavuot

The sixth of Sivan, and outside Israel the seventh, too, (except among Reform and Reconstructionist Jews) is the holiday of Shavuot. The holiday, as mentioned in the Bible, is an agricultural one, celebrating the wheat harvest. It comes seven weeks after the barley harvest and the first counting of the Omer that begins on the second day of Pesaḥ. The Talmud explains that Shavuot is also the holiday celebrating God's giving of the Torah to the Jewish people.

Shavuot is the only holiday mentioned in the Torah without a date given for its celebration, only that it comes fifty days after the first day of Pesaḥ, after the counting of the Omer has been completed. According to the Midrash, the counting from Pesaḥ to Shavuot reflects how anxious Jews were after their exodus from Egypt. They counted the days until they received the Torah.

Among the many Shavuot customs is decorating the synagogue and home with flowers and greens in remembrance of Mount Sinai, which was covered with green, growing things.

There is a tradition to eat cheesecake, cheese blintzes, and dairy foods on Shavuot. One reason given for this custom is that according to legend Moses was taken from the water on Shavuot and would only accept milk from an Israelite. Another reason commonly given is that the Jewish people first learned the laws of keeping kosher when the Torah was given. Then they ate dairy foods until they could properly clean their pots and utensils which until then had been used to prepare nonkosher foods.

There is a custom to stay up all night on the first night of Shavuot to study Torah and then to say the morning prayers at sunrise.

In synagogues and temples the Ten Commandments are read.

It is also a common custom to read the Book of Ruth, the story of a woman who converts to Judaism and voluntarily accepts the Torah. Ruth was the great-grandmother of King David, who was born and died on the sixth of Sivan—Shavuot. And the Book of Ruth is set at the time of the harvest in Israel.

In Reform temples, confirmation, signaling the end of the Hebrew school year and the graduation of the oldest students into full Jewish adulthood, is held on Shavuot.

Shavuot is a holiday with many traditions and many names. It is called Pentecost, "fiftieth," because the holiday comes after the forty-nine days of counting the Omer. Shavuot is also called Atzeret *(Solemn Assembly) because just as Shemini Atzeret is the concluding day of Sukkot, so Shavuot is considered the concluding day of Pesaḥ, with the two holidays being connected by the counting of the Omer. Shavuot is also called* Ḥag ha-Katzir *(Holiday of the Harvest),* Yom Ha-Bikurim *(day of the first fruits),* Z'man Matan Toratenu *(Time of the Giving of Our Torah).*

The Story of Ruth
adapted by Mortimer J. Cohen

The story of Ruth, of Moab, is one of the most beautiful in all literature. It describes the friendship, the love and the devotion of two women—Ruth and Naomi. It praises loyalty—loyalty to one's family. This loyalty plants in human beings the seed of confidence and faith in each other. And out of the seed of loyalty in human beings to each other grows the sturdy loyalty of people to God. As long as people live, they will thrill to the words of Ruth to Naomi:

> *"Entreat me not to leave thee,*
> *And to return from following after thee:*
> *For whither thou goest, I will go;*
> *And where thou lodgest, I will lodge;*
> *Thy people shall be my people,*
> *And thy God my God . . ."*

The story of Ruth is all the more charming because it presents a sharp contrast with the stormy times of the Judges, in which it is placed, times so dark with war and cruel deeds. But, there were years in that period when the Israelites were not engaged in war, when they harvested in their fields and toiled patiently in their little villages. The plain folk often suffered famine and sorrow and the separation of families, and even death. Without faithfulness and loyalty to each other to sustain them, life would have been far more difficult for them, perhaps even impossible. The rich helped the poor, moreover, by leaving the cor-

ners of the field and whatever fell out of the hands of the reapers for the poor to gather, that is, to glean for themselves. The right to glean was commanded by biblical law.

Ruth's Loyalty

It came to pass in the days when the judges judged, that there was a famine in the land. A certain man of Beth-lehem in Judah took his wife and two sons to live in the land of Moab. His name was Elimelech and that of his wife Naomi, and his two sons were Maḥlon and Chilion. After they had been living in Moab for some time, Elimelech died, and Naomi was left with her two sons. They married Moabite women, named Orpah and Ruth. About ten years later, Maḥlon and Chilion both died, and Naomi was left without husband or children.

Bereft of her two children as well as of her husband, Naomi set out with her daughters-in-law from the land of Moab to return to Judah, for she had heard that the Lord had remembered His people and had given them food. As they were setting out on the journey to Judah, Naomi said to her daughters-in-law:

"Go, return each of you to the home of your mother. May the Lord be kind to you as you have been kind to the dead and to me. The Lord grant that each of you may find peace and happiness in the house of a new husband."

She kissed them good-bye; but they began to weep aloud and said to her:

"No, we will go back with you to your people."

But Naomi said:

"Go back, my daughters; why should you go with me? Can I still have sons who might become your husbands? Go back, my daughters, go your own way, for I am too old to have a husband. Even if I should say, `I have hope,' even if I should have a husband tonight and should have sons, would you wait for them until they were grown up? Would you remain single for them? No, my daughters! I am sorry for you, for the Lord has afflicted me."

They again wept, and Orpah kissed her mother-in-law good-bye, but Ruth clung to her.

Naomi said:

"See, your sister-in-law is going back to her own people and to her own gods; go along with her!"

But Ruth answered:

"Entreat me not to leave thee, and to return from following after thee; for whither thou goest, I will go; and where thou lodgest, I will lodge; thy people shall be my people, and thy God my God; where thou diest, will I die, and there will I be buried. The Lord do so to me, and more also, if aught but death part thee and me."

When Naomi saw that Ruth had made up her mind to go with her, she ceased urging her to return.

They travelled on until they came to Beth-lehem in Judah at the beginning of the barley harvest.

Naomi was related through her husband to Boaz, a very wealthy man of the family of Elimelech.

One day Ruth, the Moabitess, said to Naomi:

"Let me now go to the fields and glean among the ears of corn after him in whose sight I shall find favor."

"Go, my daughter," said Naomi to her.

She went, and came and gleaned in the field after the reapers; and it was her good fortune to glean in that part of the field which belonged to Boaz.

Just then Boaz returned from Beth-lehem. He greeted the reapers and said to his servant who had charge of them:

"Whose maiden is this?"

The servant replied:

"It is the Moabite maiden who came back with Naomi from the land of Moab; and she said, `Let me glean, I beg you, and gather sheaves after the reapers.' So she came, and has continued from the morning until now, and she has not rested a moment in the field."

Ruth Meets Boaz

Then Boaz said to Ruth:

"Listen, my daughter. Do not glean in any other field nor leave this place, but stay here with my maidens. I have told the young men not to trouble you. When you are thirsty, go to the jars and drink of that which the young men have drawn."

Ruth bowed low and said to him:

"Why are you so kind to me, to take interest in one who comes from another land?"

Boaz replied:

"I have heard what you have done for your mother-in-law. May the Lord repay you for what you have done, and may you be fully rewarded by the God of Israel, under whose wings you have come to take refuge."

She said:

"I trust I may please you, my lord, for you have comforted me and spoken kindly to your servant, although I am not really equal to one of your own servants."

At noonday Boaz said to her:

"Come here and eat some of the food and dip your piece of bread in the sour wine."

She sat beside the reapers; and she ate until she had had enough and had some left. When she rose to glean, Boaz gave this order to his young men: "Let her glean even among the sheaves and do not disturb her."

So she gleaned in the field until evening. Then she beat out that which she had gleaned; and it was about a bushel of barley. She took it up and went into the city, where she showed her mother-in-law what she had gleaned. She also gave Naomi what she had left from her meal after she was satisfied.

Naomi said to Ruth:

"Where did you glean today and where did you work?"

Ruth told her where she had worked, and said:

"The name of the man with whom I worked today is Boaz."

Naomi said to her daughter-in-law:

"The man is a near relative of ours."

And Ruth, the Moabitess, said:

"Yes, he said to me, 'You must keep near my young men until they have completed all my harvest.'"

Naomi said to Ruth:

"It is best, my daughter, that you should go out with his maidens and that no one should find you in another field."

So Ruth gleaned with the maidens of Boaz until the end of the barley and wheat harvest; and she lived with her mother-in-law.

And Naomi said to Ruth:

"My daughter, shall I not try to find a home for you where you will be happy and contented? Is not Boaz a relative of ours? This very night he is going to winnow barley on the threshing-floor. So you prepare yourself and put on your best clothes and go down to the threshing-floor; but do not make yourself known to Boaz until he is through eating and drinking. Then when he lies down, you mark the place where he lies."

Ruth said to her:

"I will do as you say."

She went to the threshing-floor and did just as her mother-in-law told her. When Boaz was finished eating and drinking and was in a happy mood, he went to lie down at the end of a heap of grain. Then Ruth came to him softly. And Boaz said:

"Who are you?"

"I am Ruth your servant; take me in marriage, for you are a near relative."*

Boaz replied:

"May you be blessed by the Lord, my daughter. Have no fear; I will do for you all that you ask; for all my townsmen know that you are a good woman. Now it is true that I am a near relative; yet there is one nearer than I. If he will marry you, let him do so. But if he, being your nearest relative, will not marry you, then as surely as the Lord lives, I will do so."

When Ruth came to her mother-in-law, Naomi said:

"Is it you, my daughter?"

*Ruth's appeal to Boaz was based on an ancient Israelite custom. The brother of a man who died without leaving an heir had to marry the widow. The purpose of this custom was to perpetuate the name of the dead man and to keep his property within the family. Although Boaz was not a brother, nor an immediate kinsman, he had the right to marry Ruth, because the kinsman more closely related to the dead husband refused to do so. This custom must be remembered, to understand why Naomi advised Ruth to go to Boaz.

Ruth told Naomi all that the man had done for her. She said:

"He gave me these six measures of barley; for he said, 'Do not go to your mother-in-law empty-handed.' "

Naomi said:

"Wait quietly, my daughter, until you know how this will turn out, for Boaz will not rest unless he settles it all today."

Ruth's Marriage to Boaz

Meanwhile Boaz went to the city gate and sat down. The near relative of whom Boaz had spoken came along. Boaz called to him:

"Ho, sir! Turn aside and sit down here."

He turned aside and sat down.

And Boaz said to him:

"Naomi, who has come back from the country of Moab, is offering for sale a piece of land which belonged to our relative Elimelech, and I thought that I would lay the matter before you, and ask you to redeem it in the presence of these elders who sit here. If you will redeem it and so keep it in the family, do so; but if not, then tell me, that I may know; for no one but you has the right to redeem it, and I am next to you."

He said:

"I will redeem it."

Then Boaz said:

"On the day that you redeem the field from Naomi, you must also marry Ruth, the Moabitess, the widow of Mahlon, that a son may be born to bear his name and to receive this field."

The near relative said:

"I cannot redeem it for myself, for fear that I should lose what already belongs to me. You may take my right of redeeming it as a relative, for I cannot do so."

Now in those days this was the custom in Israel concerning redeeming and concerning exchanging: to make a valid agreement between two men, the one drew off his shoe and gave it to the other.

So the near relative said to Boaz:

"Buy it for yourself."

A Shavuot Bummer

Cheese blintzes with raisins.

And he drew off his shoe.

Then Boaz said to the elders and to the people present:

"You are my witnesses at this time that I have bought all that was Elimelech's and all that was Chilion's and Mahlon's from Naomi. Moreover, I have secured Ruth, the Moabitess, the widow of Mahlon, to be my wife so that she may have a son who will receive this land and carry on Mahlon's name, and the name of the dead be not cut off from among the people. You are witnesses this day."

Then the elders and the people who were at the city gate said:

"We are witnesses. May the Lord make the woman who is coming into your house like Rachel and Leah, the two who built up the house of Israel, and make you also famous in Beth-lehem. May your house be like the house of Perez, whom Tamar bore to Judah, through the children which the Lord shall give you by this young woman."

Boaz married Ruth, and in time the Lord gave her a son.

And the women said to Naomi:

"Blessed be the Lord who has not left you at this time without a near relative, and may his name be famous in Israel. This child will bring back your strength and take care of you in your old age; for your daughter-in-law who loves you, who is worth more to you than seven sons, has a son!"

Naomi took the child in her arms and she became its nurse.

The women of the neighborhood also said:

"Naomi has a son!"

They named him Obed. And he became the father of Jesse, who was the father of David.

Because the great King David was descended from Ruth and Boaz, the story of his ancestry is given here.

Perez was the father of Hezron.

Hezron was the father of Ram.

Ram was the father of Amminadab.

Amminadab was the father of Nahshon.

Nahshon was the father of Salmon.
Salmon was the father of Boaz.
Boaz was the father of Obed.
Obed was the father of Jesse.
And Jesse was the father of David.

The Forty-Ninth Man

by Rabbi Zevulun Weisberger

One day, Don Eldra was *davening Mincha* in his room, locked from the inside. He lived in Barcelona, Spain, in 1497 and he could be burned to death if he was seen practicing his religion. There was a knock on the door and the servant announced the arrival of Don Eldra's business manager. He completed the *davening* and went to the door where he was told, "You are needed in the fields, sir." Don Eldra mounted his horse and set out with his manager.

About halfway there he suddenly remembered something. His *siddur!* He had been interrupted in the middle of the *davening* by the visit, and he had forgotten to put away the *siddur* after he finished *Mincha.* Now the servant would probably clean the room, spot the *siddur,* and realize that Don Eldra was a Jew. This would be enough evidence to denounce him before the Inquisition (the investigation and punishment of Jews). Rewards were being offered to people who reported Marranos (secret Jews), and no servant was immune to such temptation.

Don Eldra paled. "Manuel," he said, "I just remembered something I must take care of at home. I must return at once."

You should taste my cheese cake

"But the fields . . . the men can't work until you come."

"I know, I know, I'll come right back, but I must take care of something first. It's urgent!"

With that, he suddenly turned his horse around and galloped back home. Sweat covered his face, and tension stiffened his whole body as he strained to get back before the servant entered the room.

He was exhausted and out of breath when he arrived. He ran to the room. Too late—the servant was already in the room cleaning. He must be distracted while the "evidence" was removed. Don Eldra spotted a valuable crystal vase on a small table. He "accidentally" bumped into the table, tipping it and making the vase crash to the floor. The startled servant turned at the sound of the crash and instinctively ran over to pick up the broken glass.

While the servant cleaned up the broken shards, Don Eldra walked over to the other side of the room, stealthily picked up the *siddur,* and put it in his pocket. The servant was too busy to notice and Don Eldra, in his most natural voice, apologized to the servant for the extra trouble he caused him.

Apparently the servant had not seen the *siddur.* Don Eldra whispered a silent prayer of thanks to *Hashem. "Ribono Shel Olam (Master of the Universe), let us merit being in our land, where we can pray to You without fear or danger."*

All this happened a few days after *Pesaḥ.* Don Eldra should have been a happy and relieved man that night, but he wasn't. When he got home he heard the news that his friend, Raoul, had been caught by the Inquisition in the act of celebrating the *Pesaḥ Seder.* Tears came to Don Eldra's eyes as he thought of Raoul's fate . . . and the lot of those people who were with him. They had surely been tortured and would be burned at the stake—if they were still alive. This was the risk these brave Jews took in fifteenth-century Spain. To be caught observing *Hashem's mitzvos* in that accursed country meant an awful death.

Don Eldra himself was able to observe all the rituals of the *Seder.* He and his group, fortunately, had escaped detection—but for how long? The menacing tentacles of the Inquisition seemed to be tightening around that small group of loyal, hidden Jews. Decades before, the Jews had enjoyed a "Golden Age" in Spain; now, there was only fear, sorrow and gloom.

Even at home, one spoke in low tones, as if someone were listening to his every word. Don Eldra spoke to his friend Izak, "*Shavuos* is not too far away and it is now the ninth day of the *Sefirah*. What will we do on the *Yom Tov* of *Shavuos?*"

"Well, we'll have a *minyan* as usual in our secret hiding place."

"Do you really think we should risk it?"

"On the day of *Kaballas HaTorah* (Acceptance of the Torah) we must celebrate the holiday by hearing the reading of the *Aseres*

Reflections Through the Night

*Scenes From
an Entire Night Awake
on Shavuot*

by Chaim Berger

After supper: It is the first night of Shavuot, and we've just finished our holiday meal. A little later, I plan to head to the synagogue for a customary full night awake engaged in Torah study; until then I am engaged in a fierce struggle—not to go near the couch—I don't want to risk dozing off. ("To doze, perchance to miss Shavuot night..;" where have I heard that quote?) Instead, I opt for a cup of coffee.

Late night: streams of people walking in the darkness, converging on the synagogue. The brightly-lit *shul* (synagogue) stands in stark contrast to the darkened streets and buildings around it.

1:00 A.M.: I return from the sanctuary, which has been full of people at this unlikely hour, listening to a lecture by the rabbi. The entire synagogue is buzzing, full of energy, as people sit in various rooms to study and learn. Now, I sit down with a volume of the Talmud in front of me. Facing me is my study partner, my *ḥavruta*. We work our way through a Talmudic text and commentaries, questioning, answering, discussing. The two of us have been studying together like this on Sabbath afternoons for quite a few years now. I have always felt like our Shavuot night session is a kind of anniversary celebration, marking another year of study (and the close friendship that inevitably grows out of it).

Later, I am studying alone.

My study partner has gone in to listen to another talk. I decide instead to spend some time studying the *Megillat Ruth* (Book of Ruth), read on Shavuot. After a while, I feel a bit drowsy—a hazard of studying alone. I head for yet another cup of coffee, wisely deciding to forgo the cheesecake, among the other refreshments set out. I recall the first childhood years in which I started staying up the whole night. There was hardly a more exciting and enjoyable time all year (nor another legitimate way to avoid having to go to sleep). Of course, I remember too, how hard it was for me in my younger years to stay awake for the early morning services to follow. The nights awake seem to get shorter and shorter each year—like the years themselves—as I get

Hadibros (Ten Commandments)."

"But how can we be sure of the actual date when we have to count the *Sefirah* by ourselves? We couldn't possibly have a regular *minyan* every day during the week. It's too dangerous."

"It's too easy to forget the counting when one *davens* by himself. What should we do?"

"I have an idea," Don Eldra exclaimed. "We'll use Esther's plan!"

---

older, I note with a twinge of regret.

Dark before the dawn: After some more learning, I go out for a last bit of fresh air, before the services during which we will greet the dawn, to begin soon. The lovely late-spring air mixes with the air of inside, the "air" of *gemaras* (Talmudic texts), *ḥumashim* (books of the Five Books of Moses), and other sacred texts—and of course that all-night coffee. I wish I could find a way to bottle the air of this night, and open it up for inspiration at some other time during the year.

Dawn: I cover my eyes for the first sentence of the Shema prayer, and the first rays of the sun signal the dawn of a new day. When, a few minutes later, we stand and silently say the *amidah,* the silent prayer of the service, the only sound is of the birds beginning their day outside. The noise of the human world—traffic—has not yet begun to sully the day. A pristine, beautiful moment. The sunlight begins to flood the sanctuary.

Early morning: I'm on my way home, and the quiet residential streets are slowly beginning to come to life. In our home, though, the day will not start as early as usual. A little more sleep, morning services, and long meals and quiet rest of a sacred *yom tov* holiday day will replace the rushing-about of a regular day-in-the-life. And so, I am greeted by silence as I let myself into the house.

I head upstairs to bed. As I slip between the covers I let out a contented sigh. My mind is still stimulated by last night's experience, and I am trying to will myself to sleep. I will nap this morning, while the regular holiday morning services are going on in the synagogue, and then get up for a long festive lunch at noontime with my family. Years of experience have taught me that it will take more sleep for me to get caught up. By tomorrow morning, though, after a good (afternoon and) night's sleep, I'll be back to "normal"—whatever *that* means.

I will not deny that I am proud of staying up all night. I came, I studied, I stayed awake. I have turned my sleeping schedule upside down a bit, but the pleasure's all mine. So for now, good night; or is it good morning, or should it be . . . szzzz.

He meant Queen Esther's plan in the palace at Shushan. She appointed a different maiden to serve her every day of the week. When the seventh girl appeared, Esther knew it was Shabbos.

The next day he was busy recruiting new workers for his business. It was a large group, indeed, assembled in that room when their new employer gave them the details of their jobs.

"Men, I have some special projects for you. I have to work this on a rotating basis. I'm going to give each of you an assignment. Each day another person will come to me with a report on the job. Each man will get a number; you, sir, are number ten; you are number eleven and so on."

Finally, the big day arrived. Number Forty-Nine had come the previous night; *Shavuos* had arrived!

With a secret password, the message was given about the *minyan* for *Yom Tov*. Some once brave souls decided not to take the risk of being caught. There were others, however, who could not let the anniversary of *Kaballas HaTorah* go by without *Tefillah* and *Krias HaTorah* with a *minyan*.

The men slowly gathered in Don Eldra's home. The servants were told that it was a social gathering to celebrate his wedding anniversary. In a way it really was, for, on *Shavuot,* the Jewish nation is like a *chassan* (bridegroom) and the Torah is like a *kallah* (bride).

There were only nine adult Jews present and the group was anxiously awaiting the arrival of number ten. There was a knock on the door, but it wasn't the usual signal of a participant. It was Don Eldra's daughter Shani, with a warning that a stranger had come to the house.

Don Eldra quickly left the basement room to speak to the visitor. The *minyan* was halted, and the eight men were all afraid that their unexpected visitor was an agent of the Inquisition. The men started to recite *Tehillim* quietly.

It was one of Don Eldra's "hired hands"—one of his new workers, number Forty-Nine, to be exact!

"What do you want?" Don Eldra asked in an irritated voice. "Why are you disturbing me now? Didn't we conclude our business already?"

"Of course," the man said, smiling. "It's just that I saw through your scheme. It was the forty-ninth day of the *Omer* that you were really interested in when you gave us the numbers, wasn't it?" He looked intently at Don Eldra as he spoke.

Don Eldra was flabbergasted. How had this man ever guessed what was in his mind? Who was this man?

"I'll tell you who I am," the man declared as if he had read his mind. "My parents were Marranos (secret Jews). They had to send me to a Catholic school and I grew up almost like everyone else, but not quite. Something inside of me told me that I didn't belong, that I wasn't like my schoolmates. I kept on searching and asking. Then I discovered the truth: that my parents were Jews and that I was forced to grow up differently. So I started to read secretly about my heritage.

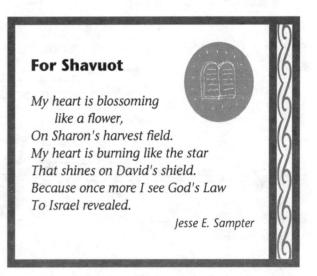

For Shavuot

My heart is blossoming
*   like a flower,*
On Sharon's harvest field.
My heart is burning like the star
That shines on David's shield.
Because once more I see God's Law
To Israel revealed.

Jesse E. Sampter

I went to Catholic services but I secretly yearned for the day when I could become myself. I knew all about *Pesach* and *Shavuos,* but I didn't do much about it. A few nights ago I had a dream. My grandfather was standing over my bed, crying. I begged him to stop crying, but he persisted, "I will mourn over you until you return to your heritage!" That's when I decided once and for all that I must act—only one question remained, "How and with whom?"

Then I realized what you were doing, because you see, I was also counting *Sefirah* (I learned about that, too!), and I knew the exact date without your special reminders. Today is *Shavuos* and I want to join you. Do you have a *minyan?*"

For a long time, Don Eldra could not answer. He stared at his guest—formerly Señor Forty-Nine. Something about the way he spoke convinced him of the man's sincerity.

He rose from his chair, stretched out his hand and said. "You have indeed come to the right place. Come, you have made our *minyan.*

Ki Mitziyon

Allegretto

N. Shachar

Ki mi - tzi - yon tei - tzei to - rah ud - var A - do -
nai mi - ru - sha - la - yim ki mi - tzi - yon tei - tzei to -
rah ud - var A - do - nai mi - ru - sha - la - yim
yim Ba - rukh she - na - tan to - rah l' - a - mo to - rah l' - a -
mo Yis - ra - el ba - rukh she - na - tan To -
rah l' - a - mo Yis - ra - el bik - du - sha - to ki mi - tzi -

*For out of Zion shall go forth the Torah and the
word of the Lord from Jerusalem.*

כִּי מִצִּיּוֹן תֵּצֵא תוֹרָה
וּדְבַר יְיָ מִירוּשָׁלָיִם

Torah Tzivah

Moderato

Torah to-rah to-rah tzi-vah la-nu Mo-she mo-ra-shah k'-hi-lat Ya-a-kov

to-rah to-rah to-rah tzi-vah la-nu Mo-she mo-ra-shah k'-hi-lat Ya-a-kov

to-rah to-rah to-rah tzi-vah la-nu Mo-she mo-ra-shah k'-hi-lat Ya-a-kov

to-rah to-rah to-rah tzi-vah la-nu Mo-she mo-ra-shah k'-hi-lat Ya-a-kov

The Torah which Moses handed down to us is the Heritage of the community of Jacob.

תּוֹרָה צִוָּה לָנוּ מֹשֶׁה
מוֹרָשָׁה קְהִלַּת יַעֲקֹב

Shavuot Crafts

Corn Husk Doll: The Biblical Ruth

Pioneers in America created their own dolls and home decorations. Making corn husk dolls is a folk art passed down from generation to generation. If you are not near a farm to obtain fresh corn shucks, you may find them in some craft or gourmet food stores (used in preparation of Mexican tamales). Grass and reeds can be used instead.

MATERIALS

corn husks
string
scissors
corn silk or thin yarn or thread
white glue
fine point black and red felt-tip pens
pieces of felt or gingham material
stalks of dried wheat

STOP!
Some of the crafts in this chapter call for the use of a hammer, scissors, or other potentially dangerous tools. Before beginning any craft, get either help or the "go-ahead" from a responsible adult.

1. To keep the husks soft and pliable, soak them in a pan of warm water, taking them out only as needed.

2. To make the head and body, wind strips of the husks into a ball (figure A). Center the ball on 1 long strip and fold over (figure B). Tie at the neck with a small husk strip or piece of string (figure C).

3. To make the arms, fold a long piece of husk lengthwise (figure D). Then fold in the width (figure E). Tie both ends to make wrists and hands (figure F). Center this strip between front and back folds of the body, under the neck (figure G).

4. Center the neck of the doll on a long, wide piece of husk (figure H). Bring 1 side over 1 shoulder, crossing in front of the doll. Bring the other side

Center Ball on Long Strip

A

B

Tie at Neck

C

D Fold in Half Lengthwise

E Fold in Width

F Tie Both Ends

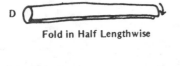

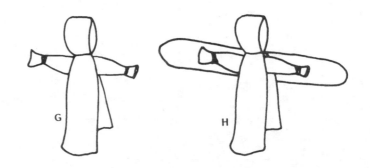

G

H

over the other shoulder, placing it over the first piece (figure I). Keep layering, until the body is as thick as you would like.

5. Tie at the waist with a wide piece of husk to make a sash (figure J). Tie the sash either in front or in back of the doll.

6. To make an even hem, trim the bottom of the dress with scissors.

7. Make hair by winding corn silk around the head. Tie it on with a strip of husk (like a headband). If no corn silk is available, glue on thin yarn or thread.

8. To make the eyes, add 2 dots with the black pen. Draw the mouth with the red pen.

9. To make an apron and a kerchief for the doll, cut out a piece of felt or gingham material (figure K).

10. Tie the doll's wrists together with string. Slide several stalks of dried wheat between the arms and body (figure L).

Hang these mock stained glass pictures against a white wall or a window. To use as a room divider, tape the pictures to each other and hang from the ceiling.

The Seven Fruits of Israel in Mock Stained Glass

MATERIALS

newspapers
7 sheets of poster board or black construction paper
black paint (if you are using posterboard)
pencil

craft knife
rolls of cellophane, any colors
scissors
tape or glue
Optional: 7 more sheets of black construction paper or poster board

1. Cover the work surface with newspapers. If you are using posterboard, paint the 7 pieces black and let dry.

2. For each picture of the 7 fruits of Israel, draw the design on construction paper or poster board. Shade in all areas to be cut out.

3. With the craft knife, cut out all the shaded areas.

4. Cut out a piece of cellophane larger than the cut-out area of the design. Tape or glue in place.

5. Construction paper or poster board with the identical cut-out design may be placed behind the cellophane so it can be viewed with a completed look from both sides. This is necessary if you want to use the picture as a room divider.

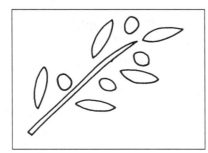

Date Honey

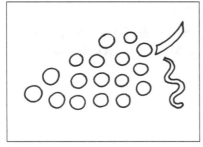

Olives

Wheat

Barley

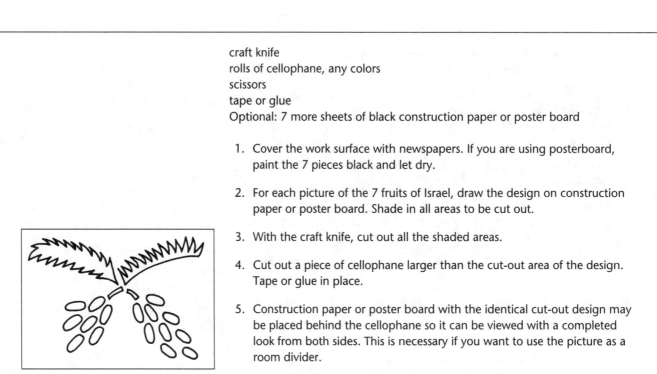

Grapes

Figs

Pomegranate

Take a trip to a hobby, variety, or craft store to stock up on floral tape, floral stems, and glitter before you make these cheerful flowers.

Egg Carton Flowers

MATERIALS

styrofoam egg cartons (each carton makes 2 flowers)
scissors
floral tape
floral stems
white glue
glitter, any color
small vase

1. Cut off the cover of the egg carton. Cut out 1 section of the cover, as shown in figure A. Cut the remaining part of the cover in half.

2. To make the center of 1 flower, cut deep fringes in half, as shown by the black shading in figure A.

3. Roll the fringed·section tightly and secure with floral tape (figure B). Set aside.

4. To make the petals of 1 flower, cut out 3 cups from the bottom of the egg carton. Cut deeply into each cup to make 4 pointed petals (figure C).

5. To assemble the petals, place each of the 3 cups inside each other. The petals of the middle cup should show between the spaces of the top and bottom petals (figure D).

6. To assemble the flower, poke a large hole through the layered petal cups. Insert the rolled fringe, tape side down, so the top shows slightly above the petals (figure E).

7. Insert the floral stem up into the center of the flower. Wrap the bottom of the fringed roll and the stem with floral tape (figure F).

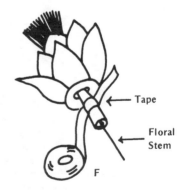

8. Repeat steps 2 through 7 to make the second flower.

9. Dip the tips of the center fringe of each flower into the glue and then dip them into the glitter.

10. Place the flowers in a vase (figure G).

Shavuot Recipes

Burekas (Mediterranean)

These burekas are made with a tasty cheese, egg, and mashed potato filling. Although the recipe calls for farmer cheese, you can use cottage cheese or cream cheese.

A Shavuot Bummer

When you eat the cardboard under the cheese cake.

CHEESE FILLING

1 pound farmer cheese
2 egg yolks
1 cup mashed potatoes
salt and pepper to taste

In a medium-size bowl, mash the farmer cheese. Add the egg yolks, potatoes, and salt and pepper, and mix well. Set aside.

DOUGH

1/2 cup butter or margarine
1/2 cup oil
3 cups flour
1 teaspoon baking powder
1 teaspoon salt
1 1/2 tablespoons white vinegar
1/2 cup cold water
1 egg, beaten with a teaspoon of water
sesame seeds

Preheat the oven to 375 degrees.

Mix the butter or margarine and oil together with the flour, baking powder, and salt in a large mixing bowl. Add the vinegar to the water, and mix well.

Roll out the pastry very thinly on a piece of wax paper. Cut it into 3-inch circles with a cup or pastry cutter.

Put some of the filling on each piece, and fold in half, pinching the edges together with a fork. Lay the burekas on a greased foil-lined baking sheet.

In a small bowl, beat the egg with the water.

Brush the beaten egg over the burekas, and scatter sesame seeds on top. Prick the top of each bureka with a fork.

Bake until nicely browned.

STOP!

A kitchen is a dangerous place. If you're not careful, you might burn yourself with splattering oil or boiling water. The recipes in this chapter are intended for older children. Before beginning, make sure an adult is available to help.

STOP

About 2 dozen

Blintzes (Eastern Europe)

You will need to use an electric mixer or a blender to make these delicious blintzes, so ask an adult for help. Be sure to turn off the mixer or blender each time you add an ingredient to the mix.

DOUGH

2 eggs
dash of salt
1 cup flour
1 cup water
1 tablespoon oil
butter or margarine for frying

FILLING

1/2 pound farmer cheese
1/2 pound cream cheese
2 egg yolks
vanilla or lemon flavoring
1-1/2 teaspoons farina
sugar to taste

Beat the eggs well with an electric mixer or blender. Add the salt and flour. Mix again. Slowly add the water. Mix well and add the oil. The batter will be thin.

Let the batter stand at room temperature for 2 hours.

To make the filling, mash the farmer cheese well; add the cream cheese, egg yolks, vanilla or lemon flavoring, farina, and sugar. Mix well.

Heat a 7-inch frying pan, and grease lightly. When the frying pan is hot, add 2 tablespoons of the batter, tipping the pan so that the batter covers the surface of the pan.

Cook on one side only, until the top is dry. Turn out, bottom side up, on a clean towel. Continue the process with the rest of the batter. (Two frying pans speed up the work.)

When all the pancakes have been made, fill each one with a tablespoon of the filling. Fold over the sides, and then roll the blintzes as you would roll a jelly roll. Fry in butter or margarine.

Serve the blintzes with sour cream, fresh or frozen berries, or other fruits.

The blintzes can also be baked by placing them on a well-greased foil-lined baking sheet and brushing the top of the blintzes with butter or margarine.

Bake in a 400-degree oven until golden brown. Do not over-bake.

8 to 10 blintzes

Cheesecake (North American)

Like the recipe for blintzes, this cheesecake recipe calls for the use of a mixer, so be sure to ask an adult for help. Be sure to turn off the mixer each time you add ingredients to the mix.

CRUST

1-2/3 cups graham cracker, zwieback, or vanilla cookie crumbs
1/2 cup brown sugar
1/2 cup butter

FILLING

1-1/2 pounds cream cheese
1 cup sugar
4 eggs
1 cup sour cream
1/4 cup flour
juice of 1 lemon
grated rind of 1 lemon

Preheat the oven to 325 degrees.

Mix the crumbs with the brown sugar and butter. Line a 9-inch spring-form pan with the crumb mixture.

With a mixer, beat the cream cheese until soft. Add the sugar. Add the eggs, one at a time, beating the mixture after each egg is added.

Add the sour cream, flour, lemon juice, and lemon rind. Mix well.

Pour the cheese mixture in the crumb-lined springform pan. Bake the cheesecake for 1 hour. Turn off the heat, and allow the cake to remain in the oven until cool. Refrigerate.

1 pie

Shavuot Fun

Shavuot Puzzles (Answers on page 275.)

In a certain community, whenever people have a Torah question, they all ask this man. Why?

The Answer Man

Eitan spent $10.00 at the bakery and bought 15 cheese danish. The danish are priced at $2.00 for the large danish, $1.00 for the medium-sized and $.50 for the small. How many of each size danish did Eitan buy?

Cheese Danish

Rearrange the letters in each group, using all the letters, to form a Shavuot word or name.
1. OATH R
2. SOME S
3. MOM CDN STEAMN
4. SHE ECE
5. REAL N

Shavuot Anagrams

A Shavuot Bummer

Planning to stay up all night to learn and falling asleep at dinner.

The Great Torah Quiz

by Barbara Spector

1. Name the Five Books of Moses.

2. The Hebrew word for the ornaments used to crown the Torah, *rimmonim,* is also the word for which fruit?

3. True or false: The Torah scroll contains no punctuation or vowels.

4. Can a scribe write a Torah in gold ink?

5. A Torah pointer is usually shaped like which part of the body?

6. The Torah (Five Books of Moses) ends with the story of the death of _____.

7. True or false: Sephardic Jews read from their Torah scroll without removing it from its case.

8. How many columns are there in a Torah scroll?

   (a) 613; (b) 572; (c) 248; (d) 127.

9. Do you have to stand when a Torah is being removed from the ark even if you can't see the Torah?

10. Should one violate the Sabbath to prevent a Torah scroll from being destroyed?

11. Who receives the first *aliyah* when the Torah is read in synagogue?

12. True or false: The Torah is put back into the ark before the Haftarah is read.

13. How many Torah portions are there?

14. Why don't we make Torah ornaments out of gold?

15. In which of the Five Books of Moses does Moses not appear?

16. Before writing each word of the Torah on the parchment, the scribe must _____.

    (a) pronounce it; (b) say a prayer; (c) bend his knees; (d) wash his hands.

17. Can the Torah be read if less than a *minyan* is present?

18. Which book of the Torah gets its English name from the census of the people in Chapters 1, 3, 4, and 26?

19. According to Jewish law, if you see a Torah drop, what should you do for forty days?

20. What should a Torah reader do if he reads a word incorrectly?

Tisha b'Av and Other Fast Days

Days of Reflection

About Tisha b'Av and Other Fast Days

The purpose of fasting is to lead us to repentance. Our rabbis learned this from the Book of Jonah.

The prophet Jonah went to the people of Nineveh and warned them that because of their wickedness, "In forty days Nineveh will be destroyed." The people of Nineveh believed in God. They fasted. It says in the Book of Jonah (Chapter 3, verse 10) "And God saw their deeds." They repented and Nineveh was saved.

The third of Tishre, the day after Rosh Hashanah, is Tzom Gedalia, the Fast of Gedalia. After the destruction of the First Temple, the king of Babylonia allowed a small number of Jews to remain in Israel with Gedalia ben Achikam as their governor. He was assassinated on the 3rd of Tishre. Following his assassination thousands more Jews were killed and those who survived were forced to leave Israel.

The fast day, Asara B'Tevet, the 10th of Tevet, comes soon after Ḥanukkah. It marks the day that the destruction of the First Temple began with the siege of Jerusalem, which lead to the eventual destruction of the First Temple.

The fast day, Shiva Asar B'Tammuz, the 17th of Tammuz, is the beginning of a three-week period of mourning that ends in Tisha b'Av, the 9th of Av. The 17th of Tammuz is the day that Moses descended Mount Sinai with the tablets of the Ten Commandments, found Jews worshiping the Golden Calf, and broke the holy tablets. During the time of the first Temple, the 17th of Tammuz was the day that services ended in the Temple. During the time of the Second Temple, it was the day that the Romans broke through the walls of Jerusalem.

The fast day, Tisha b'Av, the ninth day of the Hebrew month of Av, is the national Jewish day of mourning. It's the saddest day of the Jewish year. On that day in 586 B.C.E., the First Temple was destroyed, and in the year 70 C.E., the Second Temple was destroyed. On the ninth of Av sixty-five years later, Bar Kokhba's fortress at Bethar fell.

Many other tragedies in Jewish history occurred on Tisha b'Av. On the ninth of Av in 1096, the First Crusade began. Jewish communities were destroyed and many thousands of Jews were murdered. On Tisha b'Av 1290, King Edward I of England called for the expulsion of all Jews. This was the first of the large expulsions of the Middle Ages. On

Tisha b'Av 1306, Jews were expelled from France, and on Tisha b'Av 1492, from Spain. On Tisha b'Av 1648, hundreds of Jewish communities in Poland were destroyed and an estimated 100,000 Jews were murdered in the Chmielnicki massacres. On Tisha b'Av in 1882, there was a pogrom in Balta, Odessa, and more than 1,000 Jewish homes and shops were robbed and burned.

In the afternoon, on erev Tisha b'Av, the day before the fast if the day before is not Shabbat, it is customary to eat a hard-boiled egg sprinkled with ashes, as a symbol of mourning. Traditionally leather shoes are not worn on Tisha b'Av. In synagogues people sit on the floor or on low benches. The curtain on the Aron Kodesh, the cabinet that holds the Torahs, is removed.

Tisha b'Av and Yom Kippur are the only Jewish fast days that begin at sunset and end the following night. The other fasts begin before sunrise and end at nightfall.

Lamentations
adapted by Mortimer J. Cohen

Powerful Babylonian armies swept down on Palestine in 586 B.C.E., and their commander, the Emperor Nebuchadnezzar, captured and sacked Jerusalem, sent the Temple up in flames, killed ordinary Jewish men and women, and carried off the rulers, priests, princes, and leading citizens into what has come to be known as the Babylonian Captivity. Those left behind in the desolated land suffered terror, shame, starvation, and death.

The Book of Lamentations consists of poems of grief and sorrow on the destruction of Jerusalem. These sad poems are called elegies, or dirges, or laments. The Book of Lamentations contains five such poems describing the misfortunes, calamities, and sorrows that the Jewish people suffered when their Holy City was destroyed. Four of these poems are arranged acrostically, that is, each verse begins with a successive letter of the Hebrew alphabet.

Because Jeremiah was the last prophet in Judah, and spoke at the time of the destruction of the Jewish Commonwealth, Jewish tradition has held him to be the author of "Lamentations." Others maintain that its author is unknown. In either case, he was a profound lover of his

people, as every word of this sad book testifies. His tears are hot upon
its every page. He gave voice, too, to the eternal cry of faith in God, the
confession of guilt, the call to repentance, and the prayer of hope that
Israel might some day return to their ancestral inheritance.

The Book of Lamentations is read in Synagogue on Tisha b'Av.

Desolation and Misery

Jerusalem is compared to a widow in mourning. Her treasures and her
glory have departed. Her leaders have been slain, and her children are
in exile. Yet she acknowledges the righteousness of God. Later,
Jerusalem herself speaks and bewails her condition.

How does the city sit solitary,
That was full of people!
How has she become as a widow!
She that was great among the nations,
And a princess among the cities,
How has she become a slave!

She weeps sore in the night,
And her tears are on her cheeks;
She has none to comfort her
Among all her lovers;
All her friends have dealt treacherously
    with her;
They have become her enemies.

Judah has gone into exile,
    to suffer and endure hard slavery.
She dwells among the nations;
She finds no rest.
All her pursuers have overtaken her
    in the midst of her distress.

The roads to Zion do mourn,
Because none come to the solemn assembly;
All her gates are desolate;
    her priests sigh.
Her maidens have been dragged off,
    and she herself is left in bitterness.
Her foes have now the upper hand,
Her enemies are at ease in triumph.

For the Lord has afflicted her
    for the multitude of her transgressions,
Her children have gone into captivity,
Captives before the oppressor.

Gone from the daughter of Zion
    is all her splendor.
Her princes have become like stags
    that can find no pasture,
And they flee exhausted
    before the hunter.

Jerusalem has grievously sinned,
Therefore she has become an unclean thing.
All that honored her, despise her,
Because they have seen her nakedness.
She herself is filled with sighs,
And turns her face backward.
The oppressor has laid his hand
    upon all her treasures;
And she has seen the nations
    enter her Sanctuary,
Those whom Thou, God, didst command
    not to enter Thy holy place.

"Ho, all you who pass along the road,
    look and see,
If there is any pain like my pain,
    which has been dealt to me,
With which the Lord has afflicted me
    in the day of His fierce anger.

"From above He has hurled fire;
into my bones He has made it descend;
He has spread a net for my feet;
He has tripped me up;
He has left me faint and forlorn,
 miserable all the time.

"The Lord is righteous,
for I have rebelled against His word;
Yet hear, all you peoples,

and look at my pain:
How my youths and maidens
have gone into captivity.

"See, O Lord, how I am in distress,
how my spirit is tortured;
How my heart is shaken within me,
because I have been so rebellious.
On the streets the sword slays,
and inside the plague."

Looking Back: 1492, A Golden Age Ends
by Chaim Berger

An Age of Greatness Ended in Exile, on the Ninth of Av

Tisha B'Av of the year 1492 was more than a traditional fast day for world Jewry. It was also the date decreed by King Ferdinand of Spain for the final expulsion of the Jewish community from Spain. True to form on this inauspicious date for the Jewish people, the "Golden Age" of Spain came to an end.

Such Greatness

And what an age it was. An incredible concentration of rabbis, scholars, poets, grammarians, philosophers—not to mention sometimes also statesmen, physicians and ministers.

Can you imagine opening a newspaper to find that the Secretary of the Treasury also happens to be a renowned leader of the Jewish community and biblical scholar? Don Isaac Abravanel (1437–1508) served as finance minister to King Ferdinand and Queen Isabella. Or, how about an influential statesman who was also a renowned Talmudic scholar and Hebrew poet? That would fit Shmuel Ibn Nagdela, known, too as Shmuel Hanagid (d. 1055). Of course, we cannot leave out Rabbi Yehuda Halevi (c. 1075–c.1142), philosopher, and one of the most beloved of Hebrew poets, and Rabbi Solomon Ibn Gabirol, grammarian and poet (c.1020–1066). And no discussion of the period is complete without mentioning Rabbi Moses ben Maimon, known as Maimonides, (1135–1204). Having fled Spain early in his life with his family to escape Moslem persecution, he grew to become a foremost codifier of Jewish law and philosopher, not to mention court physician in Egypt. We have, by no means, exhausted the list of notables.

Exile, Nevertheless

To be sure, this incredible community, whose roots are believed to date back to exiles from the destruction of the Second Temple, 70 C.E., had their share of Moslem and Christian persecution, falling eventually to exile under the shadow of the Spanish Inquisition. Still,

God's Consolations

In the midst of her dark sorrows, Israel finds ground for hope in God's mercy and kindness.

My affliction and bitterness
  are anguish and misery.
I think of them,
  and I am crushed in spirit.
But this I recall to my mind,
  and so I have hope:

upon their exile from Spain, these Jews spread their learning and culture to the countries of North Africa, the Middle East, the Ottoman Empire and other parts of Europe. The *Sephardic* community (*Sepharad* is the Hebrew word for Spain) has endowed Jewish life throughout the world with its spiritual beauty. The words of its scholars live on in works on Jewish law, commentary and philosophy studied widely to this day. The phrases of its poets have been ensconced in our liturgical poetry.

So, July 30, 1492, scarcely three days before Columbus set sail for the New World with the Nina, the Pinta and the Santa Maria, was the date set for the expulsion of the Jewish community. Like the archaeological site, which contains layer upon layer of history through the centuries, Tisha B'Av, historically the saddest day in Jewish history, had another layer added in 1492.

A Parting Thought

We'd like to end on a remarkable story mentioned by Rabbi Eliyahu Kitov, a twentieth-century rabbinical teacher and author, in his remarkable *Sefer HaToda'a* (The Book of Our Heritage):

> On their trek from Spain, during the Three Weeks before Tisha B'Av, the rabbis of the time ordered that music be played for the exiles, in order to keep their spirits up. Traditionally music was not supposed to be played during the Three Weeks before Tisha B'Av, in keeping with the traditions of national mourning for the destruction of the Temple. But the rabbis, Rabbi Kitov says, wanted to make a point. They wanted to teach that Jews should never cry over having to leave a place of exile—and Spain, for all the Jewish community's glories and comforts, was still exile—we only cry over having to leave Jerusalem.

We find it an awesome and courageous thought, especially during the Three Weeks before Tisha B'Av.

The gracious deeds of the Lord never cease,
   His compassion never fails;
They are new every morning;
   great is His faithfulness.
"The Lord is my heritage," I said,
   "therefore will I hope in Him."

The Lord is good to him who waits for Him,
   to the one who seeks Him.
It is good that one should wait quietly
   for help from the Lord;
It is good for a man,
   that he should bear the yoke in his youth.
For the Lord for ever
   will not spurn him.
Though He cause grief,
   He has pity, so rich is His love;
He does not willingly cause pain,
   nor grieve the children of men.

Let us search, and examine our ways,
   and return to the Lord;
Let us lift up our hearts along with our hands
   to God in the heavens.
The sin is ours, we have rebelled,
   and Thou—Thou hast not pardoned.

I called on Thy name, O Lord,
   out of the lowest dungeon.
Thou didst hear my cry,
   close not Thine ear to my plea.
Thou didst answer my call,
   and saidst: "Fear not."

Thou, O Lord, art enthroned for ever;
Thy throne endures from generation to generation.
Why dost Thou forget us for ever,
And forsake us for so long a time?
Turn Thou us unto Thee, O Lord,
And we shall be turned;
Renew our days as of old!

It is customary to pray facing the Temple in Jerusalem. Jews living west of Jerusalem face east—mizraḥ. In many traditional homes a mizraḥ sign is placed on an eastern wall.

MATERIALS

1 sheet of black 9" x 12" construction paper
pencil
small scissors (manicure)
white glue
pages from a Hebrew newspaper (with printing, no pictures)
8" x 10" or 9" x 12" picture frame

1. On the construction paper, copy the symbols shown on this page, or draw your own. Carefully cut out each drawing.

2. Glue the cut-out construction paper to the Hebrew newspaper. Trim the edges of the newspaper.

3. You may use another page from a Hebrew newspaper as a mat when framing the picture. Place the mizraḥ in the frame and hang on an eastern wall.

Tisha b'Av Craft

Hebrew Newspaper Mizraḥ

STOP!
Some crafts may call for the use of a hammer, scissors, or other potentially dangerous tools. Before beginning any craft, get either help or the "go-ahead" from a responsible adult.

Resources

Books

Enjoy-A-Book Club
555 Chestnut Street
Cedarhurst, New York 11516
(516) 569-0324

This club specializes in children's books, games, and tapes of Jewish interest for sale at discount at book fairs and to individuals by mail. They publish a catalog.

Jewish Book Club
230 Livingston Street
Northvale, New Jersey 07047
(201) 767-4093

This club sells Jewish books for adults and children at special club prices.

Jewish Book Council
15 East 26th Street
New York, New York 10010
(212) 532-4949

Among its many services, the council provides lists of recommended books on Jewish subjects.

The Jewish Publication Society
1930 Chestnut Street
Philadelphia, Pennsylvania 19103
(215) 564-5925

Membership in the society entitles members to discounted purchases from its list of some of the best Jewish books for children and adults.

Magazines for Children

Olomeinu/Our World
5723 Eighteenth Avenue
Brooklyn, New York 11204
(718) 259-1223

Olomeinu is a monthly publication of Torah Umesorah—The National Society of Hebrew Day Schools. It features fun pages, biographies, holiday material, fiction, and more.

Shofar
43 Northcote Drive
Melville, New York 11747
(800) 643-4598

> Shofar *is published six times a year. It features fiction, fun activities, and articles on sports and Jewish personalities. Single yearly subscriptions are $14.95.*

The Jewish Parent Connection
160 Broadway, 4th Floor
New York, New York 10038
(212) 227-1000

Magazines for Parents

> *The Jewish Parent Connection is a not-for-profit magazine for Jewish parents spanning the complete spectrum of religious observance and providing an ongoing forum for the open exchange of information and ideas between Jewish parents, educators, and parenting specialists throughout the world.*

Tara Publications
29 Derby Avenue
Cedarhurst, New York 11516
(516) 295-1061

Music

> *Tara publishes and distributes a huge selection of Jewish songbooks. Tara also distributes Jewish music tapes and CDs.*

Transcontinental Music
838 Fifth Avenue
New York, New York 10021
(212) 249-0100

> *Transcontinental Music supplies Jewish music materials for home and schools.*

Answer Pages

Rosh Ḥodesh

The Shared Cookies

The one who brought 10 cookies should get all $1.50. Each friend ate 5 cookies. The one who brought 5 also ate 5. She didn't contribute any to the one who came without cookies.

Hebrew Month Mix-up

Each of the three groups of letters can be rearranged to form the words: A HEBREW MONTH.

Shabbat

Shabbat Shalom

There were 15 hand shakes and 30 "Shabbat Shaloms."

Candle Puzzle

Neither. As they burn, they each give off the same light.

How Far?

3/4 of a mile.

Two Shabbat Candles

1 hour and 15 minutes is the same as 75 minutes.

Ḥallah Riddle Answers

1. A ḥallah covered with hoppy seeds. 2. So the ḥallah would rise and shine. 3. The side you haven't eaten. 4. Your teeth. 5. Challahfornia.

Rosh Hashanah

Rosh Hashanah Anagrams

1. APPLE. 2. SHOFAR. 3. PRAYER. 4. SWEET. 5. REPENT.

A Relative Puzzle

The two people are married. They're husband and wife.

Apples and Honey

He paid 70¢ for the apple and $1.05 for the honey.

Rosh Hashanah Calculator Fun

BLISS and LIE.

Sukkah Building
It would take just 2 hours.

How Many Days?
3.

The Cohen Family
There were seven Cohens sitting in the sukkah, Mr. and Mrs. Cohen, their four sons and their one daughter.

So Many Bees
There were 4 bees in Michael's sukkah.

Party Time
24.

Simḥat Torah Candy
Buy 3 lollipop packs and 2 boxes of almonds and raisins.
(18¢ + 18¢ + 18¢ + 23¢ + 23¢ = $1.00)

How Many Grandchildren?
4.

Art Puzzle
Candies and Cookies (canned E's and cooked E's).

Simḥat Torah Scramble
Answer: A Torah hora

Sukkot

Simḥat Torah

Ḥanukkah

Candle Puzzle

Ḥanukkah Candles
Neither. All candles burn shorter, not longer.

Tu B'Shevat

Ḥanukkah **Gelt**
Dina was given 3 two-dollar bills and 1 five-dollar bill.

Ḥanukkah Anagrams
1. DREIDEL. 2. MENORAH. 3. ḤANUKKAH. 4. CANDLE. 5. GIFT.

Ḥanukkah Riddle Answers
1. Springtime. 2. Take one candle out of the box and the box will become a candle lighter. 3. Because the recipe said, "Take one egg and beat it." 4. A dreidel with hiccups. 5. Because the candles are long enough. 6. Do you give up? So did the candlemaker.

Purim

Mixed-Up Fruit Basket

The fruits in the basket are peach, apple, pear, plum, date, orange, and tangerine.

Apples

Make applesauce.

HEREST — ESTHER
MURIP — PURIM
AMHNA — HAMAN
MOSTCUE — COSTUME

Almonds, Raisins, and Dates

50 almonds, 25 raisins, and 25 dates.

Hamantaschen

It would take just 15 minutes if you bake them all in the same pan.

Purim Anagrams

1. ESTHER. 2. VASHTI. 3. PARTY. 4. MORDECHAI. 5. PARADE.

How Heavy?

The answer is not 3 pounds—it's 4 pounds.

Purim Scramble

Answer: His teeth

Pesaḥ/Passover

Yom ha-Azma'ut

Purim, Purim, Purim Answers

1. Hadassah. 2. Vashti. 3. Shushan. 4. (c) He drew lots. 5. Three days. 6. Sunrise (as opposed to Yom Kippur and Tisha B'Av, which begin at sunset the night before). 7. Haman and Mordecai. 8. Yes (because the name of God does not appear in the Megillah, so it is obvious that an image of God has not been made). 9. (b) In one breath (because they were all hanged together). 10. "Lots." 11. (b) Babylonian. 12. A festive meal held on the day of Purim. 13. (c) A Purim play. 14. Hamantasch. 15. (a) Kreplach. (They are also three-cornered.) 16. Two. 17. True. (There's also the megillot of Ruth, Lamentations, the Song of Songs, and Ecclesiastes.) 18. Iran. 19. Haman's wife. 20. Hamantaschen.

Pesaḥ/Passover Magic

It's more than just the edge of the plate holding up the wine cup. Behind the plate your thumb is supporting it, too.

Four Cups of Wine

Fill the 6-cup pitcher. Then pour from the 6-cup pitcher into the 5-cup pitcher until the 5-cup pitcher is full. Now, just 1 cup remains in the 6-cup pitcher. Fill the 3-cup pitcher and then pour its contents into the 6-cup pitcher. It will now contain exactly 4 cups of wine.

The Matzah Ball Problem

Get out the garden hose. Fill the hole with water and the matzah ball will float within Danny's reach.

Matzah, Matzah, Matzah

The Adlers have just 1 box of matzah, the large one in the dining room.

The Unbroken Matzah

Drop it from the lowest rung of the ladder.

Parade Puzzle

There were only 3 women, a woman with her daughter and granddaughter, but together they are 2 mothers and 2 daughters.

Flags

Amy had 4 flags left, the 4 she didn't give away.

Lag B'omer

Shavuot

The Drummers

The old drummer was the young drummer's mother.

The Valuable Coin

The coin is a fake. The State of Israel wasn't founded until 1948.

All-about-Israel Quiz Answers

1. Africa and Asia. 2. (c) The Romans. 3. (a) Jerusalem. 4. (c) One-and-a-half hours. 5. True. 6. No. (There are some exceptions.) 7. (c) A bearded rabbi. 8. (d) Seven gold stars against a white background. (The white was to signify the new and pure life, the seven stars the seven-hour workday.) 9. (c) Tel Aviv. 10. (a) 1941. 11. Yes. (Rina Messinger in 1976.) 12. Netanya. 13. Ashkenazim and Sephardim. 14. Great Britain. 15. (d) 2.7 percent. 16. (b) Mordecai Anilewicz, leader of the Warsaw Ghetto Uprising. 17. The Hebrew University-Hadassah Medical Center. 18. (c) Ancient Jewish coins. 19. Gene Simmons, bass guitarist of the rock group Kiss. 20. Political parties.

The Letter Box

If you begin with the T in the lower left corner and read every other letter you will find that following Lag B'Omer (the thirty-third day) is the "Thirty-fourth day of Omer."

On Target

Have 3 arrows land on 14, and 2 on 29. (14 + 14 + 14 + 29 + 29 = 100)

The Answer Man

He's a wise (Y's) man.

Cheese Danish

Eitan bought 1 large, 2 medium and 12 small cheese danishes.

Shavuot Anagrams

1. TORAH. 2. MOSES. 3. COMMANDMENTS. 4. CHEESE. 5. LEARN.

The Great Torah Quiz Answers

1. Genesis, Exodus, Leviticus, Numbers, Deuteronomy (or Bereshit, Shemot, Vayikra, Bamidbar, Dvarim). 2. Pomegranates. 3. True. 4. No. 5. The hand. 6. Moses. 7. True. 8. (c) 248. 9. Yes (Torah ornaments have bells so you can hear the Torah being taken from the ark and know when it's time to stand.) 10. Yes. 11. A kohen. 12. False. 13. Fifty-four. 14.

Reprint Acknowledgments

The author gratefully acknowledges permission to reprint the following:

"The Story of the Jewish Calendar," "Shabbat in Jerusalem" by Yaffa Siegel, "Reb Meir Bear" by David Einhorn, "If Not Higher" by I. L. Peretz, "Battle Time Bar Mitzvah" by Barbara Soferr, "Wings" by Lamed Shapiro, "1944" by Ruth Minsky Sender, "The Silver Menorah" by Moshe Dluznowsky, "Escape by Dreidel: A Legend", "The Ḥanukkah Flower", "The Date Tree" by Judah Steinberg, "Planting for Tu B'Shevat" by Jesse B. Robinson, "There Have Been Other Purims," "An Orange for All Seasons" by Zalman Schneour, "A Very Special Passover" by Sheila Gruner, "A Passover in Spain" by Curtis Lubinski, "Long is the Way to Jerusalem" by Miriam Bligh-Grotto, "Manager Jones Plays a Hunch" by M. Levin, all from *World Over* magazine and *World Over Story Book* reprinted with the kind permission of the Board of Jewish Education, New York, NY.

"Ḥanukkah in Yemen" by Leah Abramowitz, "The Sefirah Days" adapted from the Midrash by Rabbi Eliezer Gevirtz, and "The Forty-Ninth Man" by Rabbi Zevulun Weisberger from *Olomeinu* magazine and "Day School Daze" cartoon strips on pages 4, 47, 93, 133, 161, and 223 from *The Jewish Parent Connection* reprinted with the kind permission of Torah Umesorah.

"The 'Worthless' Esrogim," based on a midrash, by Gershon Kranzler, reprinted with the kind permission of the author.

"The Sabbath: A Metamorphosis," "Reflections Through the Night," and "Looking Back: 1492, A Golden Age Ends" all by Chaim Berger, reprinted with kind permission of the author and *Gateways*.

"Miracles on the Sea" from *The Case Against the Wind and Other Stories* by I. L. Peretz, translated and adapted by Esther Hautzig and reprinted with the kind permission of Esther Hautzig.

Shabbat crafts and art reprinted from *Shabbat: A Peaceful Island,* Rosh Hashanah crafts and art from *Rosh Hashanah and Yom Kippur: Sweet Beginning,* Sukkot crafts and art from *Sukkot: A Time to Rejoice,* Passover crafts and art from *Passover: A Season of Freedom* all by Malka Drucker and reprinted with her kind permission.

Ḥanukkah crafts and art © 1980 by Malka Drucker, reprinted from *Hanukkah: Eight Nights, Eight Lights* with permission of Holiday House.

Crafts and art for Yom Kippur, Simḥat Torah, Purim, Yom ha-Azma'ut, Lag B'omer, Tisha b'Av, and Shavuot and "Alfalfa Sprouts You Can Eat," "Citrus Seed Plants," "Sweet Potato Vine," "Avocado Plant," "Upside-Down Garden," and "Pineapple-Top Plant" for Tu B'Shevat from *Jewish Holiday Crafts* by Joyce Becker, reprinted here with her kind permission.

"The Apple Tree's Discovery" by Peninnah Schram and Rachayl Eckstein Davis from *Chosen Tales* by Peninnah Schram. Reprinted by permission of the publisher, Jason Aronson, Inc., Northvale, NJ © 1995.

The recipes "Sopa De Avas," "Tabooli," "Bimuelos or Loukomades," "Kofya—Wheat Pudding," "Haroset for Passover," "Albondigas De Matzah," and "Bimuelos De Matzah" by Ida Varon, Henriette Politi, Catherine Caraco Elias, Liane Donnell, Dora Olivebaum Iderne, Regina Arditti, Fortunee Abouaf, Vicki Levin, Betty Albala, and Sue Caraco from *Cooking the Sephardic Way,* reprinted with the kind permission of the Sephardic Sisterhood of Temple Tifereth Israel, Los Angeles, California.

"Chicken Soup" and "Dreidel and Dreidel Variations" from *Miracle Meals* by Madeline Wilker and Judyth Groner. "Hallah Riddles" and "Hanukkah Riddles" from *Jewish Holiday Fun* by David A. Adler. "Gittel and the Bell," from the book of the same name by Roberta Goldshlag Cooks. "Haroset," "Matzah Brei," and "Quick Macaroons," from *Matzah Meals* by Judy Tabs and Barbara Steinberg, all reprinted with the kind permission of Kar-Ben Copies, Inc.

The recipes "Hallah," "Roast Chicken," "Cholent," "Halva," "Carrot Tzimmes," "Honey Cake," "Raisin Cake," "Potato Pancakes," "Sufganiot," "Baked Salmon," "Coleslaw," "Apricot Bars," "Burekas," "Blintzes," and "Cheesecake," from *Jewish Cooking Around the World* by Hanna Goodman. "Jonah," "Esther," "Ruth," and "Lamentations" adapted from *Pathways Through The Bible* by Mortimer J. Cohen. "Purim, Purim, Purim," "The Great Torah Quiz," and "All About Israel" from *The Great Jewish Quiz Book* by Barbara Spector. "The Guest" by Sholem Aleichem translated and adapted by Chaya Burstein, "Hamantaschen," "Babanatza," "Pita Sandwiches," "Felafel," and "Tehina Sauce" from *The Jewish Kids' Catalog* by Chaya Burstein. "Size Isn't Everything: A K'tonton Story" and "K'tonton Takes a Ride on a Chopping Knife" from *The Best of K'tonton* by Sadie Rose Weilerstein, reprinted with the kind permission of The Jewish Publication Society.

Holocaust chronology from *We Remember the Holocaust* by David A. Adler, reprinted with the kind permission of Henry Holt and Company.

Photographs on pages 144, 186 through 189, 191 through 196, 197 (upper photo) reprinted with the kind permission of Yad Vashem, Jerusalem.

Photographs on pages 52, 77, 117, 197 (lower photo), 203, 205 (except upper left photo), 263 reprinted with the kind permission of the Israeli Consulate.

Photographs on pages 59, 62, and 136 reprinted with the kind permission of Dr. Asher Mansdorf.

All music was prepared by Velvel Pasternak of Tara Publications and is printed here with his kind permission.

Octopus menorah cartoon on page 97 suggested by Eitan J. Adler.

Chapter introductions, "Mendel of Chelm Captures the Moon," and all other photographs and art prepared by David A. Adler and copyright © David A. Adler 1996.

Index

About the Author

David A. Adler is the author of more than 125 fiction and nonfiction books for young readers, including the Cam Jansen mysteries, the Houdini Club magic mysteries and biographies of George Washington, Abraham Lincoln, Helen Keller, Eleanor Roosevelt, Frederick Douglass, Martin Luther King, Jr., Robert E. Lee, Simón Bolívar, and others. Among his many books on Jewish subjects are *The House on the Roof*; *A Picture Book of Jewish Holidays*, an American Library Association (ALA) Notable Book; *Happy Hanukkah Rebus*, a *Parents' Magazine* Best Book; *The Number on My Grandfather's Arm*, winner of the Sydney Taylor Award; *A Picture Book of Anne Frank*, winner of the Helen Keating Ott Award; *One Yellow Daffodil*, *We Remember the Holocaust*, *Hilde and Eli: Children of the Holocaust*, and *Child of the Warsaw Ghetto*, all selected as Outstanding Social Studies Books for Children by the Children's Book Council; and *Our Golda: The Story of Golda Meir*, a Carter G. Woodson Honor Book and on the International Relations Committee and ALA list of Outstanding Books for Children. A former teacher, magazine illustrator, and editor for The Jewish Publication Society, he lives in New York with his wife and children.